Cops, Teachers, Counselors

Cops, Teachers, Counselors

Stories from the Front Lines of Public Service

Steven Maynard-Moody and Michael Musheno

The University of Michigan Press
Ann Arbor

Copyright © by the University of Michigan 2003
All rights reserved
Published in the United States of America by
The University of Michigan Press
Manufactured in the United States of America
⊛ Printed on acid-free paper

2006   2005   2004   2003   4   3   2   1

A CIP catalog record for this book is available from the British Library.

Library of Congress Cataloging-in-Publication Data

Maynard-Moody, Steven.
Cops, teachers, counselors : stories from the front lines of
public service / Steven Maynard-Moody and Michael Musheno.
p.   cm.
Includes bibliographical references (p.   ) and index.
ISBN 0-472-09832-2 (cloth : alk. paper) — ISBN 0-472-06832-6
(paper : alk. paper)
1. Human services personnel—United States.   2. Social workers—
United States.   3. Police—United States.   4. Teachers—United
States.
I. Musheno, Michael C.   II. Title.

HV40.8.U6 M39   2003
361—dc21   2002156538

Research for this book was supported by the National Science Foundation
grant number SBR-9511169

for the storytellers

Contents

Stories

Stories

Acknowledgments

The place was different but the moment was the same: for Michael it occurred in a police patrol car; for Steven it was in the meeting room of a vocational rehabilitation office. The moment was when each of us collected our first story, and we knew we were hearing and, in our mind's eyes, seeing governing at the front lines. We were entering the world of street-level work, a world of tensions, ambiguity, and difficult—often painful—choices and judgments. At these moments we were not sure what these first stories and the many stories that followed would tell us or if they would fit into a larger narrative.

Long before these first stories had been collected, we had formed a research team and worked out the details of selecting sites and storytellers and developed interview and story-collection protocols. The original research project had a third principal investigator, Marisa Kelly, associate professor of political science at the University of the Pacific. Marisa had to pull out of the research, but her insights helped form the foundation of this project, and we remain in her intellectual debt. The research team also included two extraordinary assistants: Trish Oberweis at Arizona State University and now assistant professor of sociology at Southern Illinois University at Edwardsville, and Suzanne Leland at the University of Kansas and now assistant professor of public administration at the University of North Carolina at Charlotte. Trish and Suzy put in the long hours and attention to detail so essential in field research, but more than labor they contributed ideas and insights. They were more our colleagues than our assistants, and we owe both of them more than we can acknowledge.

These first stories were preceded by two years spent crafting a grant proposal for the Law and Social Science Program of the National Science Foundation, receiving encouraging reviews but no funding, and making revisions and eventually receiving funding. We gratefully acknowledge the NSF funding, without which this research would not have been possible. Before collecting our first stories, we had to secure permission from top officials, supervisors, and the cops, teachers, and counselors themselves. We greatly appreciate all who opened the door to us and let us enter their worlds. They gave us their time and attention for what was an explicitly theoretical and academic research project.

As we sat in the police car and voc rehab office collecting our first stories, we had, in front of us, two more years of fieldwork plus three years of trying to make sense of it all and finding the words to express what we learned. But with so much yet to do, we felt it all coming together; we felt we were on to something, although at that time we had only the faintest clues about what that something was. This research project has been a wondrous intellectual adventure, and we thank all who made it possible.

The Japanese have a worthy tradition of dedicating books to the authors' teachers. We dedicate this book to our teachers, the story-tellers. They let us into their work worlds and took the time to tell us their stories, stories that painted a multidimensional portrait of street-level work. They revealed the unseen positive and negative aspects of their views and actions. Like all great teachers, our storytellers posed great challenges to our theorizing. From our storytellers we learned—and have tried to capture in this book—a great deal that gives us confidence in the caring, good judgment, and responsible action of street-level workers. We also saw actions and heard judgments that raise concern. During discussion of the book manuscript in a graduate class, one student who worked in law enforcement commented, "You're bipolar in your view of cops." He was, of course, right.

Many of the observations in this book may upset those convinced that society and governance depend on accountability and law abidance. Their concerns are real but so, we believe, are our observations about street-level judgment. Although we may not convince some readers of the possibility of responsibility without traditional account-ability and of front-line policy action disjointed from policy implemen-tation, we do ask these and all readers to listen closely and with open minds to the stories told by cops, teachers, and counselors. The story-tellers have much to say, more than any analysis—ours included—can capture. The full text of all stories, interviews, and questionnaire data used in this research are archived at the Inter-University Consortium for Political and Social Research. We encourage others to look at these primary materials both to critically examine our interpretations and to add observations and interpretations.

Acknowledgments

This book and the research that supports it are collaborative in every sense of the term. Either of us working alone would have written a very different—and much less richly textured—book. We came to the research and writing from different (although not opposing) theoretical orientations, and each of us was confident of his views and interpretations. At times, lengthy phone calls and E-mails led to misunderstandings and disagreement, but our mutual stubbornness also led to deeper understanding. We learned much from each other and rediscovered the truth of the plural version of the writer's adage: we couldn't understand what we thought until we saw what we wrote. As we responded to each other's drafts, we found deeper understanding and agreement that our discussions often missed. This book was not, therefore, assembled like a jigsaw puzzle, with each of us fitting in his own pieces. It grew out of a dialogue of drafts in which the ideas and words of each author became so intermixed that it is now impossible to discern who thought and wrote what.

This book has greatly benefited from the close reading of many patient friends and colleagues who gave us what we needed most: encouragement that our ideas, however ill formed and poorly stated, had merit and criticism that showed us the way to greater clarity. We are grateful to Michael Brintnal, Evelyn Brodkin, Gray Cavender, Susan Coutin, Robert Dingwall, Chuck Epp, George Frederickson, David Goldberg, Zeke Hasenfeld, Steve Hebert, Michael Lipsky, Bill Maurer, Marcia Meyers, Rosemary O'Leary, Dennis Palumbo, Norma Riccucci, Michael Smith, Cam Stivers, and Dvora Yanow. Storytelling builds community, and in telling the story of our research and in soliciting help in interpreting street-level worker stories, we felt emboldened and enlightened by this community of scholars.

Kathy Porsch of the Hall Center for the Humanities at the University of Kansas convinced Steven to submit book proposals to the Guggenheim Foundation and the National Endowment for the Humanities; though unsuccessful, the proposals and Kathy's questioning forced considerable refinement of the ideas that shaped this book. Thelma Helyar, the Policy Research Institute's patient editor, helped us improve various drafts. We were also blessed with three extraordinary reviewers from the University of Michigan Press: John Gilliom, Ann Chih Lin, and William T. Lyons Jr. All three understood and supported the publication of our manuscript yet posed intellectual challenges and detailed commentary. We still get dizzy when we think of Bill Lyons's thirteen-page review. This book has benefited greatly from their comments; only they and we know how different the final book is

Acknowledgments

from the manuscript they reviewed. We are also grateful to our editor, Jeremy Shine, for his enthusiasm and intellectual engagement in our work.

Writing—even collaborative writing—is lonely work. We are both blessed with families who understand our need for quiet time to think and write and who are also a source of joy that takes us away from our preoccupations. During late nights, Birgit offered Michael insights and encouragement through the many blind alleys and meanders that mark the journey from thoughts to drafts to a book. Carey did the same for Steven during long walks. Our enduring gratitude for much more than a book go to Birgit, Micah, Carey, Bethany, Peter, and David.

Part 1. Two Narratives of Street-Level Work

1. Dealing with Faces

I can't say I follow the rules completely. I don't. But I interpret them in each situation and make the best call. Yeah, from my own value system, I suppose.

—western police officer

I don't use the cookbook method. It's all based on what people need to become as independently employed as possible. You know, not everyone requires support for eight or ten months, a year, two years, whatever.

—western vocational rehabilitation counselor

I deal with the kids one to one, whereas the administration deals with the kids as a whole. [The administrators] have to look at what is good for the building as a whole, meaning the 623 students we have here. I look at it on a case-by-case, class-by-class basis. [The administrators] are consistently telling me I have to look at it the other way, and I never will because I deal with the personalities, the faces, the parents, and the problems on a one-to-one basis, and sometimes what's good for a kid is not what's good as a general principle for the entire building or another school. I look at it on a kid-by-kid basis. I really don't care what the building policy is.

—midwestern middle school teacher

A western police officer asserts that both rules and her "own value system" are in play in deciding what to do. A western vocational rehabilitation counselor also acknowledges rules, referencing a "cookbook method" of decision making, but points to "what people need" as central to doing her job. A midwestern middle school teacher reveals a clash of values with policy and administration. The administration makes decisions on what is best for the student body, or what the teacher calls "the building." In contrast, he "deals with faces"—the

3

faces of kids and parents—and makes his decisions on a "kid-by-kid basis."

These are the voices of street-level or front-line government workers. They convey a strong orientation toward faces, or who people are, and toward the workers' own beliefs, their value systems, in explaining their decision making. At the same time, these workers make it clear that policies, rules, and administrative oversight pervade their work and are ever present in their calculations about what to do. Whether on a patrol beat, in the offices of social services, or at the front of public school classrooms, street-level workers' beliefs about people continually rub against policies and rules.

We refer to the demand that workers apply law, rules, and administrative procedures to people's behavior as the expectation of law abidance. We reference the orientation of workers to concentrate on their judgments of who people are, their perceived identities and moral character, as the desire for cultural abidance. We argue that law abidance and cultural abidance coexist in the everyday world of street-level work and that their coexistence defines the tensions of street-level work, revealing a deeper understanding of street-level decision making, or why street-level workers do what they do.

The dual existence of law and cultural abidance is evident in other studies but is rarely a central theme of works that focus on street-level decision making.[1] We think this is the case because the coexistence of these two phenomena unsettles a prevailing narrative about the state and governance. This prevailing narrative—what we call the state-agent narrative—portrays a democratic state as an edifice built on law and predictable procedures that insure that like cases will be treated alike. In this formulation, deviations from law are allowable only if workers adapt law to the circumstances of cases in a manner consistent with policy and hierarchical authority. Such deviations are referred to as discretionary decision making, and the apparatus of public administration is designed to confine and channel discretion to secure equal treatment to the extent possible.

Given the prevailing narrative, scholars and the news media alike focus on the most disturbing qualities of workers practicing cultural abidance or operating more from beliefs and identities than from law and behavior. One of the most recent revelations of the destructive elements of cultural abidance has been the discovery of patterns of racial and ethnic profiling in police officers' decisions (both individually and in groups) regarding whose cars to stop and search on U.S. highways.[2]

4

Given such revelations, it follows that any and all reliance on moral beliefs and identities destroys citizens' lives and threatens governance as we know it.

To represent attention to moral beliefs and identities as part of the everyday decision making of street-level workers asks scholars, the media, and governmental practitioners to question what they have invested in the prevailing narrative. It even asks people to accept some degree of disorder, if only temporarily.[3] To ease the inevitable discomfort, we try to bring order to workers' everyday attention to cultural abidance by offering a second narrative—what we call the citizen-agent narrative—and show the complexity of its practices and effects. Moreover, we demonstrate that this narrative operates in close proximity to, although often in tension with, the prevailing state-agent narrative.[4]

In this less settled state of affairs, some citizens receive unauthorized but extraordinary and life-enhancing help from risk-taking street-level workers. Other citizens, based on different judgments, receive what the rules and procedures allow—no more but no less. Still others are excluded from help and social benefits or, worse, are maligned and abused by front-line workers and the system in which they work.[5] Authorized or prohibited, legitimate or illegitimate, helpful or destructive, street-level cultural judgments are an irreducible element in governing the modern state. Our task is to reveal the patterns of decision making that emerge when both law and beliefs as well as behavior and identities matter in the everyday world of street-level work.

This book is based on the voices of street-level or front-line workers as expressed in their own accounts or stories. We collected and retell a wide range of work stories: stories of encounters with difficult people and dangerous criminals; stories of success and failure; stories of frustration and fear; and stories of conflict with citizens, supervisors, and other agencies. Some of these stories are long and complex, while others are brief and one-dimensional. Some stories provide what appear to be accurate accounts of events, while others are exaggerated and fictionalized. All of the stories were prompted by a straightforward question: we asked workers to tell us stories about how and when their own beliefs about fairness and unfairness helped them make decisions. We encouraged them to tell stories about times when their beliefs conflicted with formal and informal agency policies as well as times when policies facilitated workers' reliance on their own beliefs. Finally, we invited stories of worker relations as well as those that involved citizens, students, and clients. Story 1.1, like so many street-level work stories, puts a face on public service as social and cultural practice.

Story 1.1.   Midwestern Vocational Rehabilitation
"A Happy Ending"

This is a happy-ending story. This is one of those that poor [supervisor] would probably just faint away dead. This is one [the supervisor] does not want to know about. . . .

This is about a lady with severe chronic mental illness. She came through the mental health center through the support of an employment grant.

This is somebody who had been Miss Texas or Miss Oklahoma or something—you know, a real high achiever and then bang. I don't remember if it was depression or what happened. Well, anyway, she ended up in a series of mental hospitals. Somewhere along there she was married and had a little boy and was divorced. So now she is in [midwestern city], she is a single mom living with zero money practically in a real bad part of town with this little guy.

And she worked so hard to put herself back together. She was doing so well. She had picked up an associate's degree in electronics something, computer something, but had never actually worked with the degree or anything because of her mental illness.

Meanwhile, back at home in the neighborhood, her little boy was probably the only white guy in the neighborhood, and the neighborhood bullies were just beating the crap out of this little guy. The [other] parents were like, "So what?" . . . So all these other stresses were coming back on her. She couldn't move until she got a job, and she can't get a job.

Somehow she caught a ride to [nearby town] and interviewed. And they were hiring bachelor's degree people to do these jobs. . . . Somehow she waltzed in there and convinced them that she could do the job, . . . and they hired her, which was amazing in itself. And plus she had done it on her own, which was even more wonderful, except she didn't have a car.

And now she found somebody that had a good dependable older little Toyota for like $1,500. Well, if you have no money, $1,500 might as well be $15 million. Somehow, the mental health center could come up with $400, just kind of seed money. So I came up with $340 for maintenance, but that still left a bunch.

So we got creative. I wrote up enough money to cover insurance, car tags, and fees, and, you know, called them interview clothing and gas, knowing good and well that these are things she is going to need but the money is really for the car. So she went and bought her car.

So she finally moved . . . and lived happily ever after. Her little boy is still in school and is doing great. She has advanced into a better position. They love her.

Everything worked out beautiful, but if we had gone by the rule book, she would not have gotten the car, she would not have gotten the job. She would have ended up back in the hospital.

"A Happy Ending" is a simple story yet lays bare a number of the defining substantive features of the stories workers told us. First, many of the stories focus centrally on the construction of the character and identity of the citizen. In this case, the citizen is a client of a vocational rehabilitation counselor working out of an office in a core urban neighborhood. According to the worker, the client, a "lady," was a "high achiever" who came to him with a "severe chronic mental illness." Rather than focusing on her illness, the worker tells about the client's positive character traits. She is a responsible single mom with "a little boy" coping with hard living conditions, which are depicted in racialized terms: "her little boy was probably the only white guy in the neighborhood, and the neighborhood bullies were just beating the crap out of this little guy." Showing initiative, another positive character trait, she goes to a nearby town in search of work that can better her conditions and "amazingly" gets offered a job that reflects—even exceeds— her earlier educational achievements.

Second, like many of the stories, the citizen's character is entwined with the worker's decision making.[6] A worker judges a citizen, often using mainstream beliefs about good and bad character, and acts to reinforce that judgment. In this case, the judgment is highly positive, and the worker's action is strongly proactive, reinforcing the citizen's identity as a responsible parent seeking work to overcome hard times and harsh living conditions.[7]

Third, policies, rules, and administration are depicted as barriers to reinforcing judgments about character and identity or as tools for actualizing those judgments. In this case, the woman needs a car to secure meaningful work and improve her family's conditions, but the rules stand in the way. The worker "writes up money" to cover the purchase of the vehicle while reporting that the money will be used for items such as clothing and gasoline that can be purchased legitimately for a person with a disability who has secured work. The worker bends the rules to help a client of good character.

Fourth, the stories reveal that street-level workers are highly sensitive to coworkers and immediate supervisors, including those in their work sites and related agencies. In "A Happy Ending," the worker gains the support of a coworker in the mental health center and realizes that what he is doing cannot be officially acknowledged by his supervisor even though the supervisor might be supportive. It is one of those actions that would probably make the "poor supervisor . . . just faint away dead." While coworkers and supervisors are intimate characters in the stories told by street-level workers, the higher echelons of the agencies and the more formal elements of policy and procedures embedded in the organizations are lumped together as "the system," out of touch with the everyday realities of front-line work. Workers and their supervisors have to find ways to make this formal state apparatus work for them or face the task of subverting this apparatus, a responsibility they are willing to take on for the right citizen-client in the right circumstance.

Finally, the stories reveal that judgments and related actions are reached with confidence and an unblinking focus on the people who come to these workers. They deal with faces. Street-level workers do not question themselves with regard to the power they wield, nor do they seem disposed to weigh the broader implications of their actions.[8] In this story, the worker tells us that "everything worked out beautiful." The worker alludes to a neighborhood under stress but does so only as a place that his client needs to exit if she and her boy are to be better off. Her deprivation is a function of illness and, as a result, the worker does not confront the issues of race and class that operate just under the surface of this story.

The work world of cops, teachers, and counselors is a baffling terrain, dense with law, rules, and procedures; bounded by overlapping hierarchal and agency relationships; and populated with the diverse and often hard to read faces of citizens, clients, supervisors, and coworkers. It is a world where identity and moral judgments are bound up with the quotidian work of the state. This is the front line of public service.

2. State Agents, Citizen Agents

How do street-level workers make sense of their world and account for what they do? These questions guide our inquiry and lie at the heart of scholarship on the state and its workforce. Much of the existing literature converges on a viewpoint of street-level workers that focuses on how they apply the state's laws, rules, and procedures to the cases they handle. We call this viewpoint the state-agent narrative. We propose an additional viewpoint, a citizen-agent narrative, that is muted in existing scholarship yet prevalent in the stories told to us by street-level workers. The citizen-agent narrative concentrates on the judgments that street-level workers make about the identities and moral character of the people encountered and the workers' assessment of how these people react during encounters.

The two types of narrative are distinct but not discrepant, describing coexisting qualities of street-level work. The state-agent narrative is about law abidance, both of citizens and workers; the citizen-agent narrative is about normative or cultural abidance, identifying those who are worthy citizens and colleagues and those who are not. Both narratives are interwoven into the meaning and purpose of the modern state.[1] At times, the dictates of the state-agent and citizen-agent narratives exist in concert: law, public policy, and agency procedures provide a good match with the street-level workers' views of the people they encounter. At other times, tension intrudes between workers' inclinations and the dictates of the law. When law, policy, and rules are ill matched to workers' views of fairness and appropriate action, street-level work smolders with conflict over what is the right decision and what is the right thing to do.

The distinct contours of the citizen-agent narrative are most evident in these moments of tension. Many of the stories we collected revealed these tensions and conflicts, and by analyzing these stories, we seek to

9

enhance understanding of the sense making of workers and why they do what they do. Our project focuses on explicating the citizen-agent narrative as the frame or map that workers employ to understand and navigate these moments of tension and conflict. Before turning to that task in parts 2 and 3, we identify the conceptual contours of both the state-agent and citizen-agent narratives.

A considerable amount of public agency and street-level work is routine and follows rules and procedures: researchers estimate that welfare workers adhere to the standard client-intake script 75 percent of the time.[2] One fundamental characteristic of street-level work is that frontline state agents are bound by a long tether of hierarchical relationships. There is some variation—teachers are subject to fewer rules than police officers—but from the number of coffee breaks to the types of services provided to the manner an arrest is executed, nearly every aspect of street-level work is defined by rules and procedures. Rules and procedures are an essential aspect of bureaucratic life yet provide only weak constraints on street-level judgments.[3] Street-level work is, ironically, rule saturated but not rule bound. Rather than focusing on the routines of workers, the state-agent narrative concentrates on street-level discretion, or workers' adaptations of laws, rules, and procedures to the circumstances of cases. The issue is not the prevalence of discretionary judgments but the ever-present possibility of discretion.[4] The inevitability of discretion makes issues of accountability and control central to mainstream accounts of the administrative state.

According to these accounts, rules and procedures can never universally fit each case and every circumstance. Decisions must be made. In many circumstances, street-level workers must decide which rules or procedures to apply. The proliferation of rules—often contradictory rules—requires matching the case to the rule or procedure, and this process requires discretion.[5] Moreover, despite the video cameras in police cars and the detailed reporting required of other street-level workers, a great deal of street-level work remains hidden from direct supervision.[6] On a more abstract level, H. George Frederickson reminds us that discretion is inherent in all acts of administration because "every application of a law involves further elaboration of that law."[7] Thus, like putty, discretion can be squeezed by oversight and rules but never eliminated; it will shift and reemerge in some other form in some other place. This is a fact of life in the modern state.[8]

Although acknowledging the ubiquity of discretion, the state-agent narrative emphasizes the normative importance of legal and bureaucratic rules and the fit between rules and actions. It portrays the state as an edifice built on law and predictable procedure. Delineating street-level workers' subservient role in governing has a long tradition in political science and public administration that goes back at least to the classic distinction between politics and administration that describes the profound—and, to many people, disturbing—influence that administrative implementers have on the nature of policy.[9] As if good fences make good neighbors, this distinction draws a boundary separating the democratic process of making policy and law and the bureaucratic process of carrying out policy and law.[10]

Many scholars have rejected the separation of politics and administration, but the distinction returns in different forms in the revisions of the state-agent narrative. In the 1980s it returned as implementation theory, which focused initially on policy failures as defined by the wide gap between political intentions and administrative reaction. By examining the role of policy implementers, this literature highlighted the influence of front-line workers but defined their work in terms of implementing other people's policy preferences.[11] More recently, the politics-administration distinction has been reborn as principal-agent theory, which stresses the importance of hierarchy and accountability to democratic and bureaucratic control. Even when acknowledging the impracticality of top-down control of street-level workers, principal-agent theorists define "working" as conforming to rules, procedures, and orders, whereas any deviation from rules and procedures is denounced as "shirking" or "sabotage."[12]

Another version of the state-agent narrative, reflected in previous research on street-level bureaucracy, describes the patterns of local, client-by-client, offender-by-offender, kid-by-kid discretionary judgments of front-line workers as tantamount to political decisions and policy-making.[13] Rather than making discretionary judgments within or at times contravening policy, this perspective views front-line decisions and actions as equivalent to policy. By referring to street-level decisions as policy, this version of the state-agent narrative stresses its lawlike qualities, its predictability and consistency. This is true even when street-level "policy" conflicts with official policy. With regard to what government actually does as opposed to what it says it does, street-level workers are important decision makers. They deliver the services; they actualize policy. In this sense they are policymakers, at least metaphorically.

In contrast, street-level worker stories and the citizen-agent narrative deemphasize the predictability and consistency or lawlike qualities of front-line decisions. In story after story, street-level decisions lack the consistency and coherence to be called policy. A street-level worker may handle similar cases in different ways, and workers from the same jurisdiction may handle cases differently. A group of teenage boys loitering in a middle-class neighborhood may receive only a passing glance from a patrol officer, but a similar group in a core urban neighborhood of the same jurisdiction elicits intense scrutiny if not harassment.

The state-agent narrative also emphasizes that self-interest guides the exercise of discretion. This view recognizes the inevitable mix of motives yet highlights the evidence that street-level workers use their considerable discretion to make their work easier, safer, and more rewarding. They make their work easier by managing their caseloads; by focusing on easier clients; and by avoiding, dismissing, or reducing contact with unpleasant or impossible cases. In this cynical view, street-level workers look for quick-fix solutions for long-term problems and invent procedures to move clients as quickly and effortlessly as possible through the system. The workers process rather than engage clients.[14]

Street-level work is dangerous and often unpleasant. This is especially true for police officers, but teachers also fear weapons in lockers and assaults by students. The foyers of many Social Security Administration offices are separated from the workers' cubicles by bulletproof glass.[15] Applicants are buzzed past the safety barrier only after being deemed harmless; some scary-appearing applicants are interviewed through the glass, and Social Security workers are quick to recall stories like the one told to us about a knife-wielding "crazy" who got past the barrier and threatened the intake worker. Social workers recount visits to dangerous homes and scary neighborhoods. Vocational rehabilitation counselors tell of angry or unpredictable clients. These conditions encourage street-level workers to use their discretion to make their work safer and more pleasant even at the cost of providing poorer service.

Nevertheless, the state-agent narrative acknowledges that street-level workers at times go out of their way to help others. Many street-level workers entered their professions as idealists. After years of overload, uncooperative clients, an indifferent public, and dilapidated, sometimes dreadful, working conditions, they still need to preserve some meaning and value for their work. Many use their discretion to select a small number of cases or members of the public for special treatment, the kind of treatment they might provide all citizen-clients if they had the resources and energy.

At times this treatment may involve extra attention, expedited services, or cutting people a break. A social worker finds temporary housing for a family even though all the shelters are at capacity. A cop may ignore a drug stash found in the glove box of a person's car. The state-agent narrative treats these moments as dangerous acts of exceptionalism. Moreover, the state-agent narrative highlights the benefit to the street-level workers and the state they represent in accounting for these cases of exceptionalism. As Michael Lipsky summarizes, "At best, street-level bureaucrats invent benign modes of mass processing that more or less permit them to deal with the public fairly, appropriately, and successfully. At worst, they give into favoritism, stereotyping, and routinizing—all of which serve private or agency purposes."[16]

Our analysis of stories reveals that workers are constantly attentive to who their clients are, acting on their assessments of people's character and identity. Rather than exceptionalism, we find that these moments of special attention arise from the sustained tensions between legal mandates and workers' beliefs about what is fair or the right thing to do. Facing these moments as clashes of law and culture reveals judgments in which workers sometimes treat citizens as one-dimensional caricatures and sometimes operate outside the foundations of law and agency rules and procedures.[17] It also reveals judgments wherein workers see complexity in people and their circumstances and use law as a tool to serve particularities. Either way, the citizen-agent narrative draws attention to workers' constant focus on who citizens are as much as what they do.

In addition to treating these as moments of exceptionalism, the state-agent narrative concentrates on law-deviating character of exceptionalism and the need for remedies to uphold the rule of law. The customary response to the suspicion that street-level discretion is incompatible with democratic governance is to find ways to control it, to somehow tame and tether discretion with a democratic leash.[18] The most commonly tried and advocated controls on street-level discretion are bureaucratic: by increasing the extent and effectiveness of supervision and by elaborating and enforcing rules and procedures, street-level discretion can, in this view, be brought within the auspices of bureaucratic control.

This response is especially true during a crisis. Most of the time, street-level discretion is ignored and tolerated, but when discretion leads to scandal or public concern, the inexorable response is to enhance bureaucratic control. In the aftermath of the Los Angeles police beating of Rodney King, more and more police cars have video cameras installed to increase supervision. Police abuse in New York City has led to new guidelines for interacting with the public, even including pocket-sized script cards to prompt good manners. Despite these efforts, realists lament that the edifice of democratic control cannot, in the end, really limit street-level discretion.[19] More worrisome is the observation that efforts to control discretion merely push it further underground, thereby weakening control and accountability.[20]

Story 2.1. Midwestern Vocational Rehabilitation
"Slammed in the Rear"

I tried an experiment with a chronic alcoholic fellow; a double amputee in a wheelchair. . . . He keeps talking about getting a job, and I tried to get him a car [that he can operate with hand controls]. One thing we can't do is purchase a vehicle—we can repair but not purchase.

So I tried and tried. Well, I decided he was still drinking. I have had him in and out of treatment. I have taken him to treatment, and he was back home before I got home.

I have tried everything. Well, I decide to do whatever it takes to see if it will work. So I spent out of pocket about $1,000 repairing [a dilapidated van he had purchased but could not drive]. And I was hoping that through all this kind of support and having someone that gave a damn about him, [he would finally turn his life around].

I liked the guy and wanted to try something new. When we first got the car we put hand controls on it. They delivered the car over to the place that puts the controls on it, and I said, "Well just follow me home."

So I got in my van waiting to get out on the road, and all of a sudden BAAAMMM, he runs right into the back of my van. He didn't get fifty feet. I thought I converted the man, and he runs right into me. Maybe he is trying to tell me something.

People love to tell that story.

Story 2.2. Midwestern Vocational Rehabilitation
"Recycling"

Before I started the job, way back in 1988, [a vision-impaired woman named Andira][21] had already worked with our agency. They put her through tons and tons of exams and ended up buying her some equipment like a talking scale and some items that helped her as a homemaker. And she was probably, I would guess, in her early twenties at that time. And when I had first started the job, she had already come back on the caseload, come back recycled—we like to call it recycling. We don't fail and have to redo clients, we recycle them.

And she came back through. Well, this time she decided that she wanted to work, and she wanted to work in child care. So I went through her case. I wasn't terribly pleased. I went through the case with the old counselor because there were some tests in there that maybe she had some personality problems and some self-esteem problems that she needed therapy and this sort of thing.

So we started the good old evaluation process, and at that time we basically couldn't move ahead with services for that client unless every single thing that a doctor mentioned could possibly be wrong was evaluated beyond belief. . . .

Altogether, she was probably with me for five years, and a good part of that time was evaluation after evaluation. We did physical examines, we did eye examines, we did low-vision examines, we did psychological examines. The psychological examines suggested that she might have some learning deficits of some sort, and they weren't sure what, so they wanted to do a another examine, a neurological type of examine. . . .

So they did that, and it took months and months because of the case process, and I had to wait for each one of those reports to come back. I had to wait for it, and then when it came back, I had to go through it and figure out what was wrong as far as the doctor or whoever the examiner was at that time was concerned, had to relay it to the client. The client was becoming very frustrated through the whole thing, very defeated.

Her self-esteem was in bad shape. . . . So the case was moving very, very slow. She wanted to go into child care, and in the course of our examinations and in the course of our discussion, she figured out child care to her probably wouldn't be worth the money to go into it, that she would rather maybe explore computers and see if there is some kind of data entry job that she might be able to do. . . . Well, we weren't sure about buying her a computer, because we didn't know for sure what she was going to need on the job. . . .

It got to the point where I was a little more experienced on the job, and I had already picked a fight with supervisors and won a few battles. So she said, "I don't know what to do. I can't go anywhere because I don't have the equipment that I feel like I need. If I go through training—why should I go through training? Is it going to do me any good? Is it going to do anything or not?" And I said, "Well, why don't you do this?"

I got an idea and told Andira, "Why don't you call the client-assistance program in [state capital] and raise holy hell—yell and scream, do whatever you want to do, threaten lawsuits, do whatever you want to do. Because you need a computer to do your job." And I said, "You have my supervisor's number, right?" She said, "Yeah, I do." I said, "Good. Call him and tell him you are fixing to file an appeal because you are sick of the whole thing. You want a computer and you want it right now, and tell him that you are tired of messing with the agency bull."

And she said, "I have been upset with you from time to time, but is that going to get you into trouble?" She said, "I don't want to get you into trouble." And I said, "No, you will not get me into trouble." I said, "Just don't say that you heard it from me. Just do it. Just call up and raise holy hell." I said, "I will be right here waiting for my phone call, which I am sure is going to come, and I will cooperate fully with that phone call if they want me to produce a summary of your case or if they want to review your case, that is fine. I will be ready for it. I will cooperate with it. I know how to order the computer for you. I know how to go through the contract and state bid proceedings on how to order the computer. So go to it. Let them have it."

She said, "It will not get you into any trouble?" and I said, "No, they are already familiar with your case. They know what it has been through, and they almost expect you to raise hell anyway. So do it."

So she did. . . . I hang up the phone and laugh to myself, trying to figure out how long it would take for the supervisor to call me back. And [I] wait about fifteen minutes and, bingo, there he was on the phone.

And I said to my boss, "I knew she was upset, but she really called you? I'll be darned. I know, I figured she was kind of mad, you know, and like you said, if the client is upset, I'll give her the phone numbers and stuff, and that is what I did."

I said, "I think she wants a computer real bad, but I am not sure." And he said, "Oh, yeah," he said, "I think we really don't need an appeal on this." And I said, "No, I don't think so." I said, "With all the evaluations and stuff that we have done, it can get pretty nasty. I don't think I would want an appeal."

I said, "I think we might lose that one. If I were you—I don't think its a good idea. If I were you, I would just shut up and cooperate with her, you know, if you want to know what I would do." "But," I said, "you are the supervisor. You let me know. Let me know what you want to do with this thing." But I said, "I think it is going to get pretty ugly if you don't let it go." He said, "Well, why don't you go ahead and do whatever you need to do to get her a computer." And I said, "Oh, okay, well, I'll do—you know, if that is where you feel we should go with the case, I'll do it. It sounds okay. I'll take care of it."

So I called her and I said, "Well, it looks to me you must have done a pretty good job." I said, "You are getting your computer." She said, "I am?" and I said, "Yeah." I said, "Whatever you said must have been pretty good." She said, "I did my best," and I said, "You did good. You did real good."

So we proceeded to get her a computer, . . . and she has succeeded very well as a computer instructor and moved up in their system over there, and she just recently applied to me again because she needs to—she needs some assistance with training and computer equipment and upgrading her skills so that she can learn Windows applications so she can continue her employment.

I think it pointed out a flaw in the system, and part of the reason why I rebelled and pushed her to go ahead in appealing was because I knew it would push the case ahead, and I was sick of evaluating it and I was sick of wasting my time and paperwork on it. So I figured that would push the client ahead and it would allow me to move on with that case. So I figured it benefited everybody, and it did, and I got by with it.

The issues of discretion, control, and accountability that preoccupy the state-agent narrative are evident in the stories of street-level workers. Workers are keenly aware of rules and policies and clearly know when they are deviating from them. For example, in "Slammed in the Rear," the worker wanted to provide the client, a double amputee in a wheelchair, with greater mobility. The worker realized that policy prohibited purchasing vehicles and faced organizational obstacles in trying to secure funds from the agency to repair the client's vehicle. In

"Recycling," the voc rehab worker spent a long period following the protocol for evaluating a visually impaired woman; the counselor was aware that the supervisor was not going to approve certain expenditures unless the worker followed "the good old evaluation process." Still, in both of these stories, the workers saw the rules and supervisors as obstacles to doing what was right or fair for their clients. In both stories, the workers went to considerable lengths to put what they thought were their clients' needs at the forefront, facing considerable costs or risks for doing so.

Rules, procedures, and supervisors are ever present in the stories; they are, like the office or neighborhood, part of the setting. In this way, rules and supervisors constitute a feature of the social terrain that the worker must navigate to secure something for a protagonist or restrain or punish an antagonist. The stories are citizen centered more than rule centered, and the workers' judgments are more moral than legal. It is, in part, for these reasons that we named the second viewpoint of street-level sense making and action the citizen-agent narrative. Particularly when rules and beliefs conflict, cops, teachers, and counselors describe their work more as judging people and acting on these judgments than as adapting rules to the circumstances of cases.

Street-level workers see their jobs as helping the disabled who are deemed worthy, teaching those students who are willing to work or show promise amid hardship, or, in the case of the police, protecting the good citizen while getting the "bad guys."[22] Rather than relying on policy to guide so-called discretionary decisions about cases, workers first make judgments about the citizen-client and then turn to policy to help enact or, if negative, to rationalize their judgments. In "Slammed in the Rear," the counselor did everything he could to help the alcoholic client, stretching every rule, using his own money, not because it was required or even allowed but because he "liked the guy and wanted to try something new."

This does not mean that rules and policy do not permeate all aspects of street-level work (they do) or that most street-level actions do not conform to agency guidelines (they do as well). Rules and policy may commonly fit the workers' assessments of citizens and what they need or deserve. Nonetheless, in many of our stories, the workers began by acting as dutiful state agents but ultimately found that the tension between their views and the state's dictates became intolerable. Like the requirement for endless evaluations in "Recycling," rules, procedures, laws, and hierarchy define the terrain of street-level work, but rules come to the forefront in street-level stories when they conflict with workers' judgments about people and what should happen to them. When the counselor in "Recycling" was new to the job, he, like a good state agent, followed rules to the letter and in so doing failed to help the client. As he gained experience, the tension between his views and the state's dictates became intolerable. The counselor learned how to subvert the legal and bureaucratic ordering and thereby serve the client rather than the system: he became a citizen agent. The last sentence the story captures well his new citizen-agent credo: "So I figured it benefited everybody, and it did, and I got by with it." He made a decision based on what he thought was right, he acted, and he "got by with it." As expressed in this story, the distinctive voices of street-level workers are most clearly heard when there is a clash between individuals' perceived needs and the demands and limits of rules.

Street-level workers often tell stories about going the distance, even putting their careers at risk. Their stories do not reveal an intensive focus on their narrow self-interest or that of their agencies. Street-level workers tell of many cases or situations when they made their work harder, more unpleasant, more dangerous, and less officially successful to respond to the needs of the people in front of them. Like the "nice lady" described in "You Can't Win for Losing" (story 4.5) or the likeable drunk in "Slammed in the Rear," street-level workers overinvest their time and the state's resources in certain clients even though the chance of success is slim. Vocational rehabilitation counselors tell of keeping cases open long after they could be successfully closed—they postpone earning the valued "26," or case-closed code by which their work is evaluated—because the client deserved the extra service and extra work.

In a world where case closure is the bureaucratic and policy definition of success, these long-term, open-ended cases are described in street-level stories as the sources of true worker and client successes, even though they could be considered implementation failures in the state-agent narrative because of the wide gap between political intentions—get people off welfare—and street-level implementation. Teachers and cops tell of risking their safety to protect the good and punish the bad. Other street-level workers tell of jeopardizing their careers to help citizen-clients or fellow street-level workers. One vocational rehabilitation counselor acknowledges the pressure to close cases: "We have to have a certain number of closures to be considered successful and to have offers for pay raises and a chance for advancement. The pressure is incredible." Yet for the right client, the worker will keep the case open for months, even years, to assure client success. This counselor continues, "You feel like you're doing what's best for the clients, but it reflects really bad in your evaluation."

In their accounts, workers ignore orders and challenge their supervisors and agencies to help needy clients or to punish those they judge as unworthy or bad. One vocational rehabilitation counselor sued her agency to help her client, just as in "Recycling" the teller convinced his client to file a complaint against him to get his supervisor to approve the computer purchase. Cops will ignore serious offenses committed by someone they identify with and judge as a good person (for example, the marijuana dealing of a poor, hardworking immigrant who is a responsible family man) while treating harshly the trivial offenses of someone they see as a bad person (for example, a pregnant prostitute). No one would deny that street-level workers make decisions and take actions based in part and at times on their own self-interest, as the state-agent narrative suggests. But this picture is incomplete and distorts our understanding of governing on the front lines. The street-level workers' narratives focus attention on other motives and their willingness to make their work harder, more dangerous, and, in the bureaucratic sense, less successful in their efforts to help or harm citizens. This is a key element of the citizen-agent narrative.

In their narratives, street-level workers also define their work and to a large extent themselves in terms of relationships more than rules.[23] Their judgments are rendered more in the context of social relations and less, as the state-agent narrative emphasizes, in the context of formal duties and responsibilities as defined by law and policy. Street-level workers occupy specific roles in the formal hierarchy, and this profoundly shapes their work environment, but their decisions and actions are guided as much by meaning as by function. Social relations and "different images of the self-in-relationships," to borrow Carol Gilligan's phrase, shape, guide, and give meaning to their judgments.[24]

People's projections of who they are—their identities—are intimately tied to their beliefs and the self-image they want to communicate to others. Street-level workers reveal themselves as agents, as wielders of power who know what is best for other citizens. In this regard, the citizen-agent narrative converges with the state-agent viewpoint. At the same time, workers recognize themselves as belonging to racial, class, gender, and sexual groupings and as public employees belonging to professional groupings. They are citizens who connect in complex ways with fellow workers and clients, and they are agents of the state and of their moral selves.

Workers take their contingent, complex senses of identities into the field and the hallways of their workplaces. In encounters with their constituencies and coworkers, sense making and judgments are in part effected by taking into account class, appearance, work affiliation, skin color, gender, and age.[25] These groupings are ways for workers to get a fix on people, particularly when they are in the first encounter with a stranger, and to establish bonds with people in the workplace and on the streets. Because workers are agents who wield power when interacting with their constituencies, they also have a say about who people are: they can put a fix on people, assigning them a social identity or group belonging. As powerful actors in the social identification process, they may, for example, mark one person as a responsible immigrant parent deserving a break and another as a violent predator, identities with lasting material consequences. In part 2, we take up the significance of social identity and identification to sense making and street-level judgment. Here we introduce the three key relational dynamics evident in the stories that give rise to the processes of social identity and identification.

The first is the profoundly paradoxical relationship with a citizen-client. In part, workers' professions give meaning to the citizens they encounter and to the agency. Vocational rehabilitation counselors work with the disabled, who for the most part are deemed worthy of state support and intervention—the "deserving poor."[26] Police officers deal substantially with the undeserving poor, those who are most often seen as a threat to community order and stability. In human services, street-level workers' ability to do their jobs depends on their ability to persuade clients to comply with workers' wishes. Police officers are in a greater position to require, even force, compliance. Teachers lie somewhere in between in their powers to secure compliance. The various relationships between workers and citizen-clients help define how judgments are translated into actions.

These relationships provide workers with their greatest sense of accomplishment but also prove the most difficult, frustrating, troubling, and at times threatening. These relationships are enhanced when workers project their identities onto clients and the clients respond as the workers would. Moreover, working a case or having the time to get to know a client offers workers smoother relationships and more rewarding experiences.

Street-level workers also identify strongly with fellow street-level workers both within and across agencies. This second key relationship provides the workers with a primary social group of belonging. After formal training is completed, street-level workers learn their jobs from their peers, turning to those peers for advice and support when questions or dilemmas arise. Encounters with citizen-clients define the work, but these relationships are fraught with the problems of unequals and, at least initially, of stranger-to-stranger interactions. In contrast, relations with fellow street-level workers carry the security of familiarity and the expectation of mutual support.

A number of stories reveal the cultural bonds of group belonging. Other stories highlight tensions among workers that reinforce the significance of generational, sexual, racial, and gender identities in the contemporary workforce. One police officer recalled a generational clash in her department when a motorcycle cop picked a fight with a bicycle cop. Others revealed clashes revolving around sexual, racial, and gender identities, analogous to the conflicts that arise in diverse urban neighborhoods. Vocational rehabilitation counselors described organizational clashes with rigid welfare workers. In "Harder Than Brain Surgery" (story 9.6), a voc rehab counselor had a client who needed brain surgery to remove a tumor and then needed additional welfare support to keep his home during the recovery. The voc rehab counselor, acting primarily as a citizen-agent, was able to pay for the expensive brain surgery but had great difficulty getting a few hundred dollars in housing support from the rule-bound welfare worker acting primarily as a state agent: welfare support proved harder than brain surgery.

Workers also gain a sense of belonging and mutuality through their incessant low-level conflict with what they call "the system." In their stories, the system is described as an undifferentiated amalgam of other units in their agency, other agencies, elected officials, and the media. These institutions and actors are a primary focus of the state-agent narrative and represent signs of the state-agent narrative in the lives of workers. But in street-level worker stories, these institutions and actors are shadowy, diffuse figures that signify obstacles to be overcome or forces with little real understanding of the streets or workplaces. Street-level workers see themselves as moral actors working in opposition to the system and rarely describe themselves as part of it.

To street-level workers, the system provides limited and limiting resources but only loose guidance and constraint. The system intrudes into their work, often in the guise of reform, but street-level workers spend considerable effort sealing themselves off from the system's demands and dictates. They build and maintain walls between themselves and the larger governmental and oversight systems. These walls are essential aspects of the us-against-them street-level work culture. As in "Recycling," street-level workers tell time and again how they get around and battle the system to help the worthy and punish or restrain the unworthy.

Street-level workers are not idealists imposing abstract notions of morality or enforcing philosophical views of justice, fairness, and right. In the citizen-agent narrative, they present themselves as pragmatists who temper their efforts to do the right thing with a clear understanding of what is possible for individual citizen-clients in the context of their everyday lives. Their decisions are based on practical knowledge and judgments about people and are improvisational in the face of unpredictability.[27] Street-level judgment or pragmatism is forged in the three relationships discussed earlier, especially the relationship to the citizen-client. Front-line workers do not think abstractly about the deserving poor: they deal with the blind woman who qualifies for assistance but has a personality disorder that will forever limit her ability to function in society. They do not worry about the policy of zero tolerance for drugs when they ignore the small-scale marijuana dealing of a hardworking day laborer.

Street-level workers are proud of their pragmatism, their hardearned street smarts about people, their character, and what they need or deserve. Ironically and with humor, "Slammed in the Rear" tells how the events (not the agency) punished the counselor who abandoned common sense in his desire to help. The story warns that the impractical get "slammed in the rear." In the workers' view, this reality-tested pragmatism makes their judgments superior to that of other actors in the system. This pragmatism is based on both firsthand experiences and wisdom handed down by fellow street-level workers, often in the form of stories. Even hardened police officers frequently express a surprising idealism about the significance of their work, but street-level workers are pragmatists who express disdain for the ungrounded knowledge of politicians, agency officials, and intellectuals. Direct supervisors may be spared this distrust if they have risen from the ranks and retain respect for street-level pragmatism.

In the street-level workers' narratives, lawmakers and rule enforcers are often portrayed as out of touch with reality—as clueless—whereas street-level workers portray their own judgments as correct and tempered by experience. Their stories stress the superiority of street-level judgments over the cool calculations of discretionary decision making. Street-level workers see lawmakers' and top officials' abstract and often seemingly foolish decisions and policies as an annoyance imposed by an impractical and ineffectual elite for whom the street-level workers have little respect and to whom they offer little deference. By substituting pragmatic judgments for the unrealistic and untenable views of those with formal and legitimate authority, street-level workers view themselves as acting responsibly. They are taking on the burden of making moral and pragmatic judgments that alter citizens' everyday lives, justifying decisions and actions as workable improvisations of unrealistic rules, laws, and procedures.

Paradoxically, these particularistic and pragmatic judgments have profound and far-reaching consequences for individuals, the state, and the social order. For example, the decision to subvert the rules by the exasperated counselor in "Recycling" achieves lasting success for the client, who gets and holds a good job. The counselor engages in an act that redeems the state by breaking through the bureaucratic labyrinth. Moreover, the street-level workers' encounters with citizen-clients become the context where dominant community values of order, rights, and good behavior are defined and enforced.[28]

Front-line workers decide who is a good or bad person, who has rights and who is disenfranchised, and what community actions are tolerated or punished. In their narratives, street-level workers reveal themselves as empowered citizen agents who effect the state's legitimacy and convey the status of citizenship as they ration resources, provide access to programs, and sanction individuals.[29] More than demonstrating that they are enforcers or implementers of law, street-level workers' narratives indicate that they are citizen-agents who help produce and maintain society's normative as much as legal order.[30]

3. Story Worlds, Narratives, and Research

So natural is the impulse to narrate, so inevitable is the form of narrative for any report of the way things really happen, that narrativity could appear problematical only in a culture in which it was absent— absent or, as in some domains of contemporary Western intellectual and artistic culture, programmatically refused. . . . Far from being a problem, then, narrative might well be considered a solution to a problem of general human concern, namely the problem of how to translate *knowing* into *telling.*

—Hayden White

Storytelling and understanding are functionally the same thing.

—Roger Schank

Convincing narratives have a kind of weight that mathematical formulas do not. They allow us to revive moral argumentation in disciplines that, since the eighteenth century, had aimed at value neutrality.

—Stephen Toulmin

The purpose of our research is simple, even elemental: to collect and examine street-level workers' everyday work stories to uncover their judgments as they see them. This simple goal belies the challenge of the interpretive task because these stories are often ambiguous and multi-layered: they reference both rules and morality to defend decisions, reveal internalized as well as interactive conflicts, and document shifting positions over time. These stories are not philosophical discourses on law or fairness. They are pragmatic expressions about acts and identities and assertions of dominant yet jumbled societal views of good and bad behavior and worthy and unworthy individuals. At times these stories provide detailed cognitive maps about decision making; at other times they offer only faint clues. Nevertheless, they do enable an interpretation of how law and morality intersect with identities and conduct to bring meaning to street-level judgments and actions.

Details about our methods—gaining entry to our field sites, collecting stories and other data, and organizing and conducting analysis and interpretation—are described in appendix A. This chapter explores the more general issues of narrative analysis in social research. Hearing, transcribing, reading, and rereading stories is not standard social research, although interest in narrative analysis has grown in recent years. If the root question is not how much or how many but rather how do people (in our case, street-level workers) comprehend and act in their work lives, then stories are perhaps our most powerful research instrument. We regard stories and narrative analysis as a tool that is at once a microscope for examining minute details and a telescope for scanning the intellectual horizon for themes and patterns. Even the words *knowledge* and *narrative* have shared linguistic roots, leading Joshua Foa Dienstag to observe, "This common lineage suggests that at one time to know something or someone was closely linked to the ability to tell a story."[1]

Like shoe-box dioramas, narratives create miniature worlds. Viewing the scene from a cutout window will offer a perspective that differs from looking down from the top as well as from the imagined perspective of those inside the box looking out. Storytelling, like the diorama, is an act of "world-building" and "world-populating."[2] Hearing a story, we enter, if only for a moment, this created world and interact with its characters. Street-level workers' stories re-create their world as they see it and as they want to present it to outsiders. These re-creations are not photographically accurate. It is not possible to separate the storytellers' interpretations and their decisions of what and how to present the story from the events recounted (or invented) and the characters described (or imagined). Stories are not facts or evidence waiting for interpretation; from the moment they are conceived through the many tellings and retellings, they are the embodiment of the storyteller's interpretation. This is their power; this is their limit.[3]

The words *narrative* and *story* are often used interchangeably; they are synonyms but for our purposes have different connotations. Narrative is the broader category: all stories are narratives, but not all narratives are stories.[4] The various textual forms of qualitative social science, such as ethnographies, folk tales, case studies, observations, and other similar accounts, are forms of narratives. Broadly speaking, all of these forms describe events and exist within a time span, characteristics they share with narrative art forms such as film, ballet, opera, fiction, and representational painting and sculpture. Even quantitative data and formal models are meaningless until put into some narrative structure; quantitative researchers, just like their qualitative colleagues, must attach a narrative to the findings to discover and communicate meaning.[5]

Thus, distinctions among forms blur. For example, no clear line separates the open-ended interview from the story. Interviewees often make points by telling stories, and storytellers often punctuate their narration with asides of commentary that are indistinguishable in form and content from interview responses. That said, for research it is helpful to make distinctions between forms, just as a writer should decide to approach a subject as fiction or nonfiction even though these two literary forms can be increasingly hard to differentiate.[6]

Our working definition of *story* is close to the traditional everyday use of the word. (For further details, see appendix A.) We strive to collect stories that have plot lines, however simple or tenuous, and that exist in time—what Paul Ricoeur calls "within-time-ness."[7] They have a beginning that could be nothing more than an arbitrary opening sentence ("Let me tell you this story about . . .") or could be a specific initiating event ("A few years ago this guy walked into my office . . ."). Stories also have a middle, which may include one or more digressions, and an end that brings the events to their logical or surprise conclusion. The conclusion may resolve the dilemmas or issues raised in the story, but some stories end with main issues unsettled: they just stop.

Good research stories provide details about events and setting. (Our step-by-step procedure for soliciting good research stories is described in appendix A.) They also tell us about the characters and their interactions, relationships, and feelings. Details about appearance, background, motives, emotional state, and relationships are essential guides to interpretation. The storyteller often is a first-person narrator, and details about the whiny client, hapless criminal, supportive supervisor, or meddling elected official all alter story meaning. Details about events, settings, and characters often present conflicting, ambiguous portraits of the workplace and the streets and of the workers and citizens. The details that make the characters vivid are the textual embodiments of the storytellers' judgments about the characters and events. Although stated as empirical observations, the details included in a story represent the storyteller's interpretations, not replicable observations. By examining story details, researchers anchor their interpretations in the storyteller's interpretations.

Not all of the stories collected for this research included detailed portraits of people, settings, and events. A few were one-dimensional, lifeless accounts that barely penetrated the surface of street-level judgment. Such stories tended to restate official policy and procedures. They were examined as carefully as others for themes but in the end proved less useful guides to interpretation. As in all research, narrative analysis depends on the richness of the data. In contrast to more standard interviews, one benefit of collecting stories is that they are likely to include complex, thick descriptions, although such results are not assured.

Storytelling creates its own context. For us, the research was the proximate context for storytelling—we solicited rather than overheard the stories. Storytelling occurs naturally in all social settings, and it would be ideal, if extraordinarily time-consuming, to observe and record naturally occurring storytelling. Indeed, some story-based researchers argue that it is not possible to understand stories separate from the telling; they insist that the meaning is unique to the particular enactment.[8] How, when, where, and to whom a story is told—and, just as important, how, when, where and to whom it is not told—are vital guides to interpretation. Our particular approach to story-based research does less well in sorting out this kind of information—all research requires compromises—but we do ask the storyteller to describe the context for storytelling. Many of the stories we collected were well known to others in the same setting; indeed, several storytellers told different versions of the same story. Moreover, our story-collection process occurred over several months. We would collect several stories and then make an appointment to return a month later with specific instructions that in our next visit we would like to collect stories heard, told, or recalled in the intervening month.

Like all methods, story-based research has strengths and weaknesses. Stories are less obtrusive than interviews. Interviews, whether in a fixed, random survey or an open-ended questioning of elites, are powerful and evocative research tools, but they are also an artifact of research; interviews do not exist absent the research process. Interviews set up a one-way information flow from respondent to researcher, and it is generally obvious to the respondent what the researcher wants to know. Story collection, as opposed to observing storytelling, is also an artifact of the research process, and storytellers are likely to tell researchers and other outsiders only certain stories. For example, police officers are often apologetic during field observation when there is little action, particularly related to crime fighting. A number of the stories police officers told us are action oriented and include high-speed chases and the lethal use of weapons. We clearly were told only certain stories, in part because workers have an image of their work and imagine what others want to hear about it.

Nonetheless, stories, unlike interviews, may have a life outside the research process, and the researchers' working propositions are less obvious to the storyteller. Simply put, asking street-level workers, as we did in exit interviews, to discuss their views on fairness in the delivery of government services solicits more socially and organizationally acceptable answers than those revealed in the stories told on the same subject by the same individuals. William Labov observes that personal narratives are uniquely expressive in communicating the storyteller's point of view even when the purpose of the storytelling is research:

> The most effective of these techniques produce narratives of personal experience, in which the speaker becomes deeply involved in rehearsing or even reliving events of his past. . . . Because they occur in response to a specific stimulus in the interview situation, they are not free of the interactive effect of the outside observer. The form they take is in fact typical of discourse directed to someone outside of the immediate peer group of the speaker. But because the experience and emotions involved here form an important part of the speaker's biography, he seems to undergo a partial reliving of that experience and he is no longer free to monitor his own speech as he normally does in face-to-face interviews.[9]

Moreover, stories offer kinds of information that are rarely found in interviews and especially in other quantitative forms of social scientific information. Stories allow the simultaneous expression of multiple points of view because they can sustain and suspend multiple voices and conflicting perspectives.[10] (It is important to always remember, however, that the storyteller decides which voices are allowed to speak; the multiple points of view remain an expression of a single author, the storyteller.) Stories can also present highly textured depictions of practices and institutions. Rather than merely repeating the rules, a story can show what situations call for certain routines and how the specifics of a case fit or do not fit standard practices. Stories illustrate the consequences of following, bending, or ignoring rules and practices. They bring institutions to life; they provide a glimpse of what it is like to cruise a tough neighborhood in a patrol car, to teach in an urban middle school, or to work in a state bureaucracy. For example, in "Recycling" (story 2.2), the frustrations of working in a process-bound bureaucracy are palpable. Before the voc rehab counselor could proceed with services, "every single thing that a doctor mentioned could possibly be wrong was evaluated beyond belief." Instead of securing needed services, the worker and the client spent all their time scheduling evaluations, completing the examinations, and waiting for results. The counselor eventually became so frustrated with the system that he convinced the client to file a complaint to force his supervisor to approve services.

Stories give prominence to human agency, to the role and voice of individuals with strengths and flaws and to their judgments and actions. "Narrative requires the narrator's perspective," write Molly Patterson and Kristen Renwick Monroe. "It cannot be voiceless."[11] Stories are driven by characters, actions, choices, and emotions. They offer insights into how actors make choices, understand their actions, and experience frustrations and satisfactions. Stories give research a pungency and vitality often absent from mainstream social science because they give such prominence to individual actions and motives and the human condition.[12]

Stories are told to express and sustain the values of a particular society or subgroup.[13] Language does not merely reflect the social world but also shapes it. We remember stories in part because they give guidance and coherence to our confusing world. Stories often stubbornly resist change even in the face of contradicting evidence "because they continue to underwrite and stabilize the assumptions for decision making in the face of high uncertainty, complexity, and polarization."[14] Stories are cultural artifacts that hold, in compact form, the norms, beliefs, and decision rules that guide actions and choices. Though not immutable, they resist change, thereby making them even more useful to the social scientist looking for patterns. We use stories, then, to search for decisional patterns that reveal how street-level workers defend their actions when formalized rules are in tension with personal beliefs.

Moreover, stories powerfully reveal the identities of the narrator. Patterson and Monroe stress that "narrative is especially useful in revealing the speaker's concept of self, for it is the self that is located at the center of the narrative. . . . The story explains and justifies why the life went a particular way, not just causally but, at some level, morally. . . . The narrative thus becomes an invaluable tool for political scientists concerned with how such issues as identity—group or individual—influence behavior."[15] When telling stories about their encounters with and moral judgments about citizen-clients, street-level workers tag people with identities while projecting the workers' own identities. As they classify citizens as good and bad, right and wrong, worthy and unworthy, they are also revealing the complexities of their identities as citizens and state workers. Although narratives provide explanations—often what appear to be fact-based explanations—all narratives are essentially normative.[16] To tell a story is to tell a moral.

A story's value lies in revealing interpretations and meaning, yet stories are objective in the sense that they can be reproduced into a text that can be transcribed, read, argued over, and interpreted by researchers and research subjects alike. No single story text is definitive, but a single rendition can provide a common starting place and a reference point for interpretation. Moreover, these text-based interpretations are "challengeable," which, along with presenting an explanation, constitutes one of the two major elements of theory building.[17] Accepting the hermeneutic tradition's central insight that "no interpretation, no reading, can be made in a wholly neutral or disinterested fashion,"[18] a text starting place provides interpretations with a discipline that at least offers the potential for reliable and shared interpretations so essential to the intellectual tradition of social science. As described in appendix A, we developed a thematic coding scheme for the stories (the codes are reproduced in appendix E). Each story was coded by a member of the research team and then double-checked by another. Beyond this more mechanical process, we continually asked ourselves and each other for support whenever observations and themes were discussed in the stories.

Stories subtly and poignantly reveal the norms and beliefs that shape and guide choices and actions. Stories have limits as research tools, however, which is why some form of multiple methods and triangulation remains the preferred approach to any research problem. In addition to collecting stories, we interviewed participants, collected data through a questionnaire, and spent considerable time as participant observers in the field (see appendix A).

Stories are not historically accurate reconstructions of events. As Gary Bellow and Martha Minow remind us, "All tellings are unique, incomplete, and inaccurate."[19] The more often a story is told and the further the story is in time from the recounted events, the more it reflects the norms and values of the storyteller and social institutions.

Although story texts are often stable over time and many retellings, they can be subtly altered and adjusted as they are recalled and retold; details about characters and events are added, lost, and recast. Storytellers embellish narratives by including elements from other events as well as from imagination, rumors, and gossip. Ironically, the more a story deviates from historical accuracy, the more fully and richly it depicts norms, values, and beliefs because these accounts more fully embody the storyteller's interpretation of events.

Stories are misleading about prevalence. They are biased toward the memorable and, therefore, the nonroutine and the dramatic. They exaggerate the good, the bad, and the unexpected and downplay the everyday. Police stories recall when a drug arrest ended in the death of an officer or when officers overlooked the cocaine in the dresser after a fireman's suicide, not the daily grind of patrol and routine traffic stops. The state worker tells stories of when the governor unexpectedly called, not about the drudgery of paperwork.[20] Social workers tell stories about the clients they saved with extraordinary effort, not those who are routinely processed.[21] As Labov writes, "if the event becomes common enough, it is no longer a violation of an expected rule of behavior, and it is not reportable."[22]

Stories are not, therefore, a random snapshot of events and individuals; rather, they are highly selected and continually emended portraits.[23] Individuals recall those characters and events that help make sense out of the buzzing confusion of experience, and storytellers combine, distill, alter, and fictionalize characters and events as they tell and listen to stories. This process gives stories their normative power. Stories cannot, however, tell the social accountant how often something happened.

A more troubling concern for story-based research is silence. Like other text-based research that relies on interviews and documents, stories perpetuate the conspiracy of silence about certain topics or issues that are so threatening or counternormative that they remain secret. Paying attention to what stories are never told is important to understanding normative orders because, as Anthony Alfieri asserts, "Acts of silencing are predicated on a normative preunderstanding."[24] Like the White House aide who no longer keeps notes for fear of subpoena, some stories are not told even when they are well known to insiders.

Told stories, in contrast to untold stories, tend to be conservative in that, as Patricia Ewick and Susan B. Silbey conclude, they "often articulate and reproduce existing ideologies and hegemonic relationships of power and inequality."[25] One can eavesdrop on these silences when people tell a personal story that they acknowledge that they would never tell at work; for example when an in-the-closet gay cop tells of letting off a gay prostitute. Or, at times, one organizational subculture may, with some perverse pleasure or as a power move, tell the secret stories of another subculture. What is not said and the stories that are not told are strong indicators of norms at work, but these silenced norms are far more difficult than voiced norms for outsiders to uncover. Nonetheless, we collected stories that clearly expressed the views and values of groups and individuals that are subversive to the interests of those in power. For example, a lesbian told a story of bending the rules to provide family leave to a lesbian couple (story 6.3), and many other stories in all five settings reveal judgments and acts that run counter to established ideology.[26]

The characteristics of a good story are frequently conceived in terms of aesthetics rather than social science. Some of the stories we and others collect are compelling narratives that capture attention and resonate with emotions, but research stories are often dull, with poorly drawn characters and pedestrian plots. In our research, we did not select research participants based on their skills as storytellers; we selected them because they were members of a targeted work group and because of their position as street-level workers. (Appendix A recounts the details of this selection process.) In many cases, we had to convince these workers that they did not need to be talented storytellers to have important stories to tell.[27] Moreover, dull, uninspired stories, as long as they are fully rendered, may tell us as much about norms and beliefs as a powerfully told story. Characteristics of a good story for research thus differ from a good story told in other contexts.

Good research stories, like all good social scientific information, focus on theoretically interesting issues or questions. A story-based researcher can go out and collect narratives that are then retrospectively examined for theory-relevant themes. Stories are so evocative that this undirected approach may be more productive than one might expect.[28] Or the researcher could, as we have done, direct the storyteller to focus on certain issues.

Each researcher will need to balance the trade-off between storyteller-guided and researcher-guided story collection, with most research remaining a creative blend of the two. In general, the storyteller needs guidance. Storytellers need adequate instruction so that they can focus the stories on the research topic. For example, we are studying how street-level workers resolve justice dilemmas as they deliver government services. After some trial and error, we discovered that the word *justice* is loaded, especially for police officers, and its use in instructions prompted storytellers to repeat official rather than first- or secondhand stories. In our revised instructions, we asked for stories about "fairness" or "unfairness" because these more humble words more closely fit the everyday world of patrol officers, teachers, and vocational rehabilitation counselors and resulted in more theoretically meaningful stories.

To be useful for research, stories must also be fully rendered. It is normal for storytellers, especially when telling well-known stories, to reduce narratives to compact and truncated stories, or gists. Gists are easier to remember, but they become a form of coded language that is highly evocative to insiders but less meaningful to outsiders. A fully rendered story comes from the collaboration of the teller and listener.[29] In the research setting, the listener is often the outsider-researcher whose goal is to guide the development of a fully articulated story that serves the research purpose.

In our research, we guided the story development in several ways. We did not collect stories on initial contact. After instructions on the types of stories, we made our story-collection appointment three or four weeks into the future. We then left with each storyteller a notebook that described the focus of the story collection and the characteristics of a good story and provided space for jotting notes. After collecting our first set of stories, we scheduled a second and usually a third story-collection appointment. This iterative process encouraged the worker-researcher collaboration in story collection.

As in interviews, the story-based researcher must prompt and prod storytellers to provide adequate details to render the story meaningful to researchers. This prompting involves both instructions and probes—some standard, some ad-libbed—that are used in a manner similar to open-ended interview probes. In this regard, it is often preferable for the storyteller to tell rather than write the story since writing has its own inhibitions. In most social contexts, stories are told rather than written and read. Oral stories are more free-flowing and rarely follow conventions of grammar and syntax, but since they are more spontaneous, they are more likely to omit crucial details. In our research protocol, storytellers complete their initial oral renditions of stories uninterrupted by researchers, who then follow up with probes for missing and ambiguous details. After all the stories were collected and transcribed, all storytellers received the opportunity to review their stories. We discouraged wholesale revision but allowed storytellers to edit their stories to make sure, in the end, that we were examining their, not our, renditions of street-level work stories (see appendix A).

Finally, stories should be collected in adequate numbers to allow cross-story and, if possible, cross-setting analysis. Qualitative researchers constantly struggle with depth versus breadth trade-offs, and much certainly can be learned from one or two richly detailed stories. Nonetheless, much of the current story-based research relies on too few stories to allow for the examination of common themes and to ask questions regarding the influence of setting on norms and choices. Increasing the number of stories increases leverage over research problems and yields comparable observations that strengthen interpretations.[30] In our three years of fieldwork, we collected 157 stories from forty-eight street-level workers in five research sites in two states. Street-level workers from different states and work settings told stories with similar themes, allowing us to put forward the citizen-agent narrative and its coexistence with the state-agent narrative as a worker-centered interpretation of street-level decision making.

4. Physical and Emotional Spaces

Story 4.1.   Urban Middle School
"Tough Neighborhood"

[Joe] was a student I had for English two years ago. He had a very likeable personality but also a highly explosive temper, and he was very inclined to do as little as possible. Joe, like many of our students, had an unstable family life. He was living with his grandmother at the time he attended [urban middle school]. He had little contact with his father, and he only made vague references to having seen his mother.

For Joe, fairness and justice didn't really apply. By the time he reached eighth grade, he had already been manipulating the school system for some time, or so he thought. He was quite adept at talking his way out of troublesome situations, but as the year wore on, his compilations of misdeeds caught up with him, and he began receiving more and more suspensions, culminating in a long-term suspension. . . .

Some days he was receptive, and some days he wasn't. He came to school last September to tell me he was still attending [local high school], but I heard he stopped attending school and had moved to [big city in an adjacent state]. . . .

Monday, April 21, we were told by Joe's half sister that he had been shot in the chest over the weekend and was in critical condition. . . . Unfortunately, Joe's story is one of many that includes violence. I'm sure that will always be the case.

"Tough Neighborhood" is not much of a story. It has only one character, Joe, and no discernable action or plot, but in just a few lines it paints a social portrait of teaching in an urban middle school. This

36

story sets a stage on which difficult and despairing decisions are made about real kids in all-too-real situations. We know this story: the teacher is drawn to the likeable but troubled kid from a broken home, the inexorable transgressions and punishments, dropping out, the violent end. What is striking about this story is its blandness ("one of many that includes violence") and its hopelessness ("I'm sure that will always be the case"). This story does not describe the heroic achievements of the storyteller teacher; it is an epitaph for a lost kid. It also tells the listener what it is like, some of the time and with some of the kids, to be a teacher, letting your heart reach out and the inevitable feeling of loss.

The research site depicted in "Tough Neighborhood" is an urban middle school in an economically depressed, midsized midwestern city. This city is an island of poverty in an area of prosperity and growth. A thirty-minute drive in any direction will lead to ever-expanding suburbs, packed shopping malls, office parks, and prosperous rural towns. This run-down city has few shops and businesses other than overpriced convenience stores; used-car lots; pawn shops; check-cashing windows; and the tenants of last resort, federal, state, and local government offices. There are no hotels or motels and few national chain stores. Within the city limits there are places that could be called middle class, but even those teeter on the edge of viability. Many of the neighborhoods are decidedly dilapidated, especially the large public housing projects. This city has the state's highest crime rate, highest murder rate, lowest median income, highest percentage of minorities, and lowest educational level.

The middle school is a large, older brick building at the bottom of a hill. It sits between a rail yard and a housing project. The high school is at the top of a hill, with older kids hanging out near the middle school at the beginning and end of the school day. Court-ordered desegregation has split the school evenly: one-third African-American, one-third Hispanic, and one-third white. Without the court order, the school would be mostly black, with a growing Hispanic presence. Most of the teachers are white. The school is locked twenty-four hours a day, with security patrols inside and out. The eighth-grade team, regular and special-subject teachers, participated in this research.

Two other research sites are within a ten-minute drive. Near the downtown, in an old shopping mall that was converted to government offices, is the local branch of the state vocational rehabilitation (VR) office, the second site. The local parole office is next door. The VR counselors work in cubicles with curtains for doors or out in the community, visiting clients and other service providers. Further downtown is the police department, the third site. It is located in a tall municipal office building. Although patrol officers come to the base for before- and after-shift briefings—several joked that local thieves always chose shift changes for break-ins since no officers were on the streets—most of their work is out in their patrol area. The patrol area for our research site was in a destitute area of the central city that had the highest crime rate in this high-crime city.

We also collected street-level worker stories from a vocational rehabilitation office and police patrol unit in a prosperous and densely populated urban city located in the center of a western metropolis, the fourth and fifth sites. The population of the western city is ethnically and economically diverse and a point of settlement for new immigrants, including many Latinos. Still, the western city lacks the pervasive poverty or the run-down neighborhoods of the midwestern city. The western vocational rehabilitation office is located in an area with a number of governmental offices that lease space from owners of low-rise business complexes. The office is surrounded by residential apartment complexes populated by students who attend a local university and workers in service and tourist industries. Each counselor had a private office, and although caseloads are diverse, clients are not as poor as those in the midwestern city.

The western police patrol unit or work group we came to know operates in the agency's downtown headquarters, located just across the street from the city's municipal building, in the heart of a redeveloped downtown. The patrol unit works the downtown area and the surrounding neighborhoods, which include a long-established barrio, student rental properties, and renovated older homes occupied by professionals drawn to the downtown scene. In contrast to the midwestern police department, the patrol unit and its supervisors are more diverse, with women prominent in management and supervisory roles. At the beginning of the fieldwork, the patrol commander was a white woman, unusual in a still male dominated profession. Also in contrast to the midwestern site, the western department has a reputation for being innovative. The midwestern department was organized around roving patrol cars and quick 911 response, whereas the western department was among the first wave of law enforcement agencies to adopt community policing as a forcewide practice.

Our five research sites are located in two contrasting urban areas and encompass three very different types of street-level work. Teachers are respected if undervalued professionals. Like all street-level workers, they are in constant face-to-face contact with citizen-clients—in their case, kids and parents. Behind the closed classroom door, they are in charge. Although working with a set curriculum that they have little or no say in designing and under the supervision of the principal and vice principals, teachers have considerable sway over what they teach and how they treat their students and their families. In our research site, the school's external environment is dangerous, and the halls and lunchroom can be chaotic and threatening, but the classrooms are havens of control and order. Yet, as "Tough Neighborhood" suggests, the teachers are painfully aware of how little they can do for the kids who are so briefly their students.

Vocational rehab is a state-managed but primarily federally funded program for disabled citizens. Originally established in 1918 to help disabled World War I veterans return to work or be retrained for alternative work, VR now encompasses all disabled citizens—poverty is not a requirement for eligibility. Recipients must have a documented disability—the definition is continually revised, however—and need help to prepare for, obtain, or maintain appropriate employment. Like teachers, who have little influence over the design of curriculum and the students who attend their classes, VR counselors have little say over who qualifies for services. Also like teachers, VR workers have and exercise broad decision-making powers over the nature and quality of the services provided. While rules and bureaucratic processes are ever present, decisional space opens for both teachers and VR counselors as they close their doors and interact with their respective constituencies.

VR clients range from high-school-age young adults to those nearing retirement age. Some are injured on the job and need physical therapy. Others need a prosthesis, retraining, or "work hardening," learning how to avoid injuries. Still others survived crippling auto accidents or have poor health from years of hard drinking. Some clients are blind or deaf; some have congenital disabilities; many are mentally ill. Even within these categories, there is a wide range of individuals. Some are seen as heroic, the "super crips," who despite their disability retain their positive spirit.[1] Others, especially those the counselors diagnose as having personality disorders, are, as one worker put it, "a real pain." In the midwestern voc rehab office, nearly all the clients were also poor and lacked social skills and social support.

The design of police work is outside the control of street cops. Legal rules define criminal activity. Police administrators, in collaboration with local political and business leaders, federal authorities, and academic consultants, determine the basic model of policing that a municipal agency will follow. For example, the current move toward community policing has been mandated from the top down.[2] While operating in a work environment saturated with rules, procedures, and multiple levels of oversight, street-level cops have enormous flexibility in deciding who they are going to help and who they are going to subject to sanctions. This sets them apart from VR counselors and teachers, who have little control over whom they serve: clients appear in the voc rehab agency waiting rooms and kids arrive in the classrooms on the first day of school. In terms of adapting services to citizens and deciding what, if any, sanctions they will impose on actions, street cops, like teachers and counselors, have broad powers.

Police work also differs from teaching and counseling in that it is largely a territorial practice, and, much more than teachers and counselors, police officers represent and are authorized to employ the state's coercive power.[3] Cops, whose bodies are uniformed with state symbols, rely on the threat or use of force to stop, interrogate, detain, and sometimes brutalize citizens. Police see themselves as not only enforcers of the law but as moral agents, a characteristic they share with teachers and VR counselors.[4]

Whether their workplace is on the street, in a classroom, or in a cubicle, the work lives of cops, teachers, and counselors are shaped by the complex network of government organizations. Rules, mandates, laws, and procedures as well as resources and expectations flow in constant but ever-changing streams from federal, state, and local elected bodies and agencies. These countless little streams (such as a local parent group worried about profanity in reading assignments) or major tributaries (for example, U.S. Justice Department regulations regarding racial profiling by police) deposit layers of rules and procedures on street-level agencies. Every legislative investigation, every new law, every administrative change, every supervisor's good idea, and every street-level worker's publicized mistake generates a new regulation, a new procedure, and a new form to fill out.

Street-level workers constantly complain that complying with procedures crowds out work with citizen-clients. Pinned to the walls of the cubicles of countless street-level workers are faded photocopies of a cartoon of a man sitting on the toilet with the caption, "The work isn't finished until the paperwork is done." Although their work worlds differ, cops, teachers, and counselors face dilemmas that put rules and beliefs about the right thing to do into play as these workers contemplate how to act toward citizen-clients. The interplay of rules and beliefs is encrypted in the language these workers use and especially in the stories they tell.[5] In these mundane bureaucratic settings saturated with layers of rules, it may seem surprising to find a strong undercurrent of emotional engagement ranging from fear of violence to strong feelings about the character of citizen-clients.

Story 4.2.   Midwestern Police Department
"In 1983 I Was Shot"

Last week the chief called me in and jokingly asked me if I qualified my firearms weapon service for January–July. I had qualified the day before, and he knew I had, and I said, "Yeah."

He said, "Would you mind bringing in the gun so I can send it over to forensics for a comparison?" And I laughed and said, "Why?" I thought he was kidding.

He said that they had found a particular individual who was a victim of a homicide the day before, and the name of the individual was the name of a juvenile who had been one of the three juveniles who had shot me in 1983.

It turned out he was not [the same person]. [There were] two brothers, and he was not the one involved in the shooting. But it made me think back to 1983. . . . In 1983 I was shot.

I went back to that particular night. It was cold. December 3, 1983. I remember certain things. I was meeting with another officer, it was thirteen degrees below zero, the actual temperature. And it was me and another officer about 3:00 in the morning; maybe 2:30 in the morning. And a call came out about a disturbance. . . . Two units are responsible for that area. I knew that the one officer was getting lunch or breakfast at that time. He was a friend of mine, so I volunteered to take his call because he was eating lunch and I didn't want to disrupt him and it was cold.

The calls are very minimal in the middle of the night, especially in 1983. So I went to the call and talked to the lady who was threatening to shoot some people. . . . We talked to the people and resolved the situation.

We went over to our police cars and right across the street in the 900 to 950 block near the 7-Eleven. It's no longer there—it's there but it is boarded up. We drove across the street. The other officer and I got out. I pulled open the door for him, and he walked through the door.

As I stepped through the door, the door shattered behind me. And I very distinctly remember thinking that it was so cold that it had just shattered from the cold. And I started to turn to see what had happened when I got struck in the back by something I couldn't see, and it sent me into a 360 degree turn and actually knocked me to the ground. As I started to fall to the ground, I knew that I had been shot just by the feeling, the burning, but mostly it's like being hit with a very large thing, not like a point, the force of it. . . .

So the other officer asks, "Are you okay?" And I say, "No, I've been hit." He looks over and of course we're wearing all sorts of clothing over clothing and he says, "Yeah, yeah, you have a hole in your back." He got on the radio and said we'd been fired upon and officer down. . . . And the first person on the scene was the officer who had been originally sent to that call, and I think he felt very bad because I had made the call for him.

He came running through the glass and figured out where the shooting was coming from. He could see it was three juveniles that were about half a block down the street.

That's where they were. They had stolen the gun and other stuff from the houses in the area. They always frequented that 7-Eleven store, playing games, shoplifting. The manager had removed them from the store and had disallowed them from coming back in.

So in one of the robberies they stole the gun. They were going to go up there [to the 7-Eleven] that night. Why? Simply 2:00 in the morning to shoot out the windows to scare the manager or shoot the manager. I'm not sure which. When they saw two police officers pull up, they thought, "Why not shoot them as well?"

Story 4.3. Midwestern Vocational Rehabilitation
"The Loaded Purse"

I remember one lady, she had done time—done prison for shooting her husband. I got her records and the story said that she pulled a gun out of her purse and shot him at point-blank range. So there were some psychiatric things involved with her.

So, anyway, she was out of prison and on parole, and they referred her here. This was twenty years ago. She wanted to set up her own cosmetology business. She wanted to buy a bunch of equipment. With her situation and all—being self-employed and running your own business and having to deal with the public is really a lot of stress and pressure—and I had to say, "I just don't think so. You know, if you want us to help you get a job some-place, [we can], but I just don't think that setting up your own business is something that we really ought to do."

She picked up her purse up off the floor, put it on her lap, and reached into her purse. I was ready to hit the deck—"Oh, jeez. . . ." I was ready to say, "On second thought, that plan really didn't sound so bad, [Jane], you know."

And she pulls out a pack of cigarettes. But, anyway, she didn't threaten me, but I had conjured that up in my mind that it's all over.

So, anyway, she accepted [our job plan]. We didn't set her up in her own business, but this wasn't a big deal for her.

Stories create settings—physical and emotional spaces—and these settings describe how street-level workers feel about their work worlds. By exaggeration—"thirteen degrees below zero"—and repetition, "In 1983 I Was Shot" stresses how cold it was on that late-night police patrol. In a section of the story not reproduced here, the storyteller rationalizes his decision not to wear his bulletproof vest: "It was cold. If I don't wear a vest, I can wear another shirt instead." Details about the neighborhood are scant except for the pervading sense that this is a dangerous place and that the danger is lurking and unpredictable. The officer calms a potentially violent domestic disturbance and is then shot when entering a nearby convenience store simply because three kids, angered at the store manager, thought, "Why not just shoot [the cops] as well?" Acknowledging the ever-present danger, a western patrol officer admitted, "I wear body armor. If I'm in uniform, I wear body armor everywhere. That was a promise I made to my kids because they asked me to."

Fear of violence also enters the work world of the voc rehab counselor, but in "The Loaded Purse" the fear is portrayed with self-depre-cating humor. Like all street-level workers, voc rehab counselors must deal with unpleasant, sometimes scary clients. Clients are prominent features of the street-level workers' physical and emotional spaces, the foreground. All else is background. In this story, the physical setting is implied—the counselor is in his office cubicle interviewing a new client—but the emotional setting is carefully drawn. Counselors frequently conflict with unrealistic clients who the counselors think want more than the agency can offer—in this case, setting up the client in her own beauty salon—or more than they think the client can benefit from or manage. These encounters are always tinged with conflict, or latent conflict, a characteristic of street-level work highlighted by the details of this particular client: she is a violent psychotic who went to jail for pulling a gun from her purse and shooting her husband. When in the story she reaches for her purse as the counselor denies an unrealistic request, the everyday tension between client and counselor is clarified by exaggeration, and fear enters the emotional space between client and counselor. Then, wonderfully, the tension dissipates as the client "pulls out a pack of cigarettes" and proves unarmed and cooperative.

Street-level work is not antiseptic but personal and close. The emotional space created in street-level work and stories is best described by three pairs of poles: deadening routine and moments of panic, chaos, and violence; benevolence and revulsion; and hopelessness and accomplishment. These extremes describe the range of worker emotions and, therefore, the boundaries of the emotional space of street-level work. But more than marking emotional territory, street-level work often shifts abruptly from one pole to the other. These rapid, unpredictable shifts in emotion give street-level stories their edge and highlight the undercurrent of tension and apprehension rife in street-level work, which is unsettled, always churning.

Much street-level work is remorselessly routine. Workers follow set schedules and long-memorized procedures. Counselors and police officers must file lengthy reports, although most paperwork is now done on computer. Teachers repeat lessons from set curricula and textbooks bought by the district: what was taught last year is nearly identical to what will be taught this year, a routine that spans teachers' careers. All must fight boredom, but, as in "In 1983 I Was Shot," that routine is unpredictably interrupted by moments of chaos, panic, and danger. A late-night domestic-violence call ends without incident, whereas walking into a convenience store for a snack leads to getting shot. This extreme of routine and panic is more visible in criminal-justice work—police, prison, probation and parole, and immigration—but is present in all forms of street-level work.

An essential character of this emotional space is the unpredictable and rapid shifts between these poles, as demonstrated by a second domestic-violence story with the exaggerated elements of a tall tale.

Physical and Emotional Spaces

Story 4.4.   Midwestern Police Department
"The Ex-Marine on Steroids"

About February last year I responded to a domestic-violence call in a part of our city. And the standard practice is that you usually wait about a block or so away until your backup unit gets there so you don't get into a situation you can't handle.

On this particular evening I stopped, waited a block away, notified the dispatcher I was standing by. And at that time I was approached by a black male and a black female. And what happened was they were arguing and they were walking down the street and saw my police car. . . .

So I got out of my car, and he starts telling his version of the story and the whole time she's screaming, "Arrest him! Arrest him! He hit me! Arrest him!"

So I listened to his version of the story. I listened to hers. And the story was that they had gotten into a verbal argument and he had hit her. And this guy was probably six feet, three inches tall and 215 pounds, and it was all muscle. He had just gotten released out of the Marine Corps after fourteen years of service. And what I found out later that I did not know at the time was that he was high on steroids.

So my backup still had not gotten there, and I started to stall and everything. I said, "You were wrong for what you did, and I am going to have to arrest you."

He said, "You are not arresting me. I am the one who called."

And I said, "I know you are the one who called, but unfortunately, you are the one who broke the law."

And he said, "You are not arresting me."

So I notified my backup and told him to speed up. And when I went to grab ahold of [the man], . . . he hit me in the face and cut open my eye. . . . And then he got ahold of me, threw me up in the air about twelve feet, and I hit a telephone pole. I weigh 240 pounds with all my equipment on. . . . I could see him grab my gun. . . . I knew he was winning [the fight over the gun], and I knew that my backup was close, and I did not want someone else to get hurt with my gun so I rolled over and I laid on my gun and I let him beat me while I was waiting. And then . . . my backup pulled up, . . . and we were able to take him into custody.

Well, when it goes to trial, they plea-bargain it out. He pleaded guilty to a misdemeanor battery. They dropped the criminal damages, they dropped the resisting arrest. He had a $150 fine and fifty-five days in jail, five days for time served, and the rest was probation.

In this story, the by-the-book handling of an all-too-common domestic-violence call quickly and unpredictably shifts to a violent confrontation in which the outmuscled officer is attacked by an ex-Marine on steroids. The officer, in addition to the black female, becomes the object of domestic violence, taking on the victim role. It is surprising that this officer would tell such a humiliating story—machismo norms would likely silence such stories—although the exaggerated details about the size, strength, and steroid use soften the humiliation. The emotional message is clear, however. Although eventually rescued by his backup, the officer is alone in a dangerous place that unpredictably shifts from routine to violence.

Experienced street-level workers internalize this emotional dilemma. Even during routine actions, they anticipate the danger. One western police officer recalls,

After getting off the phone, I had a sense of fear setting in. I picked it up off the dispatcher's voice as he spoke to me. Just before leaving my house, I was standing at the trunk, the rear of my police car, putting on my ballistic vest. My hand started to shake and my voice quit, and my wife then told me, "Take it easy. You've done this a hundred times over. You'll be okay."

In this story the canine officer's dog is killed, an event described with the same sorrow as having a human partner killed. He was not okay, and in this story, like so many stories, the line between routine and chaos is quickly crossed.

Just as they work in environments that shift unpredictably between numbing routine and moments of danger and chaos, street-level workers are pulled between the feelings of benevolence and revulsion. Workers at times feel great compassion for citizen-clients, and the professional and the personal merge. The distance created by authority that separates counselor and client, teacher and student, and police officer and community member often disappears and is replaced by a strong, almost familial, bond between them. This close emotional space is the source of caring and concern but also of revulsion and, at times, anger. In this emotional space, the significance of who people are, their identity and character, is revealed as central to workers' accounts of why they do what they do. The importance of identity and moral judgment to the citizen-agent narrative is taken up in depth in the next two sections of the book. Here, we focus on the emotional content of the stories as context for revealing these normative dimensions of street-level work.

As will become increasingly evident throughout this book, in story after story, cops, teachers, and counselors describe their close personal bond with citizen-clients. In "Slammed in the Rear" (story 2.1), a VR counselor goes far out of his way to help a borderline client, even "spend out of pocket about $1,000 in repairing his car," with the only explanation, "I liked this guy." The counselor is punished for his over-investment when the client rear-ends the counselor's car. Another counselor became a "parking lot therapist" for a client for whom she felt a connection (story 8.1): "He was a real interesting person. Looked real tough. Dressed in black—black jeans; big black motorcycle boots; long, long hair, down to his waist, pulls it back in a ponytail; wears dark glasses; wears muscle shirts, looking real mean and tough. But he is a pussycat."

A western police officer befriends a "young gal by the name of [April]. By then she was probably in sixth grade and she was rather heavily into crystal [methamphetamine], alcohol, and was pretty promiscuous. But she was really a good kid. I know it sounds crazy when you say that, but she was a good kid." The officer and the girl became friends, "over a couple of years, if I was sitting someplace, April would show up. We would sit and chat." The story skips ahead a number of years, and "then this young lady comes up to the car window and starts talking to me. . . . I had no idea who this woman was. . . . It turned out to be April, and she was a beautiful young woman. . . . She turned to me and said, 'You know, you were the only person that cared enough to listen. . . . You're the only person that never asked me for anything. You just helped me out here and there.'" The relationship between the storytelling cop and April was more like that between a father and daughter than a cop and a troubled kid.

The close personal and emotional space shared by street-level workers and citizen-clients can also be a source of revulsion. The position or nature of their work insulates others in state agencies from the public. For example, we interviewed a state worker who processed disability claims and who said that in twenty years he had met face to face with

only one client. In contrast, street-level workers have daily, almost elemental encounters with citizen-clients. Such workers experience the
whiny clients, encounter the strutting gang kids, and receive indifferent
stares from students. Those on the front lines smell the alcoholics, deal
with angry parents, and argue with uncooperative clients, unable to
escape into the cold abstractions that characterize the thinking of others in the policy-making world. Voc rehab counselors do not think
about the disabled but deal with specific cases. Police officers do not
deal with "juveniles" or "career criminals" or other terms but confront
the people on their beats. And teachers are less concerned with educational policy issues than with dealing with their classes.

The same intimacy that engenders compassion can sour to disregard
and contempt. One voc rehab counselor admitted to her dislike of one
of her mentally ill clients:

> It's difficult to work with whiny people. [A particular client] was
> one of those people who call in, "I got this other problem, poor
> me, what am I going to do, and can you do this for me?" Every-
> one has problems, and once in a while people do need assistance
> with their problems, but with her it was a constant thing. "Oh, my
> sister came to my door and didn't have a place to live. She's my
> sister and I have to take her in, but she drives me crazy. And my
> boyfriend, he's abusive to me and I can't get rid of him." And on
> and on until I don't want to hear any more. I don't want to talk
> to her anymore. Just go away.

Finally, street-level workers are torn by feelings of genuine accomplishment (they make a profound and lasting difference in the lives of
people—often needy people) and a pervasive sense of hopelessness (no
matter what they do, it is not enough or will make little difference). The
same voc rehab counselor who complains of the difficulty of working
with "whiny people" describes how she makes lasting improvements in
the lives of others. Counselors describe how providing a new set of
false teeth, fixing a broken hearing aid, finding the right workplace,
installing a wheelchair lift, and providing the right training and emotional support change clients' life prospects.

Teachers and cops tell similar stories in which their efforts result in
life-altering changes. The teacher sees a disruptive kid and gets the
family much needed help. The cop, as in April's story, befriends a juvenile on the verge of committing serious crimes who then grows up to
become a responsible adult. Time and again, street-level workers

express their deep sense of personal accomplishment in helping individuals. They do not tell stories about efficiently implementing public policy; they tell stories about using policy and the system to serve individuals.

Story 4.5.   Midwestern Vocational Rehabilitation
"You Can't Win for Losing"

We had a lady named [Michelle] who was one of my first new clients. I took her in the spring of 1989. . . . She is a lady who used to work in insurance as a data entry person, then she developed diabetes and diabetic retinopathy, and so her eyes were starting to lose vision. . . . She wanted to have services so she could go back into that kind of work. She also needed some assistance in taking care of herself at home because she couldn't see well and her vision was going down rapidly.

So we opened a case, and we did all sorts of services. We had a rehabilitation teacher go out and assess her in her home. We provided services to help her take care of herself at home—like label her appliances for her so she could use them, you know, with braille language and large print, the microwave, the washer and dryer, and these sorts of things. We helped her learn how to use a cane.

We said she had a great need for training and vision skills, so we sent her to [a residential program] for about five or six months. She learned braille, how to use the cane safely, and learned how to use the typewriter. With the vision loss she was exposed to talking computers. It was a really good work over. . . .

She was in the hospital quite a bit, and she ended up on [kidney] dialysis. . . . Well, she didn't feel . . . that she had the stamina . . . to work a full-time job. . . . She said she wanted to try medical transcription. . . . We can get the computer equipment for her at home, so she can do it when she felt good and when she doesn't have dialysis because dialysis takes three or four hours and it really tires people out. . . . We helped her with some transportation costs and with the tuition costs of taking a few courses for medical transcription and medical technology. . . .

We finished that, . . . and then her health went down again. She had several different hospital stays, and when she was finally done, she wasn't sure she could do the medical transcription. . . . About fifteen months later her husband called and said that she died from complications from her diabetes.

She was a very nice lady, a very motivated lady, despite all of the health problems. . . . We did all we can to provide the kind of services to her, . . . but . . . we couldn't provide the kind of finish to the case because of her health. That is your "can't win for losing" story.

Individual citizen-clients are also a source of hopelessness. Sometimes this is expressed in juxtaposition with accomplishment, as in "You Can't Win for Losing." Other stories express more despair. The kids in the urban middle school are too unmotivated, their families too disconnected and dysfunctional, and the neighborhood too poor and dangerous for the teachers to make a real difference in most of their students' lives. In the midwestern city, the police officers feel that juries ignore evidence and so do not bother arresting criminals. Police officers in both cities confront people with no conscience who are what the officers call just "bad guys." Voc rehab counselors have clients who try to scam the system, are lazy, or have "personality disorders" that preclude any possibility of success. Street-level workers recognize that they can do nothing for some individuals: some cases, some situations are hopeless. How these workers respond to this hopelessness is a core issue in street-level work life. The physical and emotional setting creates a context for the importance of identity and moral judgment in street-level work, the subjects of the next two sections of this book.

Part II. Enacting Identities in the Workplace and on the Streets

Street-level workers care as much about who a person is as about what the person has done. Identity matters as much as acts. By identity, we mean how we come to recognize ourselves and each other through group belonging.[1] All of us belong to certain groups: this is to say that we occupy subject positions. For example, street-level workers belong to various occupational groups and are recognized for their belonging to racial, class, gender, and sexual groupings. Each of these group memberships (for example, working-class, white, female, heterosexual) represents what we call a subject position. Each subject position is filled with meaning, so that being hailed as a cop, a Latino, or a female often defines our expectations of who we are and the expectations others have of us. Identity, then, provides a way of organizing the social world, of endowing both ourselves and others with recognizable meaning.

There is a dynamism to identity because people occupy a number of subject positions that combine or intersect amid the shifting contexts of everyday life. For example, the occupational identity "rookie police officer" may give way to a racial identity as a cop sheds the uniform, drives through a posh business district in an upscale new car, and is pulled over by a police officer from another jurisdiction. Pulling out law enforcement identification is likely again to shift the motorist's identity. For the officer who initiated the stop, the motorist is resignified as a fellow officer; for the rookie cop, his black maleness may fill his sense of belonging at that moment.

Street-level workers have strong occupational identities. Particularly for police officers, conventional wisdom holds that the bonds of occupational identity are highly salient, creating a local culture of shared beliefs that enable cops to handle tensions in the workplace and danger on the streets. This bonding in turn produces a group loyalty and a code of silence in which officers are loathe to reveal the wrong-doing of fellow officers.[2] We find evidence of bonding among street-level workers that is consistent with conventional wisdom and existing literature. Street-level workers unite against management to push grievances and close ranks to protect the reputation of workers even when there is evidence of criminal wrongdoing. We take this up in chapter 5.

But stories and field notes also reveal that street-level workers take on their identities differently within and across professions. Cops, teachers, and vocational rehabilitation counselors offer unique markers of their occupational identities, establishing unwritten but enforceable expectations of the "good" worker and defining their jobs' key tensions and contradictions. While these expectations and work tensions are commonly understood, they are sufficiently incomplete to enable workers to fill in their occupational identities in particular ways. For example, some police officers occupy their identities on and off duty, carrying concealed weapons and positioning themselves in restaurants with a clear view of the front door. Others submerge their occupational identities the moment they put on their street clothes and take up other subject positions, such as "students" attending university classes or "coaches" of neighborhood ball teams.

Like the complex array of identities evident in contemporary public agencies, divisions are also a strong feature of the organizational environments we observed. We take up the divisive qualities of identity and identification in the workplace in chapter 6. The state-agent narrative puts workers in a bureaucratic setting where they struggle against management to retain discretionary powers and preserve their self-interests. But the stories told to us suggest that the conventional wisdom of bureaucratic division is overstated. What is more striking in the narratives is how the growing diversification of the workforce is generating identity enclaves for workers (or social and cultural space for group belonging) and redefining these agencies' internal politics.[3] Like urban neighborhoods, the urban work sites we studied are occupied by street-level workers who draw significantly on their generational, religious, class, physical, ethnic, racial, sexual, and gender identities to form bonds and declare differences in their daily interactions with one another.[4] Younger workers distance themselves from older workers who are less sensitive to issues of race, ethnicity, gender, and sexuality. Feminists and lesbian feminists have gained dominance in one of the vocational rehabilitation work sites; as a result, the few white male workers tell stories of occupying the margin rather than the center of organizational life. In one of the law enforcement agencies, lesbian officers occupy line and supervisory positions and are sufficiently networked to press for changes in the way their agency imagines family. Their gains are, in turn, a source of agitation for officers of color, who see white female lesbians as unfairly advantaged.

At least in the urban work sites of our study, the politics of bureaucratic stratification, particularly managers versus workers, is being supplanted by a complex politics of identity in which workers and managers take up belonging in one or more of the many identity enclaves. These enclaves provide a sense of place and a site for the accumulation of power. Holding these work sites together becomes more of a challenge. Workers retain a sense of common belonging related to their occupational identities. Bureaucratic norms and those who define them continue to communicate the ranks of the organization and define the structure of rewards, thus keeping people in line. But as the absolute dominance of traditional enclaves—particularly white male heterosexual networks—are challenged and power is more broadly distributed, some work sites, like some urban neighborhoods, are generating local cultures where order has to be negotiated amid difference.

Street-level workers also come face to face with difference in the many strangers they encounter on the streets, in the hallways, and across the desk. Getting a fix on who people are becomes a centerpiece of their work. Chapter 7 takes up identity and identification's significance for street-level work. Appearance, skin color, gender, and age are filled with social meanings and provide workers with quick composites for getting a fix on the people initially encountered on the street, in the hallways of an urban school, or across the desk of a vocational rehabilitation work site. In figuring out who a person is, front-line workers also can put a fix on people, assigning them a social identity or group belonging that carries with it significant meaning and consequence. Especially in first encounters where fear and danger are evident, street-level workers tend to use their powers of cultural definition to flatten peoples identities or (en)force their membership in stigmatized social groupings.

In addition, stories reveal sustained interaction's significance in how workers employ social identity and identification in making sense of people and circumstances. For example, a vocational rehabilitation worker, recognizing the multiple and intersecting identities of a client she has counseled for a period of time, uses her persuasive powers to encourage a citizen-client to change his identity in the workplace, where performing as a deaf person is defeating his career goals. With prolonged interactions, workers and citizen-clients are more likely to share languages and culturally recognizable symbols. They are more likely to understand each other, to interpret words and deeds in a larger, less stereotypical context. Prolonged interaction encourages street-level workers to see common ground, whereas short-term contacts highlight differences. Stories with short time frames, featuring one or few encounters with strangers, are about fear, confrontation, the flattening of identities and its negative consequences. In contrast, stories of sustained interactions between workers and citizens tend to offer thick accounts of who people are, imbuing citizens with complex identities and presenting positive outcomes that signify the rewards of street-level work. These stories also tend to project workers' bonds with citizen-clients, representing them as matched or at least as having similar identities.

What tends to interrupt the positive direction of sustained interaction is citizen conduct that workers deem inappropriate for the circumstances. Workers expect civility in conversation and deference to their advice. When incivility and failure to defer are evident in the stories of sustained interaction, citizens tend to be fixed with a stigmatized identity and experience negative sanctions to teach lessons in civility and morality.[5] Part 3 turns to the moral weight of street-level decision making, a pervasive feature of workers' normative orientations.

5. Workers Unite: Occupational Identities and Peer Relations

Story 5.1.   Midwestern Vocational Rehabilitation
"Bonus Check"

Back when I was an income-maintenance worker, we went through computer conversion when we converted all of our files and put them on the computer. We had all gone through training—and for some a couple of weeks training—and we came back and all had like over two hundred on our caseload. So we had all these cases to put on our computers, and of course we were still having to do our regular work. To try to do all that we were having to work a lot of hours overtime, for which we really weren't getting paid.

Well, the income-maintenance workers filed a grievance of sorts—I don't know if it was like a fair-labor-type thing. I had already switched over to vocational rehabilitation by the time that the grievance and all that was filed. Anyway, they did find in favor of the income-maintenance workers and said that was above and beyond the call of duty to have to work all those hours of overtime and that we should in fact be compensated for that. So they did it. I mean, what I got in pay really was minuscule compared to the hours that I had spent.

So I ended up getting kind of like this little bonus check that was like, I don't know, $150 or something like that. I ended up getting this little bonus check because the workers had filed like a class-action suit or that type of thing.

Story 5.2.   Western Police Department
"Getting Rid of the Cocaine"

This is an incident that occurred about six years ago. I'm not sure of the exact date, but I can certainly get that. It actually involved a local fireman. He and his wife were actually in the process of buying a brand-new home that they had saved for quite a few years. And as they went to secure the loan and buy the property, the stress level for the fireman had raised quite a bit, and because I believe that just payments and things to that effect were going to be quite a bit more than the current ones that he had on his home. And he also hadn't sold his first home, so he got in the bind of making payments both on his current home and on the property that he had just bought. And as time went on, he started to speak, uh, somewhat irrational, and his wife started to notice he seemed to be under a great deal of stress by his actions and his behavior. Well, one day she called a friend of his [who was a police officer, and he found the fireman dead].

It looked like a plain suicide, which is really all that it was—tragic suicide, but nothing really more complicated than that. They had to go through his property and things, his dresser and things of that effect to look for any suicide notes or anything that may have foretold what was to happen. As he was doing this, in a pair of the fireman's socks, [an officer] found a small vial of cocaine and instead of turning it over to the wife or letting the family know about it or anything to that effect, he just got ahold of the prosecutor and they decided just to get rid of it and be done with it and throw it away, which is exactly what happened. And here was a case where you really could have turned that thing into a big mess and said, "Look, we've got a local fireman who may have been doing cocaine," but instead of doing that, he got rid of it.

Further investigation by the officer revealed nothing as to any kind of widespread use. I believe he'd spoken to a close friend of the deceased and he said he was aware of the cocaine, but it was just a recreational, small amount, as in first-time-trier kind of thing. And autopsy reports of the blood revealed no alcohol, no drugs, anything in there, which would be consistent with what the close friend or the confidant had said of the person who had taken his life. So as far as we could tell, there wasn't any type of a widespread use of it in the fire department or anything of that effect from what we looked into.

Peer relations among workers matter. Sometimes, as revealed in "Bonus Check," workers perceive a shared sense of being wronged and unite to press a grievance, usually in response to procedural or policy changes that influence their ability to do their jobs as they see fit.[1] Cops, teachers, and counselors all tell of putting in extra hours to meet the needs of citizen-clients and yet rarely put these issues at the center of their stories about injustices in the workplace. Instead, they protest when they perceive that management practices further increase workloads while doing nothing to enable more effective handling of citizen-clients. Computerized case tracking systems are viewed as management tools for monitoring workers that achieve little efficiency but have the potential to draw workers away from direct contact with citizen-clients. The only way to avoid the trade-off is to work more, and many workers offer accounts of doing just that, challenging the state-agent narrative that portrays workers as self-interested and always looking for ways to make difficult jobs easier.

Workers recognize that they are at a power disadvantage against management and therefore rarely register grievances. In "Bonus Check," workers unite to offset the power imbalance and take on management. They also realize that resorting to legal norms and discourse may make a difference. The narrator weaves into her account references to legality in describing the workers "filing a grievance," their engaging in "a fair-labor-type thing," and her getting a check because they filed "a class-action type of thing." Her references to legality are imprecise, reflective of the discourse that citizens bring to the lower courts and mediation programs when they are trying to get the attention of officials and gain advantage over adversaries from their neighborhoods and workplaces.[2] It may appear ironic that workers invoke moral discourse and substantive justice concerns to frame their judgments for handling citizen-clients (a subject taken up in part 3) but embrace legality when struggling over work conditions. However, in dealing with citizen-clients, workers are in the power position to render moral judgments as they see fit, at least until they are challenged by citizen-clients, who themselves may draw on everyday notions of law to gain some leverage against the more powerful workers.[3]

In "Getting Rid of the Cocaine," a veteran officer tells a different tale of strong peer bonds among workers. A spouse of a fireman makes a distress call to a particular police officer who is a friend. The officer responds to the plea for help and finds the fireman dead, the victim of a "tragic suicide, but really nothing more complicated than that." In the course of looking for a suicide note, the officer or one of the other police officers at the scene comes across a vial of cocaine. The officers on the scene and a prosecutor agree that they should "get rid of it" to avoid what "could have turned the thing into a big mess." They band together to suppress evidence of criminal wrongdoing on the part of the deceased. Their decision is justified by the reported account of a friend of the deceased who says that the firefighter was a "recreational" user and by tests, conducted after the decision was made, that revealed no illicit substances in the firefighter's blood. Moreover, the narrator claims that "as far as we could tell," there "wasn't any type of a widespread use of it in the fire department." The investigative effort, however, appears superficial and informal rather than systematic and serious in intent. In the context of the story, the investigation merely confirms the officer's judgment to protect the reputation of a fellow street-level worker, even though that judgment involved the suppression of evidence.

What prompts a group of workers to bond together and suppress rather than follow the law and investigative procedures? The stories reveal that workers identify strongly with their occupation and similar occupations. When we reference "identity," we are addressing how we come to recognize ourselves and each other. In "Getting Rid of the Cocaine," workers empathized with the family and its circumstances but also recognized in the firefighter their own identities as professional, law-abiding, heroic pillars of the community they serve. The workers realized that revealing the firefighter as a cocaine user who could not handle the pressures of everyday life could be a "a big mess" for the occupation of firefighters as well. And carrying out a full-scale investigation to determine whether there was a pattern of cocaine use among firefighters seemed to be beyond the pale for the officers in this story. In a similar story, workers and supervisors in the western police department identify with a police officer who has been convicted twice for harassing his ex-wife. While policy calls for his removal from the force, the officers close ranks to save his job because they regard him as a professional officer who is susceptible to his former wife's ability to get under his skin. His problems are deemed personal rather than professional. Continuing to work the streets, he is required to undertake counseling but resists until he is threatened with a temporary suspension.

While strong occupational identity generates peer bonding, workers take on these identities differently within and across professions. Field notes reveal different ways that cops handle the social isolation, danger, and coercive powers that are self-defined markers of their identification as police officers.[4] One described his identity as an officer as follows:

> When I'm off duty at home, . . . when we go out to restaurants, I never sit where they put the menu. I always have to sit in certain spots. I have to have a good view of the door, the front door. My back has to be to a corner. It's just a type of . . . lifestyle. And that's what I am is a police officer, and I see people [when I'm] off duty that I've arrested before. A lot of times they don't recognize me without my uniform, but I carry a gun everywhere I go.

He seems unable to abandon even temporarily his occupational identity. Another officer, however, alludes to many of the same markers but handles her police identity differently when she leaves work. In field notes that address conversations with her while on ride-alongs, one of us wrote,

> She indicated that while going to the university, she found herself deceiving fellow students about her being a police officer. And, even now, while pursuing a master's, she conceals her identity as a cop. She said that being a cop "tags your identity" in the minds of others. People either really like that you are a cop and want to talk about it, or they instantly distance themselves.

The urban middle school teachers have a bipolar occupational identity. They want to impart learning but face the immediacy of their students' behavioral problems. Some students' behavior invokes fear in the teachers, who also have to deal with youth who wander in from the streets and may or may not be enrolled in school. Cops struggle with their abundance of coercive powers and are resentful when they do not get broad support when using these powers. In their stories, teachers worry that they lack the necessary coercive powers to handle perceived threats and believe that they are on their own when they act aggressively toward youth.[5]

Story 5.3.   Midwestern Middle School
"Lack of Support"

This kid is kind of spooky. He was in learning disability. I wish I had a class to encourage him—he can draw wonderfully. This kid, I gave him a picture of a black hole or something, he almost halfway knows what he is doing, he was just kind of sketching. I looked at it and say to him, "That is wonderful. Can I have that?" He could not do anything otherwise, he is just so distracted and could not focus on things. He hooked up some light circuits one time in class, and I didn't know quite how he did it, and I don't think he quite knew how he did it, but he set up Christmas lights and they were connected so he could turn one off and the others would still be on. He set up a circuit that the lights would stay on. He had some accelerated abilities, but he was learning disability and frustrated.

Another day, it is almost like a twilight zone when I walk in here. I am in the office, and I come out of the office and I see a kid with his hood up. He is just kind of walking around without a purpose, and he is just walking by all the students and not saying hello. So I am just kind of following, about four or five steps behind him. He never turns around. He goes to the gym, the lobby area, and I am walking behind him. It is only us two, and he walks into the gym lobby area and looks up into the basketball courts and just looks in the windows and leans up against the wall. I say, "Excuse me. Can I help you?" He turns around, and it is the kid who pounded on the basketball coach. I kind of backed up, and I wasn't going to touch him for fear of I didn't know what he was going to do. He says, "Oh, I am looking for my cousin" or something. He left the building, but, I mean, it just kind of gave me this, "Uh, what is going to go on here?" feeling. You can't predict what this kid is going to do.

Here it is, I am a teacher, and I have no power. I feel like I have no power to tell a kid to move. If I touch a kid, he wants to sue me or something like that, and all I can do is tell him to please leave the building. There is nothing we can do. These kids just float into the building. We feel like the administration really doesn't care about it that much. They got all these other things to do. So this safety factor becomes involved, and just as far as what is right, I don't feel like I have any control over the situation.

This story reveals all of these markers of teachers' unsettled occupational identity. In the first paragraph, the teacher tells of a student with "some accelerated abilities" who also has learning disabilities that make him "kind of spooky." The teacher finds him doing creative things and offers encouragement but doesn't have "a class to encourage him." This subplot is juxtaposed with another in which the teacher follows a youth who has "his hood up" and is "not saying hello" to other students as he moves through the hallways toward the gymnasium. In the gym, the teacher begins to question the kid, who turns out to have previously "pounded on the basketball coach." The teacher backs up and "wasn't going to touch him for fear of I didn't know what he was going to do." The youth leaves the building without incident. The story turns to a reflection on having "no power to tell a kid to move" and receiving no support from the administration: "these kids just float into the building. We feel like the administration really doesn't care about it that much. They got all these other things to do."

Other stories tell of having to choose between focusing on discipline or learning. Depending on the storyteller, good teachers are those who stay focused on the learning process or those who know how to handle the youths in the classrooms and hallways. Those who favor discipline and policing lament that their aggressive actions get them in trouble with the administration, parents, and legal authorities. In nearly all the stories, the administration is represented as out of touch with the realities in the hallways and more focused on disciplining teachers who don't toe the top administrators' line. Those teachers who try to manage the students and impart learning, like the storyteller in "Lack of Support," are filled with fear, frustration, and alienation from work. Yet they fill the void of responsibility left by the disengaged administration, a key element in the citizen-agent narrative. The next story reveals another theme contrasting the state- and citizen-agent narratives.

Story 5.4. Midwestern Vocational Rehabilitation
"I Work for the Citizens with Disabilities"

I had a counselor who told me one time, he said, "Well, I have talked to so many people this month, so I am going to cut it off because I have got my quota." I said, "Well, what about these other people?" And he said, "Well, what is in it for me?" I think, "Well, there are more people that need the service, so that is what is in it for you."

I think that we do that here in that I work for the citizens, particularly those with a disability. The agency for whom I work is really just a conduit for my paycheck, which enables me to provide services, so I have loyalty to [the agency] so long as it is accomplishing its mission, but I am not primarily an employee of [state social services agency]. Secondarily, we have counselors where it is the other way around. At any point that it ceases to fulfill its mission, it is my responsibility to change it. In other words, the system is here for the consumer and not vice versa.

The other thing is that all people should have access to basic societal services and programs without regard to income, which translates into power. And since this is not the case, advocacy becomes a big part of what we do. And unfortunately—I guess, in a perfect world we could just send somebody and say, "Go call that agency and they'll take care of you." It isn't that way, and bureaucracies and all depend on talking to the right person, asking the right question, framing the situation, you know, just so, or you do not get it. And so a lot of our folks are unsophisticated, and unfortunately a lot of the folks in agencies will see somebody coming in as a bother rather than what [the workers] are there for. So much of our work [requires that] I have to know all these people in all of these agencies, know how their system works, so I can either tell my client exactly what to ask or "Here is how you say it to open that door" or whatever because otherwise they can't get the service. It is too bad it is that way, but that is just how it is.

Nearly all of the workers define themselves as advocates on a mission rather than bureaucrats implementing policy. This is particularly evident in vocational rehabilitation counselors' stories because of their identification with clients. The counselors' occupational identities are enfolded with those of the citizen-clients with whom they work. For some, their synergistic identification with clients relates to the fact that the workers are also people with disabilities. Many voc rehab workers are disabled—especially in the area of services to the blind—but counselors without disabilities also express advocacy as a marker of occupational identity.

Rather than having their occupational identities defined by the abundance or lack of coercive powers, as in the case of police and teachers, vocational rehabilitation counselors also emphasize the importance of having persuasive powers to do their jobs.[6] In part, these workers articulate a need for persuasive skills to get workers in other agencies to do what is necessary for clients. In addition, VR workers claim that persuasion is crucial for client interaction because they know what is best for their clients—even more than do the clients and those close to them. Many vocational rehabilitation workers, both male and female, are paternalistic toward clients and are proud of being so, a subject taken up in chapter 10.

In "I Work for the Citizens with Disabilities," the male worker who grew up in the urban community where he now works strongly asserts his advocacy identity, claiming that his "loyalty" to the agency is contingent on it staying focused on the "mission." The mission is to put first the "needs" of "consumer" clients, not the "system." The dramatic tension in the story revolves around his apparent interactions with some coworkers who do not share his perspective on the job and who in fact mirror the attributes of the state-agent narrative of street-level workers. These workers are satisfied with meeting quotas and want to know "what is in it for me" if they talk to more clients than the agency requires. The narrator considers using moral reasoning with one of these workers by invoking the substantive justice notion of need: "Well, there are more people that need the service, so that is what is in it for you."[7] While he claims that "we have some counselors" who do not see it his way, his references to a client-focused worker identity are always plural, suggesting that his view is shared by coworkers. Indeed, the great majority of narrators of vocational rehabilitation stories position themselves in their stories as oriented toward advocacy and needs, often in contrast to workers they encounter in other social service agencies who are strict proceduralists in handling citizen-clients.

"I Work for the Citizens with Disabilities" also reveals the centrality of developing and using persuasive powers to get workers in other agencies to meet what vocational rehabilitation workers deem to be their citizen-clients' needs: "It isn't that way, and bureaucracies and all depends on talking to the right person, asking the right question, framing the situation, you know, just so or you do not get it." This is the nitty-gritty of advocacy work. In revealing this orientation, the narrator also shows his paternalistic orientation toward clients. Because a lot of his clients are "unsophisticated," he must tell them "what to ask, or 'Here is how you say it to open that door.'" This story underscores another central element of street-level work: strong bonds formed with some fellow workers and citizen agents can create barriers and opposition with others.

6. Organizational and Social Divisions among Street-Level Workers

Story 6.1. Midwestern Vocational Rehabilitation
"Going Out on a Limb"

There is a young woman that I have been working with for about a year now. She is really severely physically disabled—average cognitive ability, but has minimal use of her body. The family have very little money, and her parents have been unemployed off and on all the time.

I do transition work. The situation with this student is the family was having some really severe problems. She was sixteen, which means she is old enough for transition services but not normally within the age where I would open an adult case. And there is no money that goes to transition services. It is mostly referral and information and things like that.

For adults, hypothetically they need to be old enough that I can document that what I am doing will have an employment outcome. So usually I don't do it until junior year or senior year [of high school], when they are really planning to go to college or get a job.

She was a sophomore, she was young, but the family was really in crisis. They didn't have very much money. They had a van but no lift and really no way to transport this student, their child. She is very overweight, which means they couldn't even comfortably pick her up and put her in the vehicle.

So for the most part, except for when the school bus came and got her, she couldn't go anywhere and do anything. We talked about that at the IEP [individual education plan] review, and I said we would table that and look for resources.

I found out that there was a repo [repossession] list. We have a list of equipment here that if for some reason somebody dies or hasn't followed through on a plan or whatever and doesn't need a piece of equipment, it gets taken back into the agency and stored someplace, and a memo goes out to all of the counselors listing all those things. There is a van lift on the repo list, and it turned out it would fit their van. So actually I got a lot of support. I talked to [my supervisor], and she ended up having to go to her boss, but I got them to agree that since the lift was there and all I would have to do was pay for installation, I would open an adult case for the student and pay for the lift. This is an incredible amount of flexibility in the agency. I was real impressed because there was no way that I could document this was related to employment, that this was going to do what it was supposed to do. The agency was willing to go out on a limb.

After we put in the repo lift, the old van pretty much disintegrated. They had to buy a new van. . . . They had enough money for the payments on a new van, and they found one that the lift was compatible for, but they couldn't afford to install it. It was going to cost $500 to have it transferred. . . .

We looked everyplace, and there is no money. So I am going to just pay for it. . . . I'll just document her need for it, and I'll pay for the $500 to transfer it. . . . Yeah, so I'm going to do it again, but I probably will not go through [the supervisor] this time. I'll just go ahead and do it.

Story 6.2. Midwestern Police Department
"Remembering My First Arrest"

I have a nine-year-old daughter who on occasion asks me to tell her something about police work, or she'll be watching a story like last week—a civil rights story of a black girl who wasn't able to attend school with white children—and she was asking if I had any experience or knowledge of people being treated disparately because of race. And I tried to go back into my mind and remember when I was an officer and the very first arrest I was involved in.

And we were riding on patrol. And my field training officer was helping show me the people in the neighborhoods and the business owners and also the areas where we have potential of street problems. And we were driving down a main boulevard in the northeast area, and there was a guy walking along drinking a Miller beer, which was a city ordinance violation of open possession of beverages. So [the field training officer] said, "Why don't you get out and initiate contact and write him the citation, or if necessary you can take him to jail. It's discretionary to the officer."

So I get out and, of course the individual suspect, who is an African-American male, says to my officer—knows him by name and calls him by last name and says, "You're just out here screwing with me because I'm black." And my field training officer says, "That's right. I'm just picking on you because you're black." I think he was being facetious, and I don't think that it was serious, but we ended up making an arrest, and [the suspect] tried to run, and we had to chase and to take him into custody and took him down to arrest him for possession of an open beverage.

But the ride down there, the dialogue was that there was verbal exchanges between the two. And obviously it was initiated by the suspect, but the response of my training officer was very troubling to me and used words and language that hurt. And I've been raised not to think that way, . . . and if something like that happens by the training officer you work with every month and every day—

And I determined at that point that it was . . . something the officers, who unfortunately [worked] in the late 1970s and early 1980s that I think the language barriers existed were very true. That there was a lot of profanity in the streets that was still a violation of city ordinance to use inappropriate language, but the officers would digress when challenged. And if verbally assaulted, they would respond with racial slurs back to the people who was using them against them. They would immediately digress to the lowest common denominator and get right in the gutter with them verbally and other kinds of assaults.

I think it was a decision that I was raised in a Christian home and an environment where that wasn't common language or thoughts. Educationally, I was there in [this city's] school system, where I had many friends who were Spanish- or African-American and still maintain those contacts. I was affronted by the fact that people—especially people in the law enforcement system—would use that language.

The state-agent narrative puts workers in a bureaucratic setting struggling against management to retain their discretionary powers and preserve their self-interests. Many stories pit workers against managers in bureaucratic settings.[1] Workers themselves are struggling with management in an attempt to provide quality services targeted to individual citizen-clients, whereas management is interested in engaging in surveillance of workers and in processing cases relying on categorical imperatives.

But the stories suggest that the bureaucratic imperative metaphor, which groups and divides public employees by rank, fails to capture fully the environment of police departments, schools, and vocational rehabilitation agencies. Reflective of the territory where they are located, work sites appear to be more like diverse urban neighborhoods, some in flux and others relatively stable. Managers and supervisors symbolize the formal authority structure with which citizens must deal if they want something or when they step out of line. Authorities and citizens sometimes work together to make things happen and sometimes conflict over who should get what. The same is true for managers and workers operating in public agencies.

Like urban neighborhoods, the work sites depicted in the stories and our fieldwork are occupied by street-level workers who draw significantly on their generational, religious, class, physical, ethnic, racial, sexual, and gender identities to form bonds and declare differences in their daily interactions with one another. These sources of identification as particularized citizens are as defining of relationships as the bureaucratic identifiers of worker, supervisor, and manager or the occupational identifiers of cop, teacher, and counselor.

In "Going Out on a Limb," a vocational rehabilitation worker gains the full support of her supervisor, who was able to get her boss to go along with the bureaucratic function of transforming the official categorization of a sixteen-year-old "severely physically disabled" female with no capacity for work into an adult with employment potential. Ironically, however, when the van falls apart and the repo lift needs to be reinstalled in a new van, the worker decides to do it without asking her supervisor. The worker knows the limits of cooperation. All of the employees referenced in the story are women, but the narrator gives no particular weight to their gender identity as significant to the story. The ranks of employees are salient to the story, but the moral of the story is the achievement of a unification of purpose across ranks to meet the very particularized need of an individual client and her family. The worker used her persuasive powers to get her supervisor to agree and, in turn, to get her boss to go along. The worker lauds the "incredible amount of flexibility in the agency," suggesting that this kind of cooperation across ranks happens with some frequency. Realizing that she would have been unable to generate paperwork that could document her client as an "adult case" that was "related to employment," the worker concludes that "the agency was willing to go out on a limb." It wasn't her go-it-alone, discretionary behavior that enabled initial acquisition of the lift but cooperation cutting through the strata of the organization that made the difference. But the conclusion suggests that this worker was not opposed to acting without her supervisor's permission when doing so seemed necessary. Indeed, the worker's decision of when to conform to rules and procedures and when to break them and when to cooperate with authority and when to act independently is the essence of street-level judgment.

"Remembering My First Arrest" reveals some of the complexity of identities at play in contemporary public agencies. The officer recalls his rookie year and his training officer's efforts to teach the new cop how to deal with African-Americans when working the streets. When a black man is walking with an open bottle of beer, the training officer tells the rookie to "initiate contact and write . . . the citation or if necessary . . . take him to jail." The citizen knows the officer and hails him as a bigot: "You're just out here screwing me because I'm black." The rookie discovers the truth of this allegation and, although pointing out that the citizen initiated the verbal exchange, focuses on how the officer's use of "words and language that hurt" was troubling.

The cop reveals a tension between his occupational and social identities as he digresses from the incident to a characterization of officers who dominated the occupation in the 1970s and early 1980s. He offers a justification for the racist talk and actions of these officers by pointing out that they routinely faced verbal assaults from black citizens who were violating the law with their street profanity. But the narrator returns to his concern about how the officers of this generation typically responded: "they would immediately digress to that lowest common denominator and get right into the gutter with them verbally and other kinds of assaults." Distancing himself from those officers, the narrator draws on markers of his social identity: "I was raised in a Christian home and an environment where that wasn't common language or common thoughts. Educationally, I was there in [this city's] school system, where I had many friends who were Spanish- or African-American and still maintain those contacts."

In an interview, the narrator stresses qualities of his social identity and how they distinguish him from this earlier generation of officers. Like a number of officers in the western police department, he references class: "I think of myself as a working-class, blue-collar person." He claims he is well educated and, as a result, professional in his orientation toward policing. But he contrasts his professionalism with the profession of policing, which is not "as modern as we would like it to be." He sees himself as a white male because he looks "quite white and male," but he is part Cherokee and sees himself as a minority as well. These attributes in combination with his growing up in the city where he works enables him to "see the plight of the minority issues and do as much as I can."

Generational and racial divisions appear to be significant in both of the police work sites. In a story told by a veteran midwestern police officer who had to decide disciplinary action, a more senior motorcycle cop confronts a bicycle cop while they are both drinking at a police lodge. According to the narrator,

> The more aggressive officer was assigned to the motorcycle unit as a motorcycle officer, and he verbally challenged the other officer, who was a community policing officer, to get off the bicycle that the community policing officer rode and get on a motorcycle—a real bike. And basically he imputed the viability of the community policing officer's unit, of his job, of his political responsibilities—hammered it pretty hard.

A fight broke out between the officers, with one of them sustaining a serious injury. The narrator reported that the police union was split "in terms of which side to support." Stories and field observations from the work site of the western police agency revealed a split between senior patrol officers, the "old guard," and more recently hired officers over the commitment to community policing.[2] While the administrations of both agencies embrace this reform strategy, it is one source of the generational tensions between more senior officers, who resist because it pushes cops in the direction of becoming "social workers," and more recent hires, who like the gadgets and the communication that community policing encourages between police and citizens.

A senior African-American officer in the western police agency told a story that parallels closely "Remembering My First Arrest." The dramatic tension of this story revolves around differences between the narrator and a white officer who had beat assignments that frequently

69

placed them together on calls. They often differed over how to handle calls, and the narrator began to see patterns that he found disturbing:

> On calls we went on, we would go to, say, a Hispanic household, in which it was a low-income family. The house was not clean and pretty much a pigsty. Well, when this officer would show up, he would make comments about the family, and this disturbed me, because I could see that he felt they were low-class people, beneath him, and didn't respect them. And I began to see that on other calls where we had to go to black families, he would come out with the same comments. So I felt that he was racist, prejudiced against minorities. I could see it in the way he talked to people from Hispanic and black families. And it was really bothering me.

The narrator hesitated to approach a supervisor about the officer's racism because the storyteller was "brand-new" and "didn't know how the department would handle such incidents." Later, when the narrator and this same officer were at a squad baseball game, the officer, who was drinking, walked up beside the narrator and said in a loud voice, "How much money do you have, nigger?" The narrator reported the incident to the supervisor and a senior agency manager. To the narrator's dissatisfaction, the manager decided to separate the officers' assignments and to take no disciplinary action. The narrator recounts this story of disappointment to indicate the point at which he became an activist who pushes from the inside for more hiring of African-American and Hispanic officers. These divisions demarcate identity enclaves within agencies.

Story 6.3. Western Police Department
"Bending the Rule for a Lesbian Couple"

> An employee approached me and asked me about the possibility of taking family emergency leave. This city has benefits that you're allowed three family emergency days within a year's period of time for emergencies that relate to your immediate family.
>
> This employee approached me and said, "I have a problem." I said, "Okay, what?" she said, "I want family emergency leave." I said, "That's it?"
>
> "Well," she said, "It's for my significant other."

"Okay, so what? What's happening?"

"Well, my partner has to undergo some surgery, and I want to take the day off, so I guess what I'm saying to you is I think it's the right thing for us to do is that I should be afforded the same opportunities toward emergency leave for a family situation as others in this agency are allowed to do. But if I can't, what should I do about it?"

I said, "Hmmm, let me think about this for a minute."

She says, "Hmm, hmmm, hmm," and as I was mulling it over in my head for a minute, this person reminded me by way of example. A sergeant had just recently married, maybe four or five years ago. She said, "Here we have a sergeant who's been married for four or five years and he recently took family emergency leave or something. Who knows what it is? Well, I'm here to tell you that me and my partner have been together for over nine years, so I have been involved in a domestic relationship for longer than even this guy, and he gets the pay benefits. Why shouldn't I?" I said, "You're right. You're absolutely right."

If you're the happy family with two kids, you get every benefit the city has, really. If you're not, you get cut out of nine-tenths of the benefits that they offer. That's not right, and I believe that. So, I decided it was my call for the right reasons. Really, under my current supervision, I am certain that if I have to defend that I will have an issue in front of me, but support, too.

I bent the rule. If someone wants to ask, I bent the rule appropriately. The rule sucks. I probably shouldn't have said that out loud, but given the circumstances, the comment fits. As an agency, we say we're diverse and we want to encourage them to step up and be role models—I mean, this is what they teach us to say. If you want to do that, that then has to come with all the benefits and perks that everyone else gets. That doesn't mean that we invite them here and show them what others get when it comes to benefits. I know it's being reviewed, so it's not a big deal right now—I mean, it's a big deal, but I think it has a good chance of being amended.

The command staff gathered on this once. I was at a meeting where they were talking about diversity, saying, "We think there probably are, you know, gay people here. I don't know who they are. [Laughing.] We think that there are some. And we think if there are, they're going to tell us. They should be able to step up and say, 'I am and treat me like everybody else. If you do, I'll give you everything I have.'" They've become pretty good role models for other people. We don't want to have an atmosphere that makes it look like it's a bad thing to be gay. The reason is we are a reflection of our community. We have to be a reflection of our community. We don't have a lot of minority representation, either. We need to bolster that.

We probably do have a lot of gays working in this department. You know, somebody asked me not long ago about representation of the community. The national average is supposed to be maybe 10 percent of the population is gay. Someone asked me, "Do you think that's what it is here?"

I said, "Minimally, at a minimum, 10 percent." [Laughing.] Just like that. But there hasn't been anyone who's gone out and said, "Ooh! Ooh! I am!" I mean, has anyone ever asked you if you were a heterosexual? I don't think so. If we're really treating them all the same, there's no point in asking. That would be inappropriate.

Officers' social identities are a point of tension and division. In other stories, identity enclaves, or recognized social networks of shared identity, are a source of bonding that cuts through the ranks of the agency, producing comfort zones and power bases for group members.[3] "Old boy networks" and "the old guard" reference white male enclaves and their power within work sites. "Bending the Rule for a Lesbian Couple" shows a newer enclave, one that was referenced by many officers in the western police agency. A lesbian officer approaches a lesbian supervisor, the narrator of the story, asking for family emergency leave to be with her partner. (Both the officer and supervisor revealed their gay identities during the entry interviews.) The officer points out the unfairness of the current policy, which favors traditional families, by comparing her nine-year nontraditional relationship with the family status of a relatively recently married male heterosexual who received family leave.

The narrator supervisor immediately recognizes the unfairness, noting during the interview that the "example alone was enough for me," and grants the officer the leave on the spot. The supervisor realizes that if she has to defend her decision, others will back her up: "I will have an issue in front of me, but support, too." She digresses to a meeting of police supervisors where they lend legitimacy to the gay enclave that exists in the agency, although the supervisors think that gay officers should come out, apparently to serve as role models for the jurisdiction's substantial gay community. The narrator supervisor goes on to tell of another event in which she was asked if the percentage of gay officers comes close to the presumed national average of 10 percent. She affirms that percentage but makes clear that she does not support the idea of their coming out: "There hasn't been anyone who's gone out and said, 'Ooh! Ooh! I am!' I mean, has anyone ever asked [the researcher] if you were a heterosexual? I don't think so. If we're really treating them all the same, there's no point in asking."

For most workers, the issue of whether lesbians should come out is moot. The lesbian officers' power is widely recognized within the department, power which is a source of resentment for some. In "Bending the Rule for a Lesbian Couple," the narrator supervisor mentions in passing that the agency fails to mirror the community in its representation of sworn minority police officers: "We have to be a reflection of our community. We don't have a lot of minority representation, either. We need to bolster that." This is not a passing concern for some officers: the western police department's African-American and Hispanic male officers compare their low numbers with the force's substantial white female and lesbian presence. One African-American cop, very active in pushing for more officers of color, sees a hierarchy of social identity groups in the agency that is ill matched with the groups in the community: "The department is off kilter. It is predominantly white male. Then your next group would be white female, then lesbian female, Hispanic males, black males, and then Hispanic females." He, like others, sees recruitment efforts favoring white females and white lesbians over people of color. Some heterosexual males with children resent lesbian officers, viewing them as having more time to devote to career advancement. These male officers see the movement of lesbian officers into the supervisory ranks as a reflection of their "lifestyle advantage." At the same time, most of the male workers respect their lesbian supervisors as hardworking, accessible, and fair in exercising authority.

Social bonds and difference are less pronounced among the vocational rehabilitation workers and teachers. Few of their stories reveal social identities as salient to work relations. Still, generational and gender differences appear meaningful in interviews. For example, in the western vocational rehabilitation office, longtime employees distinguish themselves as a group, as do the new hires. Each generational group is a source of support, with its members turning to one another to cope with stress, to have lunch together, and to socialize after work.

All of the newer hires are women, and all work with the mentally disabled. Shop talk, particularly related to cases, is a part of the everyday interaction among network members, a grouping that is both generationally and occupationally defined.

Occupational identities provide the grist for strong peer relations among workers. Workers sometimes unite to devise legal strategies to press grievances against management. At other times, workers close ranks to protect a fellow worker in trouble. These actions appear to be as much intended to protect the occupation's good name as to help workers under fire.

Each occupational identity is marked by a unique set of attributes that its members take for granted. Cops live in relative social isolation in part as a result of to the coercive powers they possess whether on or off duty. They live with a sense of danger, and some remain on the lookout for it even when eating out or walking across a college campus after a class. Others work hard to discard their occupational identities when they leave the job, favoring strongly their social identities. Like many other people, these citizen-workers find themselves getting nervous when they see a patrol car behind them as they accelerate while driving to a local shopping mall.

Urban teachers want to spend their time stimulating young people's intellectual growth and teaching values that lead to success in mainstream American culture but also face students whose behaviors challenge teachers' authority and beliefs. Educators distinguish themselves based on whether they tend to be oriented toward disciplining students or toward imparting learning. For those who try to do both, their stories reveal emotional distress and a drift toward alienation from work. In urban schools, especially those serving low-income neighborhoods, teachers share the common goal of imparting the middle-class values of discipline, postponed gratification, responsibility, and hard work. Those who conform to these ideals are rewarded and helped regardless of their academic success, and those rejecting these values are labeled as troublemakers and are punished and isolated.[4]

Vocational rehabilitation counselors draw their identities from the clients they serve. They see themselves as advocates, not bureaucrats, requiring persuasive powers to get clients what they need. VR counselors also use their powers as state agents to convince clients what their needs are and what jobs they are best suited to pursue. Such workers are often patriarchal in their orientation toward clients and proud of being so. How they fill in their notions of advocacy, organize their persuasive powers, and define needs are contingent on the type of disability their clients possess. Many voc rehab workers are themselves persons with disabilities, a shared identity with their clients that is the source of both connection with clients who make efforts to succeed and heightened disdain for clients who are satisfied with dependence.

Differences in the ways workers take on their occupations generate tensions within the work sites we observed. Moreover, conflicts are evident between workers and managers, though the points of contention revealed in the worker stories depart from the more conventional portrayals of management-worker rifts. But the work environments we glean from the stories appear to reflect more the conditions of diverse urban neighborhoods than those of bureaucratic organizations. Some of the work environments are in flux, while others are relatively stable.

Supervisors and workers, like municipal authorities and neighborhood activists, engage in conflict and in cooperation. Like the relations across generations of residents in an urban neighborhood in flux, more seasoned and newer workers see things differently and draw on their generational enclaves for support. Tensions are evident in relations across distinct identity enclaves as brought to life by the same social signifiers that provide the grist for conflict in urban neighborhoods: race, ethnicity, religion, class, gender, and sexuality. No more the exclusive bastions of white males, the work sites—particularly the police precincts we studied—are infused with identity politics. Workers take up membership in one or more of the identity enclaves and find in them sources of comfort and sites for accumulating power.

Workers occupying the space of identity enclaves also hold onto their occupational identities and are keenly aware of their place in the organizational ranks. In street-level stories and the citizen-agent narrative, rank, a hallmark of bureaucracy, is more a marker of identity and less a definition of authority and accountability relationships as emphasized in the state-agent narrative. In addition to the stabilizing influences of occupational identities and worker roles, the work sites regain stability as newer identity enclaves acquire recognition and carve out space within the cultures of the work sites. In the western vocational rehabilitation site, workers openly display banners and symbols of gay culture, and gay and lesbian cultures are integral to work site culture. These work sites, like some urban neighborhoods, have local cultures that are relatively stable amid difference.

Other work sites, particularly the police settings, are in a state of flux as newer enclaves are gaining legitimacy while other social groupings have vocal members but have yet to achieve full recognition and strength in numbers. These work sites are afloat in a sea of difference and are getting a taste of the politics of difference after decades of unchallenged white male dominance.[5] The western police agency's command staff, still under the control of white male managers, openly discusses the presence of a lesbian worker enclave and sees strategic advantage in its existence. Gay and lesbian power is evident in the communities the department polices; therefore, having an identifiable presence on the force may serve the agency's interests. Nonetheless, the growing power of one identity enclave underscores tensions with others, such as the underrepresented Hispanics.

In work sites that are in flux, those who occupy an identity enclave must win their coworkers' acceptance. One route for achieving such support was revealed to us in our fieldwork with the western police agency. A couple of workers associated with the lesbian enclave are viewed as superior performers in their work roles, and one has demonstrated the most valued attributes of her occupation. In her first years as a street cop, the supervisor narrator of "Bending the Rule for a Lesbian Couple" was confronted by a deranged citizen who had killed another person and was wielding knives against the officer. After trying all possible means to disarm the man, she shot and killed him. Appropriately using lethal force, especially to protect fellow officers, is central to cop identity and transcends the other identity enclaves. This act secured her status as a "good cop," even among the old guard.

The officer offered a story about this incident; more significantly, however, a number of other officers, including several males, told us stories about this officer's actions. All the many versions of the story offer information about her ability to face ultimate danger and her courage in effectively and responsibly using lethal force, something that few officers face but most contemplate every day. Her shooting the "the crazy man wielding knives" has become part of the folklore of the work site, which helps to explain white lesbian officers' substantial presence and power on the force. Despite profound differences among them, street-level workers share core occupation identities, and these occupational identities shape their interactions with citizen-clients.

7. Putting a Fix on People: Identity, Conduct, and Street-Level Work

Story 7.1.   Western Police Department
"Watching the Prostitute from a Distance"

I ran into a prostitute named [Angela], and she's thirty-nine years old, she's a white female, and she has no teeth. According to her, a black guy beat her up one time and knocked her teeth out. And she's a chronic alcoholic, and not only that, she's pregnant. I had contact with her once and I made the effort to calling a pilot program that we have here called Care Seven. It is part of a master's program for psychologists and counselors. They came out and talked to her for a little bit and did no good. The very next day, I saw her again at the Circle K—well, actually I saw her out walking Vine Street. I was watching her from a distance to see if she gets picked up for prostitution. She didn't get picked up, but she ended up going to a Circle K.

While she was there, she decided she didn't like the shirt she was wearing and she was going to change it. Well, she did it in the parking lot. She wasn't wearing a bra or anything, so she exposed her breasts to everyone in the parking lot. I found a couple of victims that wanted to prosecute her for that, so I ended up arresting her for indecent exposure. She had really been drinking that day. I found an empty bottle of vodka in her purse. She drinks that because you can't smell it on her breath. You can't tell she's drunk.

I arrested her for indecent exposure and brought her to jail, and I pretty much talked her into blowing the Breathalyzer. She did and she blew a .225, which is over twice the legal limit. She said,"Oh that's not bad. I've been cutting down since I'm pregnant." Right after she said that, she kind of stuck her fingers down below her waistline and smiled and said, "Oh, he's kicking. I can feel him moving around." She was real happy about it and didn't think anything about the fact that she was drinking. She thought that she was doing good because she was cutting down.

That right there caused me a lot of problems, especially because I have a seven-month-old baby. That just really bothers me. My wife didn't touch a single sip of alcohol, didn't take any medications or anything, just because she didn't want any possible thing wrong with the baby. And this one's going to grow up with a mother who doesn't even know who the father is of her unborn child, and she's out here drinking up.

I sent a copy of my report to Child Protection Services and informed them about her blood-alcohol reading and sent a copy of the breath alcohol results. They can't do anything. I ended up talking to my supervisor, who spent a long time in detectives— she was in detectives for child crimes and molestation. I talked to her about it, and she said that she'd run into similar situations and that you can't do anything about it. The only way you can do anything about it is if they make abortions illegal. If they make a law saying that abortions are illegal, they're basically saying that the fetus is a human being. The courts would be able to rule that by drinking and doing drugs, yeah, you're assaulting and damaging that human being. The only other way to help prevent this is to give all drug-addicted females or female prostitutes a hysterectomy. This won't happen because that would be a violation of their civil rights. Apparently, unborn children don't have any civil rights.

Street-level workers want to get a sense of who citizen-clients are, get a fix on people, to decide how to handle them. In figuring out who a person is, they also may put a fix on people, assigning to them a social identity or group belonging that carries with it significant meaning and consequence and becomes unchanging or fixed. In "Watching the Prostitute from a Distance," a police officer spots a person on his beat for the second time. In his first encounter, which occurred the previous day, the officer gains a sense of who Angela is: a homely, older street prostitute. And identifying her as a prostitute, thirty-nine years old, white and toothless, seems bound up in how the officer acts toward her. He initially sees her as someone needing help and calls a pilot program that dispatches student interns to counsel people on the street and guide them to available services: "They came out and talked to her for a little bit and did no good."

Angela's identity changes from a source of pity to a source of outrage with a new descriptive detail: she is drunk and pregnant. The officer is "watching her from a distance to see if she gets picked up for prostitution." Getting a fix on Angela converges with giving Angela a fixed identity that carries with it social baggage and consequences. The officer chronicles her as a pregnant, irresponsible drunk even as Angela is "real happy about [her pregnancy]" and thinks she is "doing good because she is cutting down" on her drinking. The fact of her drinking and being pregnant angers the police officer and prompts him to pursue actions beyond her arrest. He is thwarted by the law. "Child Protective Services can't do anything," he laments in an interview, "until that baby is born" and his supervisor, while sympathetic, makes him realize that Angela has civil rights. At the end of the story, the officer no longer references Angela but instead lumps her into group categories that pigeonhole women who frequent urban streets. Referencing these stigmatized identity categories, the officer reveals his desire for harsh social consequences, including forced sterilization: "The only way to help prevent this is to give all drug-addicted females or female prostitutes a hysterectomy." Contrary to the expectation that contact encourages sympathy, the officer begins the interaction with compassion but becomes more distant—he watches from afar—and less willing to acknowledge Angela's individuality.

In the following story, a vocational rehabilitation worker also invokes social identity categories. She too realizes that social identities are packed with meaning and carry with them consequences. However, unlike the teller of "Watching the Prostitute from a Distance," who sees identities as unchanging characteristics and locks people into social identity categories as he acts on them, this counselor tells a story about the mutability of identities and using her authority to push a person to transform his identity as a remedy to his problems.

Story 7.2.   Western Vocational Rehabilitation
"Start Acting Like a Hearing Person"

[Tom] is deaf. He's from Africa—born deaf, always had access to communication. He's black, and he moved to the United States to another state on the west coast about ten years ago. He has been in the voc rehab system in this state for the last five or six years, in and out of the system. He is definitely from a deaf culture. His parents were rich in Africa, and he always had access to languages. He had complete, full support for whatever he wanted to do and whatever language he wanted to use. If he wanted to do oralism, he could be oral. His parents encouraged full involvement in the deaf community. He's also involved in deaf Olympic sports, which is international. He's a runner. So he has complete full support of his parents, instead of his parents forcing oralism on him.

Tom wants everything now. He wants comprehensive services and everything done for him. And he doesn't have a job because he's black and deaf. He is qualified to work, and he has certification training in electronics assembly and design. And every time he has a problem, it's because they discriminated against him, they violated his ADA rights and EEOC rights. He's always angry. And any time he makes a mistake, it's still their fault. He also filed a complaint against Metro Center for the Deaf because they told him he has an attitude problem. He really does have an attitude problem. I believe that previous counselors never confronted issues aggressively, as I have.

First of all, I did not send him back to Metro Center for the Deaf because they give too much help. They hold his hand through the whole part. They found him a job instead of empowering him to find a job and teaching him to take responsibility for his actions. They make sure he has a relationship established on the job. Even if there's only one person, that's done for him. What I was happy about voc rehab is that we now have employment specialists who do not give such comprehensive services. They're more or less saying, "Do this. Do that." And they just make them do everything themselves and more or less act like a consultant. And I have great one-on-one communication with employment specialists.

An employment specialist got him hooked up through an employment agency that contracts with a huge aerospace engineering firm in the metro area. The first day my client was supposed to show up for training, he was late and then blamed everybody else. I brought him in, told him that it is his fault and then said,"Let's get over the fact of all your problems in the past." I made him stop hiding behind deaf culture, saying, "You know what? You're in a hearing world at that job. They have

money. You've got to start acting like a hearing person, culturally speaking, if you want to work."

I was using the idea of enculturation with him. Enculturation
is a continuing line between two cultures. And on one end is the
deaf world, and on the other end is the hearing world. Work and
money are in the hearing world—it's not in the deaf world. And
so in order to survive in the hearing world, you must act like a
hearing person. You must follow the hearing world's rules and
play their game. Some must come out of the deaf culture and go
to work in the hearing culture. Then they go back to the deaf
world when they're no longer in the hearing world at work, then
they go home or socialize. It's that ability to go back and forth
on that fine line or the continuum between the two cultures.
Because they are two different, separate cultures with separate
rules.

Tom is well qualified for work in the electronics field but "doesn't
have a job because he's black and deaf." He is demanding and always
angry, blaming everyone else for his problems. His social identity as a
black deaf man in conjunction with his attitude stands in the way of his
achieving job security. Tom's parents fully supported his learning oralism, reading lips and speaking, as well as sign language. Despite his
strong social immersion in deaf culture, the counselor sees his diverse
linguistic skills as enabling him to transform his identity if only he has
the will to act the part. Assuming that his identity as a black man is
fixed, she aggressively counsels Tom to replace his deaf identity with a
hearing identity while at work. She tells Tom, "You know what?
You're in a hearing world at that job. They have money. You've got to
start acting like a hearing person, culturally speaking, if you want to
work."

After telling about her conversation with Tom, the VR worker shifts
ground. Tom exits the story. The vocational rehabilitation counselor
offers a brief discourse on her philosophy of how society is organized
and hints at her personal connection to clients such as Tom. She imagines a society divided into two worlds: "on one end is the deaf world,
and on the other end is the hearing world." While she says that each
world has "separate cultures with separate rules," she also sees "a fine
line between the two cultures." There is an incentive to cross this line—
"money and work." Knowing the language of the hearing world (oralism) and acting "like a hearing person" enable the crossover. But being

in the hearing world is only temporary; it is not "home." "When they're no longer in the hearing world at work, then they go home to socialize."

The counselor feels strongly that people from the deaf world must cross over if they want access to work and money. And, as reflected in her conversation with Tom, she sees instilling her clients with this perspective as a centerpiece of her work. Her occupational identity as a counselor involves creating or shaping functional identities for her clients. But why does she feel so strongly about counseling clients regarding this perspective, and how has she come to know the importance of crossing over? In an interview, the voc rehab worker makes explicit what is only hinted at in the story:

> Well, I have a disability myself. I am hard of hearing, and I have a great passion for equal opportunities for all people with disabilities. And in reality, there is no equal opportunity. There are some setbacks imposed on them by society and their rules and their attitude toward minorities and people with disabilities. And I wanted to even the playing field. And it's something that's always been deep inside of me that angered me. So I gotta turn this anger into a positive energy by doing this type of work. I've experienced so much of the things that they've experienced. I've experienced their frustrations, discriminations in the hiring process. I know I did not speak perfectly clear, but you either think I'm dumb or I have an accent, especially on the phone. And my individuals that I counsel have the same thing. I've been there but without help. I did it on my own.

This woman identifies with her clients in that she has experienced "their frustrations." But although she is like them, she is not the same because she made it on her own. She feels a bond with Tom because his frustrations parallel hers, and yet she wants Tom to become more independent and better able to act like a hearing person. She wants to make Tom like herself. The counselor is enacting her complex identity as she acts on clients. Enacting identities is a recurrent theme in workers' stories about their relations with clients, citizens, and kids. Her identity as a mainstreamed person with a disability becomes the yardstick by which she measures the motives and actions of her client. Using her own identity in this way strengthens her self-identification: the self creates the standard, and the application of the standard reinforces the self.

How does the cop enact his identity in "Watching the Prostitute from a Distance?" He clearly does not identify with Angela. Rather, he presents a social identity that contrasts sharply. He is a member of a responsible nuclear family. He is the father of a seven-month-old baby, and when his wife was pregnant, she "didn't touch a single sip of alcohol, didn't take any medications or anything, just because she didn't want any possible thing wrong with the baby." Angela's yet-to-be-born is going to grow up with a mother who is a drunk and "doesn't even know who the father is." Contrasting their identities and assigning moral weight to their differences appear to drive the police officer's desire to pursue harsh actions beyond arrest. While identity matches are associated with workers going the extra mile to help citizens, differences in identities, as constituted by workers, are often embedded in the stories that tell of withholding help and getting the bad guys, subjects taken up in part 3.

Deciding who a person is, in the context of front-line work, is an uncertain process. Cops working the streets frequently have only single encounters with citizens and therefore have little time to get a fix on a person. Even vocational rehabilitation workers and teachers have little knowledge about with whom they are dealing before coming face to face with clients and kids. The paperwork before these counselors may give rise to concern or even fear, but their work still requires that they make personal contact.

"The Loaded Purse" (story 4.3) reveals the uncertainty and fear that define some first encounters. A woman who has recently been released from prison has been referred to a VR worker. Her paperwork reveals that "there were some psychiatric things involved with her" and that she had served time for "pulling a gun out of her purse" and shooting her husband at point-blank range. The woman wants to set up her own cosmetology business, an unrealistic goal and one that the counselor sees as inappropriate for vocational rehabilitation. As he contemplates telling her the bad news, the woman "picked her purse up off the floor, put it on her lap and reached into her purse." The vocational rehab worker "was ready to hit the deck" just as the woman pulled "out a pack of cigarettes." Although told in a humorous manner, the story reveals the uncertainty and fear that may pervade initial encounters and shows that initial encounters represent the social terrain in which workers tend to identify who people are by employing stigmatizing identity categories. Preceded only by a paper trail, the woman was a disturbed and violent parolee when she arrived for vocational counseling.

For street cops, fear and uncertainty define their occupational identity, as discussed in chapter 5. On any given day, they encounter a number of strangers in situations where a significant part of getting a fix on citizens involves gauging whether they pose a threat to the officers' safety. In stories about encounters thick with fear and perceived danger, police typically dehumanize the citizens at the center of a volatile incident and recognize them as members of one-dimensional, stigmatized identity categories. Fear and danger flatten identities. For example, one cop working in the midwestern city tells a story of subduing a "lunatic crackhead" at a family Christmas gathering without harm to other family members or to himself. Another cop in the western city who has responded to a number of domestic disturbance calls in a Hispanic barrio recognizes all Hispanic males as "incestuous predators" and "lazy alcoholics."

Urban teachers in the midwestern city presume that male youths walking the halls between classes are violent predators. With this identity in mind, some avoid all encounters with male youths outside their classrooms, while others approach roving youths in anticipation of confrontation. Some stories about hallway encounters confirm the expectation of violence, while others do not. Nevertheless, like many of the police stories about street encounters, most of these teacher stories reveal the use of stigmatizing social identity categories in conjunction with the fear and uncertainty of first encounters.

Line workers, including police officers, also have opportunities for substantial exposure to people through a series of interactions that extend over time. Teachers spend long periods with students in the classroom and in extracurricular activities. Vocational rehabilitation workers meet numerous times with many clients to develop service plans and to provide counseling. Cops who do investigative work come to know suspects; their families, friends, and acquaintances; and informants who provide reports about what is going on in the streets. Many street cops spend time getting to know their beats, learning about who does what within patrol areas; these officers, too, develop a cadre of informants as additional eyes and ears. Indeed, with the advent of community policing in many jurisdictions, including the western police department, street-level officers are expected to cultivate relationships with the full range of citizens living and working in their beats.

The stories that tell of sustained interactions with clients, citizens, and kids tend to offer thick accounts of who people are and describe how street-level workers imbue citizen-clients with complex identities.

Moreover, these stories offer themes quite distinct from those that line workers report on first encounters. Rather than emphasizing fear, confrontation, and negative consequences, these stories tend to stress good things happening to citizen-clients and, for workers, to offer accounts of the rewards of street work, as the following story reflects.

Story 7.3.   Western Vocational Rehabilitation
"The Sunshine Lady"

At the time of the interview, [Janet] was approximately fifty-eight or fifty-nine years old, and she was living in a boarding home in [the southern part of the city]. She is a divorced, white female—ethnicity unknown. She was diagnosed with schizophrenia. When I first interviewed her, she was very guarded and pretty disheveled. Her hair was cropped really short. It was uneven, as if she had cut it herself. Frankly, Janet looked like a bag lady.

Talking with Janet, I found her to be a delightful person. I discovered she was originally from the Northeast and she has a master's degree in secondary education. She majored in mathematics and worked as a bookkeeper for many years in New York. Prior to our meeting, Janet had been homeless for some time. She didn't tell me much about being homeless, as it appeared to be very embarrassing to her. However, I did find out some additional information from a caregiver at the boardinghouse in which she lived. The caregiver said she used to call [Janet] the Sunshine Lady because every day Janet would walk to the same street corner and stare up at the sun all day long. As a result, Janet now has retina damage.

Janet and I began working together on a vocational plan. We decided to try to use her mathematical ability and her bookkeeping experience, as she demonstrated she was still very good with numbers. However, we concluded that bookkeeping today is more or less computerized, so she would need to update her skills by learning how to use a computer. Through vocational rehabilitation, Janet went to the county skills center and took a few accounting and computer classes. After she finished school, VR sent her to have her hair done and to purchase some new clothes for interviewing. Janet's self-esteem started to build, but no matter what we did to help, she still looked like a bag lady. Janet did not have a lot of stamina, so she only wanted to work sixteen or seventeen hours a week. VR contracted with a job-developing agency, but after many hours of service, the job developer could not find Janet a job.

Janet and I decided to switch to a new job-developing facility. The second job developer did a wonderful job of finding the right setting for Janet. The first job he found did not work out as the employer felt that Janet was too slow. Then he found a bookkeeping position, sixteen to twenty hours a week at a small construction company. They were aware that Janet had a disability and she could not tolerate a full work week. The employer was so pleased with Janet's work he asked the job developer if he had any more people he could send to the company—they wanted more employees like Janet. Janet's self-esteem was boosted further when the employer picked her up so she could attend the Christmas party, which was held at one of the nicest steak houses in the city.

This tale could recount nothing extraordinary—a voc rehab counselor helps a client with substantial job skills find a position that benefits both the client and her new employer. But, according to the counselor, "there is more to this story."

Story 7.3, *Continued*

During this time, Janet discovered that she had inherited $48,000 and was never told. Her daughter who lived in California was appointed conservator. Janet was upset since she had been living in boarding homes in [the city] and living on the bare minimum. She was also upset that the reason for the appointed conservator was the belief that Janet was too sick and could not handle her own money.

For assessment purposes, I completed a psychological evaluation at the beginning of our working together. Janet obtained a lawyer who was requesting a psychological evaluation, which Janet could not afford. I believed it was in Janet's best interest to get a new evaluation rather than using one that was a couple of years old, especially in light of her obvious improvement. Although assisting with a second evaluation did not appear to be directly related to Janet's vocational plan, I found that the process of proving competency in order to get her inheritance was causing her a great deal of stress, thereby affecting her employment. During this same time, Janet relocated to her own apartment in a safer area using Social Security money she was able to save, and she became employed.

The results of the second psychological evaluation were very favorable. Janet's functioning improved overall and her IQ level increased significantly. This, along with the steps she had made to become more independent, helped her prove competency, and she was granted control of her inheritance. It's been about two years since I closed Janet's file as successfully employed. We still have lunch once every six to eight months. She is still working at the same place, and she is doing well. Professionally speaking, Janet is special to me. As I look back on it, I see how much she has grown and where she is now. She has a good life. She has the life she wants.

When Janet needs an updated psychological evaluation to take control of an inheritance, the counselor draws on state funds to provide such an examination, offering the following account of her decision: "Although assisting with a second psychological evaluation did not appear to be directly related to Janet's vocational plan, I found the process of proving competency in order to get her inheritance was causing her a great deal of stress, thereby affecting her employment." The counselor had formed a strong connection with her client and knew the circumstances of her life.[1] The VR worker recognizes that ordering a second psychological evaluation is an extraordinary act and develops an elaborate account to enfold her moral judgment with her legal obligations. Her actions are further justified in accounting for the normalization of Janet's life: Janet is not a schizophrenic bag lady but an independent woman who is gainfully employed and living in a safe part of the city. "She has a good life. She has the life she wants." The worker helps transform Janet's identify from a documented schizophrenic to an independent, working woman.

Like "The Sunshine Lady," most accounts of extraordinary acts include a reference to stigmatized identities that are rejected by line workers as they come to know the complexities of people's characters and life circumstances. Another vocational rehabilitation counselor tells a story about a Hispanic female, a former stripper with a history of alcohol and drug abuse who sought help to become a welder. The psychologist who evaluated the potential client concluded that she did not have a learning disability but did diagnose a post-traumatic stress disorder. The evaluating doctor wanted the counselor to question the potential client's goal of becoming a welder. In the course of several meetings and the accumulation of documents, the VR worker learns that the woman has gone through drug rehabilitation, is taking care of her son, and has enrolled in a trade school. Her responsible conduct matters to the counselor. Furthermore, at several points in the story, the counselor says that she identifies with the woman, referencing her quiet demeanor and her strong desire for "her own space" to deal with "her lack of trust of men and women." The vocational rehabilitation counselor decides to write a plan for her client, providing tutoring services to help with the schooling to become a welder.

Street-level workers' actions reinforce citizens' attempts to live "normal" lives. That is, the citizens who receive extra help or are cut a break are in the process of meeting their responsibilities as family members and/or as productive workers. Legal and bureaucratic reasoning is offered to justify extraordinary actions, but these justifications often appear as a rubber band stretched around moral decision making, binding but not determining the decisions. While using state resources for questionable purposes or cutting citizens breaks may put workers in jeopardy with their supervisors, these accounts are happy tales about work in which citizen-agents reveal a bedrock of enthusiasm for their professions, subjects examined further in part 3.

Street-level workers also see themselves as professionals who know what is best for citizens, clients, and kids. These workers are sensitive to the way people conduct themselves during encounters, expecting civility in conversation and a willingness to listen and, in many instances, defer to the advice offered. When line workers interact with citizens, clients, and kids, they are in the power position, using their bully pulpits to engage in moral suasion. Doing paperwork is a necessary part of the jobs but is rarely as fulfilling as "good" conversation, communication that is respectful of their power and knowledge.

Line workers refer to the conditions of conversation, revealing whether citizens meet these norms of conduct. In "The Sunshine Lady," the VR worker states simply her satisfaction with Janet's conduct: "I found her to be a delightful person." In a story about "a stripper" who defiles a neighbor's apartment with red lipstick, a police officer tells of forging a plan for the stripper to clean the apartment. He becomes unhappy with the neighbor, who wants to watch the stripper scrub the apartment, and warms to the woman, who is willing to do whatever it takes to put the incident behind her. The officer decides that the cleaning will take place without the neighbor present "to deal with the humility of scrubbing the door while they laugh at her or something like that." Moreover, he spares the stripper of criminal damage charges. In both "The Sunshine Lady" and this tale, conforming conduct trumps stigmatized identities, and line workers respond with extraordinary actions.

Other stories reveal the opposite. In these narratives, citizens have positive social identities, but their conduct is unacceptable to street-level workers. Workers also tell stories of defiant citizens and of withholding services that might be offered were their conduct judged appropriate. For example, one vocational rehabilitation worker tells of a woman who worked in haircutting salons and who is eligible for assistance because she has a personality disorder. The woman wants to switch careers and become a massage therapist. The worker tells the client that she already has skills and that the office is not in the business of arranging career changes for clients. But the woman is insistent about her career goals, so insistent that the worker decides that the client has a "personality problem": "She can be overbearing and very talkative, and I think she has trouble with authority." Rebuffed by the worker, the woman finds a job on her own, takes out loans, and goes to a school for massage therapy at night. Despite the woman's work ethic and demonstrated independence, the worker is not impressed: "So I think even if she gets her message certificate and she gets out there, she's probably not going to stick with it very long."

Line workers tell stories of defiant citizens who recognize that they are at a power disadvantage and act to offset their weaker positions by seeking third-party support. These citizens are cast as a particular social identity group within the work sites and are called complainers or letter writers. In the vocational rehabilitation settings, defiant clients who seek outside support for their causes are sometimes tagged with psychological disorders to explain their human agency. One vocational rehabilitation counselor who is proud of his political activism against management offers such an account.

Story 7.4. Midwestern Vocational Rehabilitation
"The Letter Writers"

I don't want to stereotype, but oftentimes the clients—there is a type of client that is a letter writer, you know, and I am not saying that it is not their right, but you know that writing letters to every agency and every congressman, to the senator, to the mayor, to everybody saying, "You know, this isn't fair" and this and that or the other thing and they've got—you know, there is always an issue. They're always not satisfied with something, and usually we are justified in what we did. . . .

It is more of a life issue and, you know, personality factors, and they have written letters to everywhere and oftentimes rambling and sometimes they just feel powerless or feeling like the agency or the system has shafted them or whatever. And I am not saying there are not those cases like that where it is true, but there are also folks for who that is kind of their hobby, you know.

Or if someone is acting strangely or exhibits psychiatric problems or personality problems which can appear to be psychiatric problems, [someone says,] "Why don't you go down there [to vocational rehabilitation] and see those people, see if they can't help you?" And you can't say, "You know, I am sorry. I can't take your application because this is really your problem." So you have this delicate situation with a personality disorder, by definition they can't—they can't understand what they have contributed to the problem. That is the definition of a personality disorder, you know—they don't get that. It is all, it's all society's fault or somebody else's fault, the FBI's fault, the government, you know—voc rehab and every other damn bureaucrat.

According to this VR worker, although some clients have legitimate reasons for complaining to third parties, a lot of letter writers are exhibiting traits of a psychological disorder by registering complaints. The result is a "delicate situation" in which counselors must work with clients who as part of the disorder that qualifies them for services may turn on workers who are trying to help and issue a barrage of complaints against them.

Teachers sometimes explain away student accusations by placing the complainers in a social identity group whose behavior is alien to the teachers or contrasted with the behavior of another grouping of youths. For example, an African-American girl goes to a middle school social worker and accuses a teacher of racial prejudice. Tipped off by another social worker that a complaint is in the works, the teacher reflects on his behavior by saying that he is used to working with younger kids and has yet "to figure out the whole adolescent thing." He realizes that he has been giving out more punishments to black adolescents than white adolescents, but "that is because those black kids were talking more."

Workers have devised cultural schema to explain away defiant individuals who turn to third parties to make their defiance stick. While distinct to the occupation and work setting, the cultural schema are similar in that complaining individuals are given social identities that enable workers to explain away complaints and attach blame to the social grouping they construct to identify troublemakers. At the same time, the stories about defiant individuals who complain to third parties are distinct from tales that focus on offending individuals who succumb to the power of street-level workers. In the former, the workers emotionally defend their actions and put a cultural fix on defiant complainers but do not tell of getting back at these individuals. In the latter, workers make it clear that offending conduct is met with actions that carry both cultural weight and material consequences.

Street-level workers need to get a fix on who they are dealing with when first encountering a citizen, kid, or client. Appearance, skin color, gender, and age are filled with social meaning and provide workers with quick composites of the social persons they deal with every day. But street-level workers are authoritative players in assigning social meaning to human traits. In some stories, workers use their powers of cultural definition to lock people into social identity categories that the workers have a hand in defining. In "Watching the Prostitute from a Distance," the police officer constitutes the meaning of "street prostitute" while he locks Angela into that social grouping. In other stories, the workers see identities as mutable and use their persuasive powers to get citizens to change their identities as remedies to their problems. Engaging citizens to transform their identities is evident in story 7.2, in which a vocational rehabilitation counselor tells of pushing a deaf black man to "Start Acting Like a Hearing Person." In both stories, the workers appear to be enacting their identities as they act on the identities of citizen-clients.

The stories reveal the potential significance of temporality in how workers employ social identity in their decision making. Fear and uncertainty are evident in the stories of first encounters with citizen-clients. In this context, workers are likely to employ stigmatizing social identities to get a fix on a person and in so doing put themselves on the defensive, keenly attuned to their own safety. In sharp contrast, stories of sustained interactions between workers and citizens tend to offer thick accounts of who people are, imbuing citizen-clients with complex identities. Rather than emphasizing fear, confrontation, and negative consequences, these stories stress good things happening to citizen-clients and offer accounts of the rewards of street work. "The Sunshine Lady" exemplifies those stories in which cops, teachers, and counselors work overtime on cases, offer complex depictions of citizen-clients, and stress positive consequences for workers and citizens alike.

Regardless of who they encounter, workers expect civility in conversation, a willingness to listen to their views of the situation, and often deference to their advice. Conduct in this manner can trump the negative social identities affixed to citizens on first encounters. When civil and deferential conduct is revealed, workers show benevolence and sometimes go well beyond the scope of their duties to improve citizen-clients' conditions. When citizens conduct themselves contrary to these expectations, negative consequences may result—services may be withheld, arrests otherwise unanticipated may be made, and positive social identities may be erased as workers enforce their moral authority over citizens. Some citizens are defiant and recognize that they can press their definitions of situations only with the help of third parties. Workers have devised cultural schema to identify and explain away defiant citizens. In these stories, however, workers do not tell of getting back at these citizens. In these instances, the cultural schema devised by workers to tinge the identities of defiant citizens appear to lack the punch or carry the material weight evident when citizens remain within the orbit of street-level workers' power. Fixing identities is closely tied to street-level workers' moral judgment, the subject of the next four chapters.

Part III. Normative Decision Making:
Moralities over Legalities

Street-level decision making is complexly moral and contingent rather than narrowly rule bound and fixed. A fundamental dilemma—perhaps the defining characteristic—of street-level work is that the needs of individual citizen-clients exist in tension with the demands and limits of rules. This does not mean that rules do not permeate all aspects of street-level work (they do) or that most street-level actions are not consistent with law and policy (they are). The most common situation may be that the rules effectively fit the complexity of workers' judgments about citizen-clients. When the rules and standard procedures fit the situation, street-level work is not problematic—there is no conflict, no dilemma, and, not incidentally, no story. As discussed in chapter 3, stories are inspired by and help storytellers and listeners deal with ambiguous and conflictual situations, not routine events.

Thus, the fundamental tension that drives many street-level work stories is the conflict between the needs and character—the identity—of the citizen-clients as defined by street-level workers and the demands of rules, procedures, and laws as understood by street-level workers. To deal with this tension, street-level workers focus on their judgments about individual citizen-clients. As discussed in chapter 2, the issues of discretion, control, and accountability that have so dominated the literature on public organizations rarely appear in our stories. These issues are not prominent for street-level workers. Rather, their moral judgments about citizen-clients are made in the context of face-to-face relationships that enacts the identity of both worker and citizen. Rules, procedures, and laws are put into play to enforce these judgments.

Moral judgments about citizen-clients infuse all aspects of street-level decision making. To street-level workers, fairness has little to do with the bureaucratic norm of treating everyone the same or even fairly implementing laws and regulations. To our storytellers, fairness and justice mean responding to citizen-clients based on their perceived worth. More than enforcers of law, street-level workers—in our study, cops, teachers, and vocational rehabilitation counselors—are producers of values and character that embody mainstream notions of moral worth and productive membership in society. At first glance, these observations reinforce the negative portrait of out-of-control workers, but the stories offer a more complex, multidimensional—and more hopeful—portrait of street-level judgment. Street-level workers do not see citizen-clients as abstractions—"the disabled," "the poor," "the criminal"—but as individuals with flaws and strengths who rarely fall within the one-size-fits-all approach of policies and laws.

What, then, are the dimensions of worthiness and unworthiness that street-level workers reveal in the stories? And how do street-level workers treat citizen-clients after making judgments about their moral worthiness? We turn to these issues in the next four chapters. It is important to underscore that the various dimensions of worthiness and unworthiness that emerge from these stories are not discrete. They bleed and blend into each other, just as the world of street-level work is not one of simple categories and hard-and-fast rules and definitions.

In general, street-level workers respond to citizen-clients in one of four ways or a mixture of them. The first is normal, routine, bureaucratic treatment. Teachers follow the rules and curricula. Voc rehab counselors follow standard diagnostic, service, and case-closure procedures. Police officers enforce the law and go by the book. In most cases, normal treatment is good treatment. Although in the narrow quantitative sense, normal treatment may be the most prevalent, it is not problematic for the street-level worker. No one tells stories about following rules, bureaucratic response, and standard treatment, although many stories begin in this manner and then shift to another mode of response.

Street-level workers in all settings tell stories about extraordinary services given to those deemed worthy, the second mode of response. Identifying the worthy citizen-clients is a complex, multidimensional judgment and the subject of chapter 8. How police, teachers, and counselors respond to the worthy is taken up in chapter 9.

The powerful bond between worker and citizen-client that characterizes these stories of extraordinary care and involvement is not always present, however. Street-level workers' responses are often dominated by what is practical or possible rather than what is desirable or best. At other times, compassion and caring give way to conflict and tension about goals and control. Much street-level work requires gaining cooperation and compliance from citizen-clients. This is especially true in police work but is also present in schools and human services. Street-level work demands pragmatism. It cannot be guided by idealism alone, and simply doing what can be done, given all the constraints and limits, guides much street-level work. This third mode of response is examined in chapter 10.

Some citizen-clients receive less than what pragmatism would allow. Police officers unabashedly talk about "getting the bad guys." This is more than just finding and punishing lawbreakers: the "bad guys" may have committed the same crimes as the "good guys" but do not deserve a break or second chance. In schools and vocational rehabilitation offices, some kids and some clients receive as little as the rules allow. So much of what is provided in schools and human services is subjective that street-level workers can comply with rules and procedures yet withhold service. In many ways, strictly following rules allows street-level workers to discourage, delay, and as soon as possible dismiss unworthy citizen-clients. The overt conflict between workers and citizen-clients and often negative responses of workers to citizen-clients deemed unworthy is the subject of chapter 11.

8. Who Are the Worthy?

Story 8.1. Midwestern Vocational Rehabilitation
"Parking Lot Therapy"

I had a male client who came in for service. He had a physical
problem. He was an upholsterer—this was his profession. He
had a back injury, and he was having a lot of trouble because he
had to lift furniture and a lot of pulling with his hands and
arms. I think he probably got a worker's comp settlement out of
it, but he wanted to go back into that type of work. He wanted
to know what could be done for him so he could go back.

I sent him to "work hardening," where they teach you how to
lift properly and do exercises to strengthen your muscles. He
went through it successfully and he was able to go back to work
in his profession.

To this point, "Parking Lot Therapy" describes a routine case handled
routinely. A client with a work injury and the goal of returning to work
is given appropriate treatment. He returns "to work in his profession,"
the efficiently achieved and desired end of a case. This is a textbook
vocational rehabilitation case, a success for the client, the voc rehab
counselor, and society. This is what the policy envisioned. But the
story does not end here.

This description of a routine case becomes the prelude, the calm
before the storm, to a much more complicated case. It is as if the storyteller is saying, "This is how it is supposed to work. Now let me tell
you how it really works." This shift in story content and emphasis
transforms this bland story of a routine case into a multidimensional
story illustrating the complexity of street-level decision making. The
story becomes a tale of a street-level worker going well beyond what is

required, even beyond the responsibility of a voc rehab counselor. The client is in many ways a marginal individual, but as the story unfolds, this street-level worker finds this man to be worthy of extraordinary service.

Story 8.1, *Continued*

But in the middle of all this, he was . . . always getting himself into trouble. He had a live-in who had children. This man had never been married. He was in his early thirties. She was an older woman. She had two or three kids.

He was a very interesting person. Looked real tough. Dressed in black—black jeans; big black motorcycle boots; long, long hair, down to his waist, pulls it back in a ponytail; wears dark glasses; wears muscle shirts, looking real mean and tough. But he is a pussycat.

He is a rescuer. He is a rescuer, he feels sorry for people. This woman didn't have a place to live, and she had a story of woe and problems, and he took her into his home with her kids. They got romantically involved. There were constant problems.

She got involved with some other guy while she was living with [the client]. He was going through emotional problems and grieving. He came in and was telling me all these things, and he was very agitated and crying.

So I said, "I think you could benefit from some individual therapy so you can deal with all the problems you are having. I can take you over to the mental health center. I'll call ahead. I'll take you over there and get you set up."

He said, "Okay."

At this point, the story takes another detour. The emotionally distressed upholsterer and the overinvolved counselor confront an unresponsive, bureaucratic mental health agency.

Story 8.1, *Continued*

I drive him over there. He wants me to go in with him because he has never had to deal with anything like this before. I go in. There's an intake worker. She's not the warmest, friendliest person. I talked with her a while. She sends us to the business office.

"How are you going to pay for this? It's fifty dollars an hour."

And [the upholsterer] says, "I can't do this. I can't pay for this."

"Well, then you are going to have to write something about your financial situation to see if we can reduce your costs."

We go back to the intake worker and talk to her a while. "Well, I can schedule you for an appointment in two weeks."

[The upholsterer] is getting very angry and agitated. I kept saying, "It's okay, it's okay. Take it easy."

He said, "This isn't going to work. I'm not going to do this." He was getting very agitated.

So I said to the intake worker, "We need to leave now because he needs to talk to someone right now."

We went out to my car at the mental health center parking lot, and I sat there approximately two hours doing crisis counseling because he needed it right then. He couldn't be put off; he was angry and agitated. He was in such an emotional state that I said to myself, "Okay, I'll do it." I knew that I was going to have to do it because he needed it right then, and there wasn't anyone else who was going to provide that service to him.[1] . . .

Eventually, I closed his case because he went back to work, but I hear from him every six months. He gets himself into trouble, and he'll come back. We'll go through the crisis counseling, and he's fine until next time.

Going beyond routine service by providing extraordinary care is perhaps expected in the helping professions, in which "doing good" is a prominent norm. Deciding who is worthy also permeates the harsher world of criminal justice. In this next story a police officer makes moral distinctions among drug dealers, a distinction based largely on work ethic.

Story 8.2.   Western Police Department
"Bad Dealers, Good Dealers, and Stray Bullets"

This incident occurred a couple of years ago. There was an individual that had been involved in a lot of criminal activity, including shootings, and his name was [Steve]. Steve never really seemed to be able to do anything that was aboveboard. He never seemed to have a job. When he did have a job, he would steal from the employer. What he eventually started doing was dealing small amounts of marijuana. He had a cousin by the name of [Cory]. Cory is a black male. Steve is a mulatto.

Well, Steve and Cory met with another individual who was a Mexican guy. He had a wife, and she was white. He had been a laborer all his life. He was a Mexican guy from Texas. This guy's name was [Francisco], and Francisco had been a hard worker.

When I talked to Francisco, he had chemical burns on his arms and back, and he explained to me that one time he had lived in a rural area and had to carry this chemical container on his back to spray weeds in these huge fields, and it was a difficult life. He came from a migrant worker's family in Texas and he came to [big city] and settled down. He had a wife and a baby and wasn't able to make ends meet. So he started dealing small amounts of marijuana, which is, of course, against the law.

He started dealing with Steve, and he thought that Steve was his friend. Steve was selling small amounts of marijuana for him, and one day Steve and his cousin Cory decided that they were going to rip Francisco off.

So they drove over to Francisco's house. It was a duplex in a residential area. It was a nice little neighborhood. I wouldn't have expected problems to have occurred in that neighborhood. . . .

The cousin showed up, went into the house and he had a loaded, high-capacity nine-millimeter handgun. He confronted Francisco, took all that Francisco had, and marched him through the house. . . .

Francisco's wife was at work. She was a waitress. So [Cory] put the gun to Francisco's head. He took him back out to the living room, and, while holding Francisco at gunpoint, he started closing the blinds in the living room, and he ordered Francisco down on his knees. Francisco knew then that he was going to be executed.

Francisco was about five feet, eight inches tall and weighed about 220 to 230 pounds. He was a stout little guy. Cory weighed about 130 and he was about five feet, eight inches tall. . . . When he had the opportunity, Francisco grabbed the gun with both hands and forced it up and got Cory off his feet and started swinging him from side to side across the room. And he threw him into a kitchen table and collapsed the table. It was enough to make Cory release his hold on the gun.

Cory then ran and . . . suddenly his high capacity was being used on him. Well, he took a couple of rounds through his mid-section, but he kept running. Francisco was right behind him, and Francisco fired at him across the parking lot. Cory ran to where Steve was waiting to drive getaway. Francisco shot through the back of the car. . . . They left at a high rate of speed, bounced out into the roadway, . . . and Francisco continued to shoot this high-capacity nine-millimeter. The gun had about a sixteen-round capacity. And some of the bullets went directly across the roadway and hit a house across the way.

They fled to the hospital and we started to receive phone calls at the police department about a residential burglary. . . . Well, of course, the supervisors came to the scene and they said, "Okay, we're going to arrest the driver of the car. We're going to file charges on the wounded suspect."

At the same time, this Francisco, who was traumatized and upset, said, "Yup, I do deal with small amounts of marijuana. I'm scared. He was going to kill me. I was afraid for my life."

The supervisor decided to arrest him for endangerment for shooting the gun and having it cross the roadway. . . . The supervisors were adamant that Francisco be arrested. I think to them Francisco was seen as a semiliterate Hispanic. . . . Francisco had come clean with us. . . . He was terrified and trauma-tized. . . .

Ultimately, what happened was I didn't file a case against him. The other two went to prison, and I didn't file anything else. I thought personally that Francisco had been through enough. . . . He was fearful for his life and he was just defending himself, period.

This story does not end with the teller's decision to disregard the supervisor's orders to arrest Francisco. There are three pages' worth of repetitious details about the three main characters, details that justify the police officer's moral distinctions among these three drug dealers: "Francisco wasn't a bad guy. . . . Francisco was just doing the best he could. . . . He was raising his little sister." "Steve, on the other hand, deserved trouble." "His cousin Cory had taken a gun and threatened a young girl with it back when he was in grade school."

In "Parking Lot Therapy," a voc rehab counselor goes far beyond her job requirements to provide a disabled upholsterer with psychological counseling. Rather than closing the case when he returned to work and turning her attention to the next disabled worker on her too-long case list, she spent hours providing parking lot therapy and informally kept the case open long after it was officially closed. In "Bad Dealers, Good Dealers, and Stray Bullets," the police officer ignores or disobeys (the story is not clear) the supervisor's direct order to arrest the small-time Latino drug dealer who shot up the neighborhood because "Francisco wasn't a bad guy." What about these citizen-clients encourages these street-level workers to go well beyond the demands of their jobs or to risk their jobs by ignoring orders? Who are the worthy?

In schools and human services, worthy students and clients have genuine needs that extend beyond qualifying for services. Three of our research sites were in a low-income, midwestern city, and need beyond eligibility usually included poverty. Middle-class or wealthy disabled people—a rare occurrence in the midwestern voc rehab—certainly received appropriate, routine service, but the counselors reserved their extraordinary care for those who lacked the financial resources to help themselves. In many cases, worthiness began as socioeconomic triage.

Themes often emerge by negative example. One VR counselor recalled a time when he had been temporarily reassigned to a nearby well-to-do community: "The first guy I had call me had some back problem and wanted me to buy him a hot tub. I thought, 'Oh, my first [wealthy] county person wanted a hot tub.' It's like, 'Can you fix my Mercedes so I can get the nanny?' [Laughter]" Voc rehab counselors and teachers cannot dismiss out of hand the unworthy client, such as the wealthy person asking for a hot tub. Street-level judgment lies more in the nature and extent of the services delivered and less in the intake decision. Intake decisions involve whether to accept citizens as clients by making them part of the worker's caseload and are tightly constrained by eligibility rules. Judgment enters more in terms of the character of the services provided, not who receives service.

Rather than consistently seeking the easy cases to reduce the overwhelming demands for their attention and service, street-level workers often feel that their work is demeaned by the citizen-client with superficial or one-dimensional needs. The upholsterer in "Parking Lot Therapy" received appropriate and professional service for his job-related injury, but the counselor did not provide extensive services until after she discovered his emotional turmoil. She could have legitimately ignored all of those issues: she had gotten him back to work; she had done her job. This pattern is repeated in case after case in schools, where teachers are drawn to the kid from the broken home or tough neighborhood or with a disability. But genuine need is not by itself enough to qualify someone as worthy of extraordinary services.

Police rarely take on long-term service roles with citizen-clients as teachers and counselors commonly do, but officers bend and sometimes break the rules for some individuals while going out of their way to enforce the rules for others. The criteria for their judgment are remarkably similar to those used by other street-level workers. In "Bad Dealers, Good Dealers, and Stray Bullets," the investigating officer ignored a direct order to arrest Francisco, a decision that could have cost the policeman his job. In the storyteller's eyes, the details of the story justify this insubordination: Francisco was not just a small-time Latino drug dealer but a hardworking family man who had risen from a difficult life and deserved a break. To the police, good people who have had a difficult life but are unlikely to become career criminals—people like Francisco—often are allowed to break the law, at least once.

In vocational rehabilitation the source of the disability also influences the judgment of moral worth. In "You Can't Win for Losing," (story 4.5), the voc rehab counselor provided extensive and expensive service to a "nice lady" who was going blind. She had not caused her disability. If clients are responsible for their disabilities—driving drunk and causing an car crash, for example—they are deemed less worthy than someone disabled by birth, disease, or accident. "The Squeaky Wheel Is the One That Won't Shut Up" (story 11.1) offers an example: although a quadriplegic clearly deserves all the compassion and services society can muster, the reason for his disabling condition ("He got really loaded and tried to fly his car over some trees, and it didn't quite make it.") and his demanding personality ("He still thinks if he wants it, he should get it—and he does.") preclude him from the ranks of the worthy.

Based solely on the man's disability, the street-level worker would be expected to do whatever possible for this quadriplegic client—to stretch the rules, to find a way to provide the services. For someone who cannot turn the pages of a newspaper or hold a cigarette, having an attendant provide those life routines is not unreasonable, but this client is not deemed worthy of such compassion. His recklessness and self-centeredness caused his disability, and he is troublesome. Although paralyzed from the neck down, this man was unworthy of compassion, and the begrudging counselor provided services by the book whenever possible.

The reasons for citizen-clients' problems or difficulties are less important than their motivations, however. If people are disabled because of years of heavy drinking, their motivation to improve can transform them into a worthy client. Cops will give second and even third chances to ex-offenders who used to sell drugs but are now working and trying to stay straight. Similarly, teachers see motivation to change as central to their judgment of their students' moral worth. Motivation clearly makes a client, ex-offender, or kid much easier to handle, since street-level workers typically define motivation in terms of cooperation. The motivated citizen-client is nonetheless deemed morally superior to the unmotivated. Conversely, the unmotivated, regardless of their need or circumstance, are deemed unworthy: "If someone is really trying, I will bend over backwards for them. I'll do whatever I can to help them out. . . . Then you get someone in here who has all the potential in the world, and they choose to blow it all, and it makes me angry." As another voc rehab counselor concluded, "The most difficult [cases] are the ones who don't try, and I just cut them off after a while." With these words, street-level workers reflect a deeply held American value in the moral standing of effort?[2]

Street-level construction of moral worth has a third dimension: morally worthy citizen-clients do not try to con or scam workers or the system. VR counselors, teachers, and cops see their work as virtuous. Citizen-clients—even those, like the quadriplegic, with profound and genuine needs—who try to manipulate the system for undue advantage are labeled troublemakers. Some try, usually unsuccessfully, to con the workers by being helpless: "She's real whiny and real dependent, and she is going to try to hook you and suck you in—'Poor me. I need all this help. You're the only person who can help me.'" Others, like the quadriplegic, are more demanding. In either case, legitimate and justified services are not withheld; nor are legitimate and justified complaints ignored. But cops, teachers, and counselors do not go out of their way to help the con artists and overly demanding. Gossip and rumors about troublesome and manipulative citizen-clients spread across schools, agencies, and police departments as street-level workers warn others to watch out for scams and demands. These difficult citizen-clients are often assigned to workers with reputations for taking the least guff.

Who Are the Worthy?

Contrary to the state-agent narrative, the teachers, counselors, and police in our study were often drawn to the hardest cases, the cases that made work more difficult, more dangerous, and less officially successful. Street-level workers do not consider normal clients as warranting special attention: they are effectively but routinely handled. One storyteller who works with disabled high school students acknowledges that she gets overinvested in the hard cases: "The kids I get really attracted to . . . are really vulnerable, the ones who don't have a lot of support. I probably get more involved in their lives than I should."

But challenge is not enough. To be worthy of extra investment, clients must be able to respond. In "Slammed in the Rear" (story 2.1), the storyteller overinvests in a client he knows is unlikely to change. The result of this experiment in treating an unworthy client as if he was worthy was the punishment of the counselor: he was "slammed in the rear," not by the agency or his supervisor but by the alcohol-abusing, wheelchair-bound client. Moreover, the storyteller concludes by saying that "people love to tell that story" because its negative (and humorous) outcome reinforces how important it is that street-level workers make careful and not just heartfelt judgments of worth. This judgment must be based on more than "I liked the guy."

In human services, worthy clients are also realistic. Unrealistic clients make the counselor's job impossible: those who try to achieve unrealistic goals fail; those who achieve more realistic goals are not satisfied. Most street-level workers assume a "father (or mother) knows best" attitude toward their citizen-clients, an issue examined in chapter 10. While ostensibly there to meet clients', kids', or families' needs, street-level workers believe, with considerable justification, that they are better suited to determine what is realistic. The workers are the experts; they have the experience. A worthy client is realistic, someone who "doesn't want to be a nuclear physicist, just community college." Unworthy clients are, for example, "someone who is mentally retarded and wants to become a computer analyst."

Client worthiness also has a material dimension that is tightly entwined with its other dimensions. Street-level workers do not see themselves as working for the state or ultimately accountable to elected officials. They insist that they work for citizen-clients rather than supervisors, agencies, or officials. Nonetheless, street-level workers take seriously their fiduciary responsibilities: "They're our tax dollars too," as one put it.

Worthy clients are good investments. In one story, a police officer befriends a troubled girl who years later as an adult helps the officer catch a major drug dealer. Voc rehab counselors are ready to pay for costly and long-term training if they feel it will end in a secure and adequate-paying job. They resist recent efforts spurred by welfare reform to push clients into low-paying, dead-end jobs if the workers believe that clients will benefit from expensive treatment. Counselors are willing to spend money to meet client needs—and to spend more than legislators and top officials may want—but only on those clients who are believed to have the capacity to repay the investment.

This material dimension of worth is a summative judgment: if citizen-clients have genuine needs, are of good character, and are motivated to respond to treatment, then they are likely to repay society for street-level workers' investments of time, effort, and money. Or, in the case of police, the worthy perpetrator, like Francisco, will repay society for his break by not committing other crimes and by continuing to take care of his family and handle the day-to-day difficulties of life at the low end of the economic order.

The material dimension of worth is the most tangible expression of how street-level judgments alter the distribution of government services and sanctions. These judgments can mean the difference between a few weeks of training followed by a referral to minimum-wage service jobs—what VR workers generically call "McDonalds jobs"—and several years of tuition and support at a community college with the possibility of a well-paying job with medical benefits (the most important job benefit for the disabled) and a future. It means the difference between an arrest and likely jail time for reckless endangerment and simply ignoring the crime. When street-level workers extend or withhold services and sanctions, when they go out of their way to help some citizen-clients while ignoring or punishing others, then street-level workers are making normative judgments about who gets what from government: they are simultaneously fusing the performance of the state with the construction of the social order.

9. Responding to the Worthy

Story 9.1.   Western Police Department
"Borrowed Pants and a $12,000 Credit Card Bill"

This is an incident that occurred about three years ago. I was
working as a detective at a school. . . . It's a predominantly
white school—I would say 99 percent white. Even [Flores], one
of the two suspects in the case I'm going to describe, though she
had a Hispanic name, seemed white. . . . It's an upper-middle-
class school. . . . Smart kids, mostly kids that are college bound.
. . . The people in this case were no exception. All three of them
were pretty affluent. . . . It was a lot nicer neighborhood than I
live [in], with lovely homes and a bunch of horse property, so I
would say all of them were upper middle class. . . .

So I was assigned a case where a girl by the last name of
[Adams] had lent her pants, believe it or not, to another girl by
the name of [Catherine Lloyd]. In her pants she'd accidentally
left the wallet, and in that wallet was a credit card that her
mother had given Adams to buy some things. She mistakenly
left that credit card in there when Lloyd borrowed the pants.

So a few weeks later, Adams's mother got her credit card
statement with about $12,000 worth of charges on there.[1] There
were charges to a . . . restaurant with $300 bill. . . . Several
charges to go to another popular restaurant . . . at $400 or $500
at a time. . . . Several charges came from some of your more
expensive clothing stores.

Obviously, when Adams's mom got it, she thought that her
daughter had charged up all the bills and things. She said, "No,
Catherine Lloyd had the pants that contained the credit card for
a week before I asked for it back, and that's when all these
charges were made."

I contacted Catherine Lloyd, and she was seventeen years old at the time. She adamantly denied everything. She says she never touched the credit card and doesn't know what I'm talking about. We went around and around and around about it and she continued to deny it.

Adams told me that there would be another friend with Catherine Lloyd named [Susan Flores]. I contacted Flores. She denied it, denied it, denied it.

So I started to go back to the different stores, sequentially going back in order so I could see if they remembered who charged these things. All of these stores remembered because it was such an elaborate bill and they remembered that the kid who paid for it was kind of young to have a credit card, but they didn't check anything.[2] They all described exactly what Catherine Lloyd and Susan Flores look like. [A detailed investigation followed, including photo lineups, interviews, and handwriting analysis.]

So I went back to [Lloyd] with all of that evidence, and she still denied it. And she denied it and said, "It wasn't me. It wasn't me. . . ." It was the same with Flores, "It wasn't me. It wasn't me. It wasn't me. . . ." [A former boyfriend then confesses that he had let Lloyd charge clothes at a boutique where he worked.] I go to Lloyd with that evidence, and she still denies it and says, "It wasn't me, wasn't me. It wasn't me."

At that point, I went to Lloyd's home and talked to her parents. . . . I explained the whole situation, presented the evidence, and really kind of made a pitch for her to tell the truth. . . . If she continued to lie like this, she was going to be convicted of a felony, because that's what that is. . . . Still, she denied it, denied it, denied it, and I left.

The next morning . . . Lloyd's mom and dad march Catherine into my office with all the items she had charged up. She broke down and started to cry and said that in fact she had charged all these things and now wanted to repent. I asked her who was with her when she did all these things, and she said it was Susan Flores.

We bring Flores down, and Flores still denied it and denied it and denied it. She said, "It wasn't me. It wasn't me."

At that time, Lloyd was about seventeen and about nine months. In our juvenile system, if you're within six months of being eighteen, they try you as an adult, typically. With that you

can be convicted of a felony, so she would start her adult life as
a convicted felon. Flores was the same age. . . .

I had some say as to whether it should remain in juvenile
court. If they remained in the juvenile court, really all they had
to do is pay back what it was that they stole and then their
record is basically sealed. . . .

I came to the conclusion that Lloyd . . . had changed. . . .
Somehow, somewhere in there she came to a revelation that she
shouldn't have done that. What I did was I asked . . . to keep
Lloyd in juvenile court and sent Flores to the adult court. I
really got the impression that Flores had really no sense of right
and wrong. . . .

Lloyd's parents were so cooperative, and they believed what
their daughter was accused of. Flores's parents were a divorced
couple. I never saw the mom and dad at the same time. I'd
always have to see them separately. They were very adamant
that no matter what, their daughter didn't do it. . . .

We kept Lloyd in the juvenile court, and we sent Flores to
adult court. . . . Lloyd's mom called me or I ran into to her or
something. She told me that [Catherine] was going on to college
. . . and was doing really well. I think Flores started to kind of
move in a different direction. If I'm not mistaken, I don't think
that Flores graduated [from high school]. I think it was kind of a
turning point for both of them.

This long story uses the narrative device of repetition. Because the
teller stretches out the details and repeats the two girls' incessant
denials, the listener feels the officer's weary frustration. All the story
details, exaggerations, meanderings, and repetitions give greater
impact to the police officer's judgment that gets to the heart of street-
level moral reasoning.

These two girls were the same age, committed the same crime, initially responded to being caught with the same denials, but received
vastly different treatment from the police officer storyteller. As discussed in chapter 8, different treatment was justified by the different
identities. The two girls began the story with the same identity—
spoiled rich girls who do not take responsibility—but one girl's identity
is transformed, while the other remains fixed. The first girl, in the religious terms of the storyteller, "repented" and came to the "revelation"
that she had done something wrong. She confessed. The second girl
never expressed a "sense of right and wrong."

The families of two girls also responded differently, highlighting the moral distinctions between the two. Catherine's parents, however rich and privileged, acted morally and responsibly: "Her mom said after I left that she not only took a hard look at her daughter, but she took a hard look at herself." The contrasts with Susan's parents. "You couldn't have more evidence, but even her parents stepped up for her and said, [echoing Susan's own denials], 'It wasn't her. It wasn't her.'" Adding yet another layer of moral judgment, the storyteller adds the detail that Susan's parents were divorced.

The decision to treat the same crime differently had, in the context of this story, lasting material consequences. The repentant Catherine went to college; the unrepentant Susan never graduated from high school and went "in a different direction." The difference in the treatment of these two girls was not based on the rules that guide police work or in the nature of the offense but rather on the officer's judgment of their varying conduct in the face of questioning and comparative worthiness as judged by the street-level worker. The following tale is much simpler: a special education teacher refuses to comply with budget-cutting administrators "downtown" because she believes a kid needs services.

Story 9.2.   Midwestern Middle School
"Ignoring Orders"

There was a cutback here about a year to a year and a half ago. The social work staff was cut due to a budgetary problem.

There was a student who was on my [special education] caseload [and] was receiving services from a social worker, and only the most severe students from the time of the cuts would be served by a social worker.

One student I thought needed to be seen by a social worker a couple of times a month, just to talk out issues—behavioral issues and social issues. Downtown told me to get his mother up here and have her sign a consent form to relinquish service, and I said, "No."

He needed continued services, and they said, "No, he is not a SED kid," which is a severely emotionally disturbed kid. Those are the only students who are going to be seen by social workers, the SED students.

I said, "Well, that is not fair to him, because he needs help also."

Well, they said, "Get his mother up and have her sign the consent to have him released from social work."

And I said, "Yeah, fine," not wanting to do it.

So his mom came up at the annual IEP [individual education plan, a legal requirement for special education students] meeting, and I didn't give her the paperwork to sign the release of consent. I filled out the paperwork and forwarded it downtown.

They said, "It is all fine, but we need a release from social work."

So I said, "Okay, fine."

So, meanwhile, the kid still gets service. The law states that unless the parent or legal guardian signs the release, you cannot stop service. Anyway, I never contacted the mother again. I kept on forwarding the paperwork back downtown, and they eventually took it, and he is still getting social work. That is my way of saying, "Screw you guys."

Citizen-client worthiness is a continuum, and many citizen-clients— like Francisco (story 8.2), the upholsterer (story 8.1), and Catherine— are a mixture of worthy and unworthy traits. Similarly, the street-level workers' response to worthy citizen-clients is a continuum. In many cases, these street-level workers will stretch and bend rules and procedures but need not break or violate them to help worthy clients. Discretion in the rules for charging juveniles as adults permitted the dissimilar treatment of the two girls in "Borrowed Pants and a $12,000 Credit Card Bill." Early in the story, the teller stresses the ages of both girls—closer to eighteen than seventeen—to underscore the discretion in how they were eventually charged. At other times, savvy street-level workers use rules and procedures to obviate legitimate demands, as in the case of the teacher using the rules about special education services to ignore her supervisor's direct order to terminate social work services. Sometimes helping a worthy citizen-client requires little more than exceeding bureaucratic expectations, as in the next story about providing $1,500 worth of dental work to an angry woman.

Story 9.3. Western Vocational Rehabilitation
"A Little Self-Esteem Will Do It"

I met [Carol] for the first time at the . . . clinic. She was a very angry woman who hated systems and didn't want to ask for help. . . . As Carol was saying different things, she would often cover her mouth when she attempted to smile. At one point I noticed that Carol was missing several of her teeth—two in front and three on the side.

In an effort not to embarrass Carol, I decided to give Carol a laundry list of services that VR is able to offer. . . . When I mentioned dental exams, her eyes lit up and she smiled—immediately covering her mouth with her hand—and said, "Oh, I didn't know you did dental stuff."

I went on to explain that sometimes when people have missing teeth, it affects their confidence level, and they tend to be socially withdrawn. Carol agreed and said she gets so embarrassed by her teeth that she doesn't want any friendships and feels she can't compete with coworkers. . . .

As Carol's case progressed, I set her up for a dental exam. She was very anxious yet excited. It was determined that a partial denture would be the best option. . . .

She landed a job as a sales representative for a home-improvement company. She has constant contact with the public and loves every minute of it. She smiles all the time and has made several friends with her coworkers. . . .

Sometimes counselors need to find out about the person as a whole before judgment is made that they just can't keep a job. To get $1,500 worth of dental treatment from the agency can be risky. Comments I've heard . . . are, "She doesn't need teeth to work." "How do we know she won't quit?" "She won't appreciate it."

Although my beliefs conflicted with the agency's policies, I felt Carol deserved a chance. . . . I feel that $1,500 is a small price to pay for a life-altering change.

In this story, as in so many others, the street-level worker pushes the system to serve the worthy citizen-client. The worker didn't break any rules, disobey orders, or undercut agency policy, but she did stretch the eligibility rules as far as possible to serve a client who she thought was worth the risk. Given the woman's poor job history and chip on her shoulder, others may have disagreed and not offered the expensive dental work, and the pattern of low self-esteem and unemployment might well have continued. (One of the counselors at the midwestern voc rehab site told a nearly identical story with the added twist that the client had lost her false teeth and the counselor had to buy a second set.) One special education teacher articulates well the attitude of street-level workers toward rules:

> I'll kind of use the system and tweak the system to get more benefits—not so much for me, but for the kids on my casework. . . . I'll not file certain things, or I will file more than enough things to get the best for the nineteen students that I am responsible for. Its just a general feeling I get. It's a personal thing. I like to do the best that I can, and I'll bend the system, and occasionally I'll snap it in half.

As these stories suggest, one common and fundamental response to a worthy client is, in the street-level workers' phrase, "to give them a break." A break can mean overlooking an offense, such as a minor drug offense or even something major, like shooting up a neighborhood. A break can involve providing false teeth to an angry out-of-work woman or a police officer befriending a troubled teenager simply because "she was a good kid." At other times a teacher decides to forgive a kid who hits him, against the wishes of the vice principal adhering to the current zero-tolerance policy for violence. Sometimes giving someone a break requires the street-level worker to get creative with the rules, as in "You Can't Win for Losing" (story 4.5).

At other times, bending the rules a little is not enough, and street-level workers provide extraordinary services for a select few citizen-clients. Those on the front lines will go so far beyond the expectations of rules and policy that they are essentially providing a new, unauthorized service. A western vocational rehabilitation counselor told a story she titled "Determination" about an out-of-work former plumber and truck driver who abused drugs and alcohol and routinely lost his temper with supervisors—not a likely candidate for extraordinary services. In the eyes of this counselor, however, his determination—"He was just so motivated to go out and work"—erased all the negatives. Returning to work as a plumber would have required numerous, expensive tools:

> I literally spent probably two weeks trying to get all these tools for him, trying to write in a hurry because I had to write up the whole written rehabilitation plan and put it into the computer. So I had to order the tools from Sears in Houston. I had to fly them here, and it was like an extra $150 to get them here two-day air.

Then we had to add another vendor because Sears didn't carry it all, . . . and it was like another $500 somewhere else in tools that he got besides that. Just the whole thing took forever. It was a major fiasco to try to get all this stuff organized and make sure we use the right vendors, but he's working.

For this citizen-client, the street-level worker was not trying to cut corners to make her job simpler and easier.[3] To the contrary, she made her job more complicated and harder than was required, and the services to this disabled plumber did not end there. She made the newly equipped plumber promise to call her every other week just to tell her how things were going and told him to call right away "if you get mad at work—you're going to call me first, before you quit your job, and talk to me about it." For the worthy few, the street-level workers put no limits on services. They are also willing to break the rules, as the next story testifies.

Story 9.4.   Midwestern Vocational Rehabilitation
"Hearing Aids Conk Out"

I had a young woman who came to me who needed hearing aids—not totally deaf, but very severely impaired. The catch was, she was working. Voc rehab had initially helped her with hearing aids to get the job years ago, and the aids finally conked out, and we are talking over $1,000 for two hearing aids. So that is pretty expensive, and insurance does not cover hearing aids. So we are talking out of pocket, and this was someone in a clerical-type job who does not have that kind of money, period.

Under "order of selection" [the term for strict eligibility rules from the federal government that were in effect at that time], she was not eligible because she needed only short-term service. . . . So in order for her to be eligible, she had to not get the hearing aids, lose her job because she could not perform her job, and not have a job. Then she could come back and apply for service to get the hearing aids to get help finding a job. . . . To get help you have to lose the job, but losing the job defeats the purpose because the hearing aids are to keep the job. So it is a vicious circle.

So what I did to help her out was just to invent some services

on paper that were beneficial but, you know, kind of marginal—
more just to put it on paper to get her what she needed, which is
what she did.

And she is still working, and she is doing fine.

Providing extraordinary service, overinvesting in a few individuals,
and breaking rules can come at the expense of other citizen-clients.
Street-level workers are painfully aware of their limits in time and
energy and their agency's limited resources: not every citizen-client
receives an exception to the "order of selection" and $1,000 hearing
aids. With the time needed to write the rehab plan, find and order the
tools, and set up job counseling, it was as if for two weeks the counselor had just the one client and an unlimited budget. The counselor in
"Parking Lot Therapy" (story 8.1) dropped, if just for an afternoon,
her other responsibilities—her other cases, appointments, and the endless reports—to take the distraught upholsterer to the mental health
center. When the workers there proved unresponsive, she provided several hours of unplanned crisis counseling. Such counseling was not
part of her job yet constituted an additional and continuing service she
provided to this troubled man long after the case was officially closed.

In "Slammed in the Rear" (story 2.1), a different voc rehab counselor repeatedly tried and failed to help a hapless client, even paying
$1,000 out of pocket to fix the client's car. In "A Happy Ending" (story
1.1), the street-level worker wrote up a series of expensive but fabri-
cated services for the former beauty queen so that she could use the
money to buy a car, a purchase that is not authorized by voc rehab.
These select few clients receive the street-level workers' compassion,
creativity, and ability to manipulate the system. It is as if by overinvesting in the few, the workers compensate for all the cases they cannot
reach because of personal, practical, or policy constraints.

For the worthy clients, street-level workers are also willing to trade
bureaucratic failure for client success. In human services, bureaucratic
success is measured in case closures. The sooner a voc rehab worker
can enter a "26" (the code for case closed) in the computer, the greater
the measured success. Agencies with too many cases dangling open for
too long are considered failing. Rapid closure means that more cases
are processed. Prolonged cases are expensive, like this example, which
lasted for at least six years.

Story 9.5.   Midwestern Vocational Rehabilitation
"The Life and Times of Doug"

A guy named [Doug] went to a rural school district in the area.
. . . They didn't provide, or chose not to provide, or said they
didn't have the funds to provide—whatever excuse you want to
use—the proper services for him. . . . He had a major vision loss,
and they didn't provide the proper reading materials for him,
the proper equipment, and he was flunking. So they brought
him down here to the state school [for the visually impaired],
and he very quickly picked up and was turning out to be an A
student, very bright. . . .

So he was at the school for the blind, and [voc rehab] did an
intake on him. Basically what he wanted from us [was] services,
education, necessary computer, and so on so he could go to college. The job goal was not real clear at that time. . . . So we put
computer programmer for the job goal, just to satisfy the
bureaucracy.

At this point in the case, the rules of the agency would have strongly
encouraged, if not required, the counselor to develop a short-term
training plan that would lead expeditiously to a job and a case closure.
The counselor took another path—a long, meandering, expensive
path—for this bright, motivated student.

Story 9.5, *Continued*

He was bright enough that he had potential and that college
would be a good risk for him. So we sent him off to [state uni-
versity]. We paid for all sorts of services along the way. . . . His
grades were consistently good, usually 3.5 to 4.0.

It was a long case—he was with me for about six years. He
went into the direction of computer information systems and
ended up completing that program. We also ended up purchasing a laptop computer for him because he needed access to the
school mainframe but needed to be in large print. . . .

We started a job placement for him . . . and we had to do a
lot of counseling with him to keep his spirits up. . . . I made several trips to meet with him, and he did finally land a job. He
started making $28,500 a year plus plenty of benefits, which is a

heck of a lot better than I was making at the time. . . . So he was
a successful client.

Based on the people-processing standard of moving cases quickly
and at low cost from intake to closure, this case was a failure. Or, at a
minimum, policy accountants would not likely consider it cost
beneficial. But from the street-level worker's point of view, this was an
example when the system worked or, more precisely, when he made the
system work for the client. A worthy client received extensive and long-
term services that eventually enabled the near-blind young man get
and keep a good job.

Helping a worthy client may at other times require doing battle with an
often rule bound and penurious system. For the worthy few, street-
level workers become client advocates. Advocacy often involves prolonged, difficult, tedious, and conflictual encounters with "the system."
Street-level workers can become pushy and uncompromising on behalf
of certain individuals. By taking the moral high ground, they place others in the system in awkward positions. For special citizen-clients, such
workers strain their peer and professional relations, burning bridges
that may be needed to help other clients. Good working relations with
others in the complex warren of social service agencies is a resource
that street-level workers are willing to spend, even squander, for worthy clients. As the next story attests, these encounters can prove
"Harder Than Brain Surgery." Although the story is truncated here, its
length speaks of the Sisyphean efforts and frustration the street-level
worker endured.

Story 9.6.   Midwestern Vocational Rehabilitation
"Harder Than Brain Surgery"

We have had some problems with getting services approved
through the consultant in [state capital]. Several years ago—I
had only been here a couple of years—I had a client who was
diagnosed with a brain tumor who had surgery and also a learning disability.
    In my speaking with him through several appointments, it
was clear to me that the thing that he was most concerned about
was that he was going to lose his home because they recommended brain surgery. He was extremely concerned that he was

going to lose his home. I think they had seven children: three of his, three of hers, and one of their own.

So I wrote an "exception to policy" to the agency because he did not meet the income guidelines because he was drawing unemployment. He was over the $375 guideline, so I wrote an "exception to policy." . . .

So I got all these questions. You know what it is like: "Please answer this, why this, why this, why this" type of thing. So I sit down and I answer them all, and then we run across the street and fax it. We did this for a couple of weeks. . . . I probably answered twenty-five to thirty or forty additional questions as to why we needed to do this for this gentleman.

The agency finally agreed after all this going back and forth that they would pay for three months of his mortgage payments, which were not that grand—it was like $420 or something a month. When you consider what I could have paid for the brain surgery without needing approval from anyone, which would have cost thousands of dollars. . . .

So anyway they answered. They finally came back after all this back and forth, back and forth on the questions.[4] They said I could pay for three months. They also had a half a month of arrears or something like that.

So I called up and said "Well, that's fine that you have done this," but I said, "I need you to also state that I can pay for all his arrearage."

Well, one of the bigwigs in [the state capital] told me, he said, "Well that is really against our policy. We don't pay for things that have already occurred. . . ."

I said, "Yes. That is why this is called an exception to policy."

Those were my exact words, and he became offended at that statement and would not, did not, agree to do that. He became offended by my attitude, I guess, and so he went and told my boss's boss, who called me about twenty minutes later.

He goes, "[The bigwig] was really upset and said you were rude and had inferred that he was an idiot."

I said, "I never called him an idiot."

He said, "Well, do you think you might want to apologize to him?"

And I said, "For asking him to do his job?" . . .

So finally I got [my boss's boss] cornered [at a meeting] the next week. I said, "Well, look, either we are going to do this or not. Either we are going to help this family or not. We are not going to halfway help them because halfway isn't going to solve the problem for them. Either give me a yes or no, but don't give me a half yes." So then [the boss's boss] went out on a limb and told me I could pay [the arrears on the mortgage].

[The brain surgery was only partially successful.] In fact, when he came out of the surgery, he couldn't even read or write. . . . So he got a lot of physical therapy and speech therapy and that type of thing but was just not able to return to work. . . .

Well, I kept the case open probably a couple of years past the point of the surgery—you know, checking in with him. . . .

"The system"—that amorphous collection of agencies, rules, procedures, supervisors, and supervisor's supervisors—creates absurd, Kafkaesque constraints, as in "Hearing Aids Conk Out." Or the system places endless steps, procedures, and levels of approval that can exhaust and discourage even the most diligent street-level worker. Like the voc rehab counselor in "Harder Than Brain Surgery," one teacher recalled his earlier efforts to help a psychotic kid in New York:

I don't know if you know anything about New York City, but the Board of Ed is just a gigantic blob that just keeps growing and growing. It takes on a life of its own, and kids do get lost. Staff gets lost too. So it was just a matter of one person—me—acting as an advocate. . . . So I was the one that kind of pushed and kept on pushing for about three or four months until she was admitted to the pediatric ward at [a mental health hospital].

Street-level workers cannot fight the system for every citizen-client or even every deserving citizen-client. Advocacy is one of street-level workers' scarcest resources. They lack the time, the tolerance, or the goodwill of their supervisors to push and push for everyone. They reserve this resource for the worthy few.

It is never easy for street-level workers to make judgments about which citizen-clients deserve a break, should receive extraordinary services, or justify battling the system. There are no unambiguous criteria to discern citizen-client worthiness. These judgment calls are complex and subtle—gray, not black and white. Although experienced street-level workers learn to make these nuanced judgments, distinguishing the worthy from the unworthy is never simple or straightforward, even for the experienced. In response, street-level workers develop a norm of suspending judgment. They often begin contact by providing routine treatment or response, but if they see the elements of worth, they start testing the client.

In many ways, the judgment of worth is based on a courtship of street-level worker and citizen-client, but it is a courtship of unequals. Police officers, teachers, and voc rehab counselors do not make snap judgments: experienced workers have been burned too often. Instead, they offer what one street-level worker called "little pearls" and watch how citizen-clients respond. As kids, clients, or even offenders pass or fail these little tests, street-level workers elevate them to the status of the worthy, demote them to the rank of the unworthy, or leave them in the vast middle ground of normal or standard treatment. When Francisco admitted to his minor drug dealing (story 8.2) and Catherine finally admitted to the credit card fraud (story 9.1), they passed the crucial test of honesty, and their status was transformed.

To illustrate this evaluation process, one voc rehab counselor told a story of a thirty-year-old man who dropped into the office just before lunch. He was scheduled to start community college the next week but had just learned that his financial aid, a Pell Grant, had been held up because he had failed to register for the military draft when he was eighteen. The counselor recalled,

> The system normally would say that "I can't talk to you right now. I got to make an appoint for you to come in 'cause it is about 11:30. Besides, school starts next week and there is no way."[5] We legally have sixty days to determine eligibility, and so, "I'm sorry we can't do this."

In other words, he should respond as "the system" would require by following the standard procedures, but to respond bureaucratically would not help the client. As the story unfolds, the client had many strikes against him: "He never worked and was pushing thirty. He had been incarcerated more than he had been out." Nonetheless, as the storyteller adds details, the client became more than just an aging loser. He was clearly disabled but had the ability to succeed in community college. He was eligible and realistic in his goals. He admitted his problems and had already tried to turn his life around. "'I have been incarcerated. I have gotten into drugs, but I am a born-again Christian'— that is the way he described himself. 'I don't do that anymore. I have gotten myself together.'" He was motivated to change but needed help.

The story, like much street-level work, presents contradictions and dilemmas with the client simultaneously having traits of worthiness and unworthiness. The counselor responds by testing. He gives the walk-in a doctor's form to document the disability and says that the client needs to get it back by 3:00. The client returns by 3:00 with the form completed. "So, I've satisfied myself that he is really disabled [genuine need], . . . and he appeared to have the ability to go to college [worthy of investing resources]. . . . He doesn't have this big pie in the sky—'I don't want to be a nuclear physicist, rather, you know, a reasonable thing' [realistic]—and it all sounded good to me." In four hours, the client proves his worth, and the counselor responds by cutting through the red tape so that the man could start college.

> So we set out with all the forms and did all the stuff on the computer and certified him, did this work for an individualized plan. And I did an authorization for school for tuition and books for the first semester and handed it to him and he was out of here at 3:30 on the same day that he dropped in without an appointment at 11:00.

Like this walk-in, many citizen-clients present a complex mixture of traits, some that would demote them to being considered unworthy of extra help or concern and others that would elevate them to the status of the worthy. In "Determination," the counselor dropped everything to get the expensive tools for a plumber who had a poor work history and an explosive temper. In another story, "The Rehabilitated Alcoholic," the street-level worker goes into considerable detail about a fifty-year-old with a long history of drug and alcohol abuse and many years in prison, an unlikely candidate for extra help. But he had changed and was ready to take advantage of the assistance offered. He was ready to work. A former stripper, drug abuser, and con in another story also received special attention from her worker because she had kicked her drug habit, was now a good parent, and wanted to become a welder—good, hard, unglamorous work.

Like the walk-in, the alcoholic, and the ex-stripper, citizen-clients who are deemed worthy receive extraordinary service and attention from these street-level workers. Their cases are kept open long after the rules would permit (and the supervisors would prefer), postponing the bureaucratic measure of success, the much-valued 26. To achieve success for the client, street-level workers may jeopardize their own measure of success, a situation that can put the agency and agency director at some risk if they collectively fail to meet their monthly quota of case closures. (Reviewing the status of case closures is the primary agenda item at midwestern vocational rehabilitation agency's monthly staff meetings.) Agencies and counselors are under constant—and, with welfare reform, increasing—pressure to close cases.

Street-level workers will work unpaid overtime for the worthy client. They will give breaks to hardworking drug dealers and repentant perpetrators of credit-card fraud. They may even ignore orders to follow the rules to provide breaks for the worthy. Street-level workers will let other cases slide and postpone the all-consuming paperwork. They drop whatever else they are doing, as in the case of "Parking Lot Therapy" (story 8.1). They come in on weekends to help a client move to a better apartment. They spend their own money, provide a shoulder to cry on, and battle the bureaucracy on behalf of worthy clients. In one story, a voc rehab counselor even sues her agency to get needed services for a worthy client, an action that eventually helps the client but risks the unforgiving anger of the state bureaucracy.

Except in "Slammed in the Rear" (story 2.1), overinvestment in clients leads to genuine and not just bureaucratic success. In these stories, street-level workers may not quickly meet the bureaucratically defined measures of success, but citizen-clients are profoundly and permanently helped. These stories end like "Parking Lot Therapy" and "Borrowed Pants and a $12,000 Credit Card Bill": years later, the citizen-client continues to work or remains law-abiding. Stories of the services and breaks given to worthy citizen-clients show how street-level workers can make lasting differences in the lives of at least a few clients. These workers describe their jobs as callings, and these few citizen-clients call out to the workers and make worthwhile their difficult and often unrewarding work. Worthy clients make street-level workers feel worthy as well. The citizens also benefit because these clients are genuine success stories: they are the citizen-clients who deserved help, received help, and are now productive, nondependent, lawful community members.

Other individuals call out to street-level workers but become sources of frustration and low-level conflict. In these instances, the desire to provide extraordinary help or consideration gives way to pragmatism and realism, the subject of the next chapter. Indeed, "The Big Bad Counselor Strikes Again" (story 10.1) begins with a clear admission that street-level workers often should and must impose their wiser views on reluctant and impractical citizen-clients.

10. Street-Level Worker Knows Best

Story 10.1. Midwestern Vocational Rehabilitation
"The Big Bad Counselor Strikes Again"

This story is kind of an example of—it reminded me of this yesterday because [the vocational rehabilitation counselors] were talking about how in some organizations some people are angry at us because they feel that we decide for the client what they are going to do and we don't let them do what they want to, and our answer to that is, "Well, sometimes we don't let them do what they want to because it would not be practical or it would not be feasible."[1]

An example of this came to my mind. This person named [Mary] came to me and she wanted to buy a computer system and vision aids for her and she wanted to go to college, to complete a two- or maybe a four-year program and then go back to work as a secretary or something like that. Well, this is all fine and good until we get records up for her and we find out that she is mentally retarded, that her academic abilities are basically low primary school, and she had a hard time even learning to take care of herself, to walk around her neighborhood, and things like that. And yet she comes to me with all these things.[2]

I told her, "These are the services that we can provide you. We can make sure that we have the equipment that you need and the training that you need to take care of yourself in your home. We can help you find a job—maybe at a workshop or in the community, maybe as an assembler, or maybe even as a receptionist at a fairly simple job where you don't have to do a whole lot." But it was stuff that she would be able to do as much as she is able to do.

123

Well, she didn't want to do that. She wanted me to get this stuff for her, to help her go to school. And I said, "Well, we are not going to be able to do it."

And the next thing I know, I get a call from our local state representative on our client's behalf saying, "Why are you doing this to this person? Why doesn't she have, you know, a chance to succeed? Because she is a black woman in a poor neighborhood? Are you going to hold this against her and discriminate and not provide services to her?" Of course, this is a black representative, which didn't help any.

As it turns out [the black representative] was a real big help on this case. But, you know, he sort of hinted that maybe this was a problem, which just sort of got my attention and kind of led me to wonder, you know, how some of the people think in the legislature: that not only do [voc rehab counselors] hold clients back, but if they are black or impoverished, we rip them off even more, we cheat them even more.

So I told him what was going on, and he wanted information about it. So I got the release that I'm supposed to get from Mary and sent him all sorts of information from the case letting him, letting [the black representative], know what is going on— her abilities, her intelligence level, her work evaluation that we did to support the fact that she would probably be best placed at a very low level of employment due to her abilities.

We did all that, and he looked at them for a while, and he called me back and he said, "Well, it looks to me like you all have done a really good job in providing services to her." He said, "I have talked to her, and I want her to learn to take care of herself at home so that she is not dependent on the system." He said, "I don't think you are going to be able to get her in college because it looks kind of obvious on the report that she is not going to be able to do that, that she is not going to benefit from a computer system." And he said, "I have talked to her, and I have told her to cooperate with you and what we should do. I don't see how you can do it any differently." And he said that, and we left on good terms and that sort of thing.

So I wanted to share that to kind of illustrate the point that even when some clients get angry they might call the TV, the local TV station; I have talked to [a local TV reporter] two or three times. And even sometimes they go right to the governor—

if they're mad, they go right to the governor's office, they go right to the senators. We got a few calls from [U.S. senator's] office when he was in power.

Even though all these people might get involved doesn't change the fact that we try real hard to meet people's needs and help them the best we can. And at this point, it was really nice to see somebody else—a state legislator—come back and agree with us on what we are trying to do.

Street-level workers and citizen-clients do not always agree and do not always get along. In an important twist to this story, the legislator eventually confirms and supports the counselor's judgment, agreeing that the street-level worker knows best. Street-level wisdom and pragmatism is also the theme of the next story, although in a different setting and dealing with different issues.

Story 10.2. Western Police Department
"Cut the Power"

The call comes out, and it has to do with this loud music complaint. I get dispatched to the apartment complex, a two-story complex. . . . The complex fits, I would say, thirty units. It's a block construction type, a fairly new complex. I go in the area of where the music is supposed to be coming from, and as I approach the front door, I can hear some very loud heavy-metal-type music just blaring. As I knock on the door, I don't get a response.

I knock on the door again, and I can see a subject sitting in a chair. He was maybe, I would guess, about fifteen feet away from the door, kind of sitting directly in front of the living room area. . . . He was a white male. His hair was kind of long. . . . And what I could see out of the shadows, he was probably mid- to late twenties. That's all I could tell.

I knock on the window, and obviously he looks at me and he notices that I'm standing there and just yells out, "Fuck you," and continues to play the music and he laughs.[3] So I pound on the door again and on the window, trying to get him to come to the door, but he just continues to cuss me.

I wasn't concerned for my safety because he didn't do any movement.[4] He just sat there, and, I guess, basically just the impression I got is that he was sitting back and there wasn't anything I could do. He knew that I couldn't really touch him, so he was safe in there. . . .

I go up to the complainant—the girl who called us lived directly above him. So I go up to her apartment. She's a college student, white female, and she says, "I'm trying to study for my midterms and this guy—I don't know what his problem is. He does this every so often, but today he's, you know, really loud. Today you can even feel vibrations on the walls." Which I did. I touched the wall, and I could actually feel the vibration from the music coming from down below.

She said, "I wish there was something you could do about that." So I asked her if there was an on-site manager, and she said that there wasn't, that there was no one else.

So I go back in and knock on the door, and the same thing happens. The guy just totally ignored me and would not come to the door and continues to swear at me. At this point, then, I started to get a little agitated because I can't get him to come to the door. So I sit back and decide what I'm going to do.

I decided to go to the electrical box leading to his apartment. So I go back there and cut the power to his apartment, and I could hear him screaming, hysterical. This time he was calling me a motherfucker—"You son of a bitch." I waited for him to come, but he never came out. . . .

At that point, then, I walked up to the door and knocked on the door and said, "I'll tell you what. If I have to come back again, I'm going to kick the door in, and I will take action. You will go to jail. I'm tired of this. This thing is over NOW. I hope we understand each other." And I left.

About this same incident, it was a year or two after this thing occurred, we had the administrators come and talk to us. The session that we were in was advanced officer training. . . . There was about sixty, maybe seventy, officers in the room. The main speaker was basically trying to get us to start thinking about community-based policing, our train of thought, to be creative and not be afraid to test the waters. I brought up this incident of the loud party call and of what I had decided to do. I solved the problem: I cut the power to the apartment.

The administrator, he kind of rolled his eyes and said, "You know that really isn't quite what they were looking for. That wasn't the kind of problem solving they were looking for."

Maybe it was a little out of bounds, but, myself, I thought, "I did what I had to do to solve the problem for the other citizen." The guy didn't go to jail, so as far as monetary-wise, he didn't suffer there. But from that time on I didn't hear any recurrence from him. . . . Sometimes we have to go out there and make decisions to take care of things. To me, I felt that, you know, I solved the problem, and I don't feel bad about it. . . . I could see that the lady was stressing on her level, the complainant. I just felt inside that I needed to do something.

In story 10.1, the self-described "big bad counselor" admits, "sometimes we don't let [clients] do what they want because it would not be practical or it would not be feasible." There are times when the street-level worker knows what is right for the client, and in this story even the meddlesome state legislator eventually agrees and supports the counselor's pragmatic wisdom. Pragmatic improvisation guides police work as well. After evoking public criticism from an administrator in front of sixty or seventy fellow officers, the street cop reflects on his actions and provides a working definition of street-level pragmatism: "Maybe it was a little out of bounds, but, myself, I thought, 'I did what I had to do to solve the problem for the other citizen.'"

Street-level workers cannot create an ideal world where all citizen-clients respond to workers' best efforts and where policies and procedures effectively guide decisions and respond to individual needs and circumstances. These men and women work in a world of often painful accommodation and compromise. In the stories and circumstances discussed in the previous two chapters, the interests of the citizen-clients and the street-level workers converged. The workers and citizen-clients were allies fighting to achieve the best for worthy clients in opposition to indifferent agencies and cumbersome procedures. Yet, importantly, in these stories, success in helping the worthy proved an ultimate success for the policy and the state, even though these successes often required postponing the bureaucratic counting of success. This and the following chapters explore the different circumstances when the views and interests of the workers and the citizen-clients do not converge, when they exist in tension and, all too often, in conflict.

In such circumstances, street-level realism eclipses idealism. Street-level workers trust their own definitions of situations and their judgments over those of supervisors and citizen-clients. And in such circumstances, workers rely on pragmatic improvisation, not following rules, which provide only general guidance, assuming an idealized

127

world of predictability and clear categories, a world far removed from street-level work. As these stories testify, street-level workers believe that they know better—better than supervisors, better than policymakers, better than citizen-clients.

Pragmatism eclipses idealism when a wide array of circumstances intrude on the relationship between worker and citizen-client. These intrusions come in many forms in street-level stories, so many different forms that it is perhaps more accurate to observe that pragmatism and realism are the dominant norms and the idealism discussed previously is the exception. Yet in many stories, pragmatism and idealism are tightly interwoven, suggesting two interdependent strands of street-level decision making. At times pragmatism is required because of the direct conflict between the worker and citizen, as in "The Big Bad Counselor Strikes Again" and "Cut the Power." At other times, as in the next story, the nature of the policy and conflicts with other agencies place barriers between workers and citizens and their ability to achieve ideal results.

Story 10.3. Midwestern Vocational Rehabilitation
"Take Your Social Security and Go Home"

Another story is about a small, nonprofit organization. They contract with the federal government to provide the janitorial services for federal buildings. . . . The program required them to have a certain percentage of disabled individuals within this program. . . .

We referred somebody that had chronic seizures, so much that she wore a helmet at all times. Because she wore a helmet, it was pretty obvious that she would be discriminated against. . . . This is the job: janitorial-like cleanup of bathrooms. . . . If she had a seizure, it is not threatening to her. It was perfect.

So she is doing this, and she started having seizures. And so they would find her in the hall. In fact, one time it was so bad they called an ambulance for her, but we were talking how that's not necessary. . . . If things were too bad, she could go home. But they were panicking. . . . They were talking about firing her, and I said, "Let's talk about this first. First of all, you know, you are a facility for disabled people, and you are telling me that you are going to fire her because she is disabled."

So I went over there and talked to her supervisor. She was the big coordinator of the whole program. And we all sat down, and the supervisor herself seemed to have problems with the idea of seizures. In a way, they scared her. She did not know what to do about it. And so we tried to create a routine. "So here is what you do. . . ."

You could tell all along that her superior was not fine with it. This woman was not going to work out: "And I don't want her to work out. I want her out of here. This bothers me"—you know, that kind of thing. I tried to level with the [supervisor], and I could talk logic with her until I'm blue in the face, and she is not going to get it. . . .

And finally, the front-line supervisor . . . would say things to [the disabled woman] like, "Why don't you just take your Social Security and go home? You are disabled. You don't have to work. Why don't you do that and save us all a lot of trouble?"

And so eventually my client decided that she did not want to stay there. She said she could not stand the [the supervisor], and so she quit the job.

In many ways, this story parallels those describing workers' responses to citizen-clients deemed worthy of extraordinary care: the voc rehab counselor goes to bat for a woman who wants to keep her job. But despite patient arguments and accommodations, the counselor cannot break through the supervisors' prejudices and fears, and the client is ultimately harassed into quitting. This is a story of honest efforts met with indifference. It is a realistic story warning that best efforts cannot always vanquish prejudice, a story of resignation and sadness told to underscore the frustrations of street-level work. This story resembles "Harder Than Brain Surgery" (story 9.6), but here heroic efforts do not lead to success. The indifference of the employing agency makes street-level work impossible.

For teachers and voc rehab counselors whose clients are children or dependent adults, working with families can create unique barriers and conflicts. Many vocational rehabilitation workers are fully comfortable with their paternalism and show no hesitancy in redirecting their clients' lives, even against the wishes of people who have much stronger bonds to the clients. A female vocational rehabilitation worker in the western city tells about her dealings with a young client and his mother: "[Joe] is a high school graduate who is technically deaf and should be using sign language, but oralism has been forced on him by his mother. It's a pathetic situation. . . . This story is not unusual at all." The counselor describes the client who is intelligent yet depressed and angry. He is "about as deaf as they come" and doesn't have enough residual hearing to lip-read or speak intelligently, yet his mother insists on lipreading and oralism. She ignores and resists the counselor's advice that he learn sign language. The story contrasts the worker's expertise with the mother's ignorance: "His mother has been insistent that he should be oral. The reason he's not oral, in her words, was 'He has a deficit in him.'"

In a meeting, the worker-narrator and the mother accuse each other of trying to convert Joe to their respective positions. The worker does not deny that she is trying to influence Joe and clearly feels that she knows better than the mother and the rest of the hearing community: "The hearing community thinks they know what's best for the deaf community." The mother never sees the wisdom of the counselor's advice, complains bitterly to the counselor's supervisor, and eventually moves away with her son. The worker is powerless and laments, "I didn't see it as a success. I see it as very sad." When circumstances intrude, street-level workers must reluctantly temper their hopes and ambitions to accommodate what is possible.

Conflicts with families are especially difficult for street-level workers because they must rely more on their power to persuade. They have less clout and cannot as effectively battle families as they often can other agencies. Conflicts with families sometimes arise over values or professional judgment, as in the story about oralism versus sign language; at other times, the conflicts concern crass self-interest. One midwestern voc rehab counselor told of wealthy parents who would not pay for special schools for their disabled but talented teenager. In this story, the parents were more concerned with keeping the A student home as a tax deduction than with encouraging independence. In a different story, the social worker protagonist gives up trying to help a man because his sister, who is the payee on his disability check, is unwilling to give up the extra income. In a similar tale, a midwestern VR counselor provides job training for a disabled but dependent adult. When the client is ready for independent living, his family balks because they want him at home doing housework.

In all these cases, the street-level workers try to overcome the resistance of the other agencies and families, reasoning, arguing, attempting to do whatever possible for clients. But as the workers acknowledge their limits, realism overcomes hope, and they pull back. They do what they can but accept with anger and sadness that much of the time they can do very little. These stories may be told to remind street-level workers of their limits.

In other stories, it is not conflict with other agencies or family members that demands pragmatism; rather, it is the characteristics and circumstance of citizen-clients and the relationship between workers and citizens. "The Big Bad Counselor Strikes Again" bears the overt message that street-level workers must enforce realism on unrealistic and uncooperative clients. Street-level workers also adopt the "I know best" attitude because they see clients as acting irresponsibly. Clients can also be foolish and childlike, as the following humorous story underscores. In this tale, the special-needs client is a caricature of the hapless mentally retarded adult who requires the counselor to act as the parent: someone must do so because others lie in ambush to take advantage of the client. The story also mocks the policy of greater independence and thereby reinforces the perceived need for workers to control citizen-clients.

Story 10.4. Midwestern Vocational Rehabilitation
"New Truck, No Money, No License"

This will show you some more of the problems that exist when working with clients.

We were trying to get this client to be more independent, but I guess he was taking this pretty liberally. He was out, so he stops at an area car dealership and buys himself a brand-new pickup truck.

And there is only one thing wrong: he does not have a driver's license, so he can't even drive the thing. And he has no way to make the payments.

So we get this call from the car dealership, and I say, "Is something wrong?"

And he says, "Well, he does not seem to know what is going on here. He just bought a truck from us."

And I said, "What? He just bought a truck from you? What kind of truck?"

"Well, a $5,000 truck."

"Do you know he does not have any money? He is not working. Don't you check credit?"

[The client] just gave them my name. So me and another

counselor went out and talked to them together because we were both kind of outraged that they sold him the truck. We had to undo the selling of the truck because there was no way he could pay this. And it was stupid. You might as well repossess it now.

It must be interesting for businesspeople because, you know, [the client] could just walk in and it was like a lollipop or something, "Yeah, I want the red one over there."

He probably said only ten words—he does not say much. And [the car dealers] probably just said, "Well sir, we can pull it right up front for you." No negotiation. The salesman probably says, "That will be $500 a month payment or something." And [the client] probably said, "Fine." And the salesman said, "Let's go. Bring it out there, and we are ready to go."

Other stories make the point with less humor: street-level workers all too often find citizen-clients frustrating, demanding, and uncooperative—"a pain in the ass," as many workers commented. Citizen-clients are most often a mixture of positive and negative traits, at once both worthy and unworthy of help and attention, leaving workers the task of deciding which traits predominate. A western voc rehab counselor describes an out-of-work woman who is trying to find a job so that she can get her kids back, the positive motivation that often encourages counselors to extend themselves to help. But [Louise] was also very difficult. She was described as having a "personality disorder," a catchall diagnosis for people who cannot get along with others. First, Louise wants to be a paralegal, but that does not work out because, "she doesn't get along with people well." Then she switched to dog training but dropped out because of conflicts with the school. Louise was "one of those people who can push all your buttons," and despite her recognized psychological problems and her worthy goal of reunification with her children, the counselor stopped investing effort in the case. It was frustrating and hopeless.

Clients like Louise who continually change their minds pose barriers to service. Workers and clients develop plans, but before they can be enacted, the clients decide they want something different. The workers feel they are spinning their wheels: they get started but have to start again; they make no progress and give up; they do the minimum and try to close the case as quickly as possible. One storyteller describes a "very, very nice man" who proves wearying. Using repetition to underscore her frustration, the counselor admits, "He's just very hard to deal with because he'll tell you, 'This is exactly what I'm going to do. I know exactly what I want to do. This is what I'm going to do.' And then two hours later, I find out its changed." After enduring these endless changes, the counselor pulls back: she becomes formal, follows all the rules, and schedules appointments only at her convenience.

Street-level workers have even less patience for demanding and manipulative clients. One western voc rehab counselor describes two such clients. "Start Acting Like a Hearing Person" (story 7.2) concerns Tom, a deaf African with many positive attributes, and, like most stories, presents a complicated picture of individuals with good and bad traits, with the narrative tension forming around which set of characteristics will ultimately prevail. Tom's family is wealthy, and he has a good education that lacks the stigma often associated with deaf schools. He can communicate and is athletic. But he is "always angry" and demanding, "wants everything now." He blames everyone else for any problem or difficulty. The counselor responds by becoming strict and bureaucratic.

Like Tom, the second demanding client needs little help, which, ironically, reduces the worker's investment in the case. This second story opens with the storyteller recalling a phone conversation with the client's previous counselor, "who was glad to get rid of her. That was the first warning sign I got, but I was not going to be basing how I treat her on that." The client next comes in, not for an appointment but because she has found a job working for a deaf agency that contracts with the vocational rehabilitation office: "She became my vendor and my client." The counselor wants to close the case since the woman has a good job. The client demands continued service but is unwilling to have the hearing tests that are required for services. A few days later, she calls and says, "I'm enrolled at the state university. I need tuition support tomorrow." The storyteller responds, "Well, that's great. I don't even have a plan written on you, and I have to get approval because the chances are I'll go over my budget."

In these cases, unlike the treatment of the worthy, there is no stretching or ignoring of the rules. Street-level workers constrain and even punish demanding clients by strictly following the rules. The deaf woman disappears but then, without warning, calls for more tuition support for a different training program. There is no plan, no testing. The rules are not followed, and the counselor answers, "No way. Forget it." The deaf woman calls again, asking for a paid interpreter so she could attend a workshop. Again, the answer is no: "There is nothing I can do about it. It is not in the agreement." The frustrated counselor sends a letter saying that the deaf client needs to come in for an appointment but receives no response. The counselor then writes to the woman to tell her that her case will be closed in fifteen days. The client calls, but the counselor says, "I left strict guidelines for my secretary that I would not bend over backwards for this girl. . . . She will be coming in at 8:30 Monday morning."

These issues echo throughout many voc rehab stories. Clients who do not respond or do not follow workers' leads are cut off. The workers use the policies and procedures to limit services. "One of Those Wishy-Washy Cases" tells of just such a case.

> I really thought he was going to be a good client—I mean, as far as being a good client being you get them a job, and you wait sixty days, and you close the case, and it looks like you have succeeded at what you are supposed to be doing. But for some reason, his behavior and his inability to focus and his [lack of] impulse control had kept him from succeeding. So finally, after spending a lot of money on maintenance and job searches and things like that, he blew off appointments too many times and I closed his case.

In these preceding voc rehab stories, counselors pull back, limit services, and close out demanding clients, however real their needs or understandable their difficult behavior. One counselor observed, "It's classic deaf behavior," before dropping a case. They understand but still do the minimum and construct them as unworthy clients. In other cases, lack of cooperation between workers and clients escalates to conflict. Conflict in its milder forms involves citizen-clients challenging or not acknowledging street-level workers' expertise and practical wisdom, not accepting the premise that street-level workers know best. Conflict escalates further when the citizen-clients challenge or do not acknowledge street-level workers' legitimate authority as state agents. This level of conflict, discussed in detail in the following chapter, is especially problematic in policing, where such challenges to police authority are a precursor to violence.

In "The Big Bad Counselor Strikes Again," the mentally limited woman would not accept the VR counselor's realistic advice. The worker's judgment was based on his own knowledge and expertise, bolstered by careful evaluation and diagnosis, which even the elected official recognized as correct. This story tells of more than just a client's wishful thinking: the tension arises because the client does not acknowledge and behave in accordance with the worker's expertise.

The stories that express this conflict often exaggerate the gap between knowledgeable and wise workers and unrealistic citizen-clients: the person of limited intelligence who wants to become a nuclear scientist, the substance abuser who wants to become a long-haul truck driver, or, as in the following story, the disabled welder who wants to be trained as an emergency medical technician.

Story 10.5.   Midwestern Vocational Rehabilitation
"I'm Disabled but Want to Be an EMT"

I got a phone call from somebody this week who said that some-one referred him to voc rehab, and they want to get him into training. And I said, "Okay, what is your situation?"

"Well, I was a welder, and I hurt my back, and now they say that I have limitations on my lifting and bending and getting around in awkward positions to do welding, and I want to go to school."

And I go, "Well, what do you want to do?"

"Well, I want to go be an emergency medical technician."

And I said, "Well, an emergency medical technician. What are you going to do when you have to help carry a three hundred pound person down three flights of stairs to get them out of a fire or whatever?"

"Oh, well, I always thought that I would have somebody to help me."

And I said, "Well, you might and you might not, but even so, a very heavy person on a stretcher with two people going down a flight of stairs or going in and getting them on the stretcher and loading them in an ambulance." I said, "That would be an inappropriate job for somebody with a bad back, you know."

Well, he hadn't thought about it, but he just really wanted to do it, and he was just kind of irritated with me. . . . I wouldn't be doing him justice by putting him into something that I felt [wasn't right for him]. He really didn't understand that. He just saw [EMT work] on TV and thought it would be neat or, you know, whatever.

He said, "Well, I don't think my back condition is going to be permanent."

And I said, "Well, if its not permanent, then you're not eligi-ble. If it is a temporary back condition, you can go back to welding. . . . If you don't have a problem, you're not eligible. If you do have a problem, I am not going to do what you want." I said, "If you want to explore other alternatives, if it looks like your back condition is going to be permanent—talk to your doctor. If it is permanent, and you want to explore other things, then I'll be glad to do that. But, no, I am not going to authorize EMT training for a person with a bad back with limits on lifting, bending, and twisting."

So he went, "I don't know."

You could see he was kind of deflated from that because that is not what he wanted to hear.

Every detail of this story underscores the correctness of the counselor's judgment and the ex-welder's lack of realism. In contrast to the public management idea of putting the customer first, the story underscores that the worker knows best. In this story, the disagreement over the best service plan ends in stalemate as the dissatisfied client disengages. At other times, the disagreement over who knows best escalates from annoyance to antagonism. Police complain about citizens who demand special attention and consequently do not permit officers to decide priorities or how to handle cases. Other street-level workers complain about the complainers, a group called the "letter writers" in story 7.4.

Complaining is more than a rejection of advice; it is a challenge to workers' authority, which is a broader issue for those at the street level. In schools, challenges to authority take the form of a generalized climate of disrespect for rules and the teachers. In "Lack of Support" (story 5.3) tells of a middle school teacher who confronts a student who was suspended but repeatedly reappears in the halls. Vocational rehabilitation clients express disrespect by subverting the process. Uncooperative clients sometimes go out on their own and find jobs, perhaps even in fields inconsistent with the counselors' recommendations. Rather than begrudgingly admitting that in these cases the client may have known best, counselors retain their view of the clients as troublemakers and confidently predict failure. For example, in one story a woman comes to see a western voc rehab counselor for money to pay for massage training. The request is "staffed" (reviewed in a staff meeting), and all the counselors agree that this is a bad choice. The request is denied. Rejecting the counselors' expert advice, the client returns to her old job and takes massage therapy classes at night on her own. Rather than praising the client's self-determination and offering some support, the storyteller insists that the counselors were right in their decision and predicts failure for the client: "So I think even if she gets her massage certificate, . . . she's probably not going to stick with it very long." Street-level workers know what is right for their clients, and the clients need to conform to those judgments.

When citizen-clients do not acknowledge or conform to street-level workers' expertise and authority, low-level conflict typically ensues—more of a tug-of-war than a fight. In these circumstances, street-level workers use rules and procedures to enforce their preferences about how situations or cases should be handled. Workers apply the rules and procedures to manage—that is, to control and manipulate—recalcitrant citizen-clients. As the VR counselor admits—even asserts—in "The Big Bad Counselor Strikes Again," sometimes "we decide for the client."

The tug-of-war between nonconforming citizen-clients and unbending street-level workers heavily favors the workers, who bring to this contest of wills the power and authority of the state. It is not a fair fight in part because the state offers few incentives to serve citizens: if anything, the incentives encourage minimal effort and rapid case closure. The same street-level workers who told stories of breaking the rules, who ignored procedures and direct orders from supervisors, who challenged their agencies' decisions and authority to serve citizen-clients deemed worthy now become strict and ardent rule and procedure followers to assert their authority over uncooperative citizen-clients. Workers make sure that appointments are kept, that treatment plans are rigidly followed; if cooperation is not forthcoming, the case is closed. When challenged by citizen-clients, citizen agents become state agents, rule breakers become functionaries.

This battle of wills between unequals is not static, however. Citizen-clients who relent and conform to street-level workers' expertise and authority may yet achieve the status of worthy clients. Such instances reinforce workers' self-justifications that they know what is best for citizen-clients. As discussed earlier, "One of Those Wishy-Washy Cases" repeats the familiar story of a voc rehab counselor closing a case because the client would not cooperate. But the story does not end there. The client calls back, receives a second chance ("little pearls"), and cooperates with the worker, who then stretches the rules that she previously enforced rigidly:

I told him that he needed to get back in touch with me [when] he was going to be mature enough to do what is needed. He did call me back, and I gave him little pearls, where he had to come to every single appointment and then I would open the case. So I have reopened his case. He is pretty much following through on what he needs to be able to do.

As story after story indicates, when citizen-clients do not comply, street-level workers disengage and move on to other cases and other situations. Even if this disengagement meets the bureaucratic standard of success—a case is closed, a kid is promoted to the next grade, a police call is handled—workers do not perceive these cases as successes. Unlike the overextension and risk taking for the worthy client, these cases provide no affirmation, and the low-level conflict and disengagement are sources of frustration and sadness.

Challenges to authority can also lead to more intense conflicts. Conflicts can build gradually after weeks of frustration as workers try unsuccessfully to get citizen-clients to conform to the workers' definitions of proper treatment, education, and/or behavior. Conflict can also flare up, as when a cop asks a suspect to stop or open the door and the suspect fails to comply. "Cut the Power" is unique among the police stories in that the officer avoided escalating the conflict, which may be why he proudly repeated the story during a training session. When conflict between workers and citizen-clients escalates beyond the tug-of-war over goals, authority, and expertise, the relationship between workers and citizens can deteriorate into confrontation. As conflict escalates, workers begin to see citizens as "bad guys," not just pains in the ass, and pragmatism gives way to hostility.

11. Getting the Bad Guys

Story 11.1.   Midwestern Vocational Rehabilitation
"The Squeaky Wheel Is the One That Won't Shut Up"

This is not a whole story, just kind of a problem with the system, but it kind of centers around a particular client.

I have known this guy, [John], for probably five years now. He's a quad. He was one of those wild kids who thought the world was his, and if you drink enough and take enough [drugs]—well, he got really loaded and tried to fly his car over some trees, and it didn't quite make it, so now he is a quad. The catch is, he still thinks if he wants it, he should get it—and he does. . . . An example is attendant care.

John is always going to need attendant care. Period. But John pushes the wire, you know. If you give him two hours, he wants ten. So John gets what I think we can allow: twenty hours a week for attendants. Attendant care is supposed to be for bodily type things, you know, dressing, bathing, bowel, bladder, that kind of thing.

Well, John's idea of an attendant is to do those things and go get him a newspaper and cigarettes and light a cigarette, stick it in [John's] mouth, and stand there and turn the pages. Go to class [for John] and take notes. Drive him here and there. You know, we are talking darn near personal slaves, minimum-wage slaves.

So, John insists he has to have at least ten hours a day. Well, that is more than twenty hours a week, and the counselor says, "This is all that is allowed, period."[1]

Well, since that was not good enough, he promptly called [his U.S. senator]. So the next thing we know we are getting a call:

the [state welfare] commissioner is calling the rehab commissioner who is calling the supervisor who is calling my old supervisor who is calling me, and now John has got all the hours he wants.

So what happens is, I can sit here and say, "This lady has got to have a car to get a job. She's got the job, everything is set, but she needs $1,000."

"No, that is not something we do. We don't buy cars, period."

But [the decision to give ten hours a day of attendant care] comes down from top down. So what happens is if you yell enough at the right people, and you know the system, then they don't like that, so they will fix the problem just to shut [the complainer] up.

So on this one particular guy, we have spent a fortune. Before he gets out of school—he is working on a four-year degree, and he is like year five and a half—we will have spent probably $100,000. He has van modifications. He has two computers. He has all these attendants. He has had hospital stays, and the bottom line is, I don't know if he will be able to go to work because what employer is going to put up with this crap? He can't go yell at his boss, you know. So it is just kind of mind-boggling priorities.

The squeaky wheel is the one that won't shut up. So the poor little nice guy who is just kind of sitting there, they get whatever crumbs or whatever happens to come along that we can do. But then we have got somebody like this guy who honestly does not deserve all the help.

I feel sorry for the man. He has got a hell of a hard time ahead of him. But at the same time, he's got an attitude, and it is not going to work.

This is somebody—I got a call from a social worker who said, "Did you know that John is in jail?" Ha Ha.

"Hello? What are you talking about? He is supposed to be at [state university] going to school."

Well, apparently he and one of his attendants had gotten busted for selling pot. And the judge felt sorry for this poor little disabled guy and just gave him house arrest. And John did not bother to tell me—he just forgot, just a little detail, because he wasn't convicted, he was just arrested. . . . The case has never been settled.[2]

There is a regulation that one of the concrete rules is if you are using an illegal substance, that is not something we can condone, period. He got some doctor to say that John was using marijuana because it helped with his spasticity. I don't know who his attorney is, but he is good. I want this guy if I ever get in trouble. And John knows if he is convicted for this—John just flat out told me that he has been using pot since he was a kid and he is not going to damn well stop now because he likes it, thank you very much. Well, it is his word against mine, you know.

And he is smart enough to know that if he is convicted and having told me this that he is out and he is losing all of these wonderful goodies. So he also told me his attorney knows all this and that they will do whatever it takes to postpone this until John has finished school and has gotten a job.

And that is interesting, too, because last year he could have used addiction to get disability, but now there are no benefits there, and I'm sure he is aware of that.[3]

His mom and dad have money, but they won't put that kind of money towards a personal attendant. John got a big insurance settlement at the time of his accident, and their house was a split-level ranch, and John couldn't get in. He could get in the garage door, but he couldn't get anywhere. John bought the house from his parents [with the settlement], so the house is in his name. And they remodeled and they turned the whole bottom layer into his very own little apartment—totally modified. It is beautiful. I mean, technologically he can control the air, the heat, everything, from his wheelchair computer. I mean, it is amazing.

You know, everything has really fallen in his lap, more than most people ever dream of. He is just so crooked. I had to slap his wrist. I found out when he was [at the university], he was in the hospital. He had been in the hospital a week and was probably going to be in for another two weeks because he had sores on his butt because he doesn't take care of himself.

He has been in the hospital more times because of those sores. They almost get healed, and then they will let him come home, and he doesn't take care of himself, so he is right back in the same shape.

He had been in the hospital for a week, and I don't know who, someone from the dorm called and wanted to know something about his meal payments. And I just had no idea John was in the hospital. He had been billing me with his attendant hours while he was in the hospital.

And I called him and said, "What the heck are you doing? I can't pay for attendants in the hospital, for God's sake. They are supposed to be providing those things while you are in the hospital."

He says, "Well, no, they don't, so I have to have my person. They can brush my teeth better."

And, it's like, "Oh, for God's sake, John."

"Well, the hospital people won't get me cigarettes."

"You don't need cigarettes. You are in the hospital. Grow up."

He had a fit because I would not pay for his attendants.

He said, "Well, they have to go to class for me to take notes."

I said, "No, they don't. Attendants don't go to class and take notes. You need a note taker, and we will get you a note taker. That is not an attendant."

On the surface, "The Squeaky Wheel Is the One That Won't Shut Up" has much in common with stories about helping the worthy or coping with the less-than-worthy citizen-client. The nature of the disability calls out for compassion, understanding, and patience, but the tone and details paint a darker relationship between worker and client. They indicate a narrative corner has been turned from the compassion and help given to the worthy and the tension and accommodations for the merely difficult. The counselor considers John unworthy and wants to give him just the minimum of service, but "the system" forces the counselor to treat this client as if he was worthy. This is the source of the storyteller's anger.

The line between those deemed worthy and unworthy is thin and imprecisely drawn. There are no reliable, external criteria differentiating the two. As the story describes, John was irresponsible and self-centered before his auto accident paralyzed him from the neck down. His new status as a quadriplegic did not change his "me-first" personality: "The catch is, he still thinks if he wants it, he should get it—and he does." He is spoiled and demanding and abuses the system. The disability counselor describes him as corrupt, ungrateful, and unlikely to hold a job, the ultimate failure to a voc rehab counselor. (But contrast this to the treatment of the "very nice" lady in "You Can't Win for

Losing" [story 4.5], who received extensive and loving care even though she was not likely to return to work.)

This story sustains tension between the listener's expectations of compassion for John and the counselor's unforgiving narrative. As in so many stories, the disability counselor might be expected to stretch the rules to provide the extra years of schooling. Having someone to help with the newspaper, drive, and hold a cigarette and even smoking marijuana are normal life pleasures that could easily be allowed or forgiven for a worthy citizen-client. Not for John. The storyteller made a moral judgment that John was unworthy, and all these behaviors are thereafter interpreted as additional evidence of moral failure. Even his use of his insurance settlement to renovate his house to accommodate his disability is characterized as undeserved: "You know, everything has really fallen in his lap, more than most people ever dream of. He is just so crooked. I just had to slap his wrist." It is as if he won the lottery rather than had a severely disabling accident. Once someone is labeled a "bad guy," then every infraction of the rules, every character flaw, is used to limit service, to punish even slight misdeeds, and to confirm the street-level worker's moral judgment of the individual, a pattern reinforced in the next story.

Story 11.2. Midwestern Police Department
"Paperwork the Rest of the Night"

Me and an officer got dispatched on a disturbance where a boyfriend was beating up on his girlfriend. We get there. The mother was in the other part of the house, and while she is explaining, he is up there beating on [the girlfriend]. You can hear it: bouncing off the walls and screaming, and she is crying.

So we said [to the mother], "Wait right here."

So we go up and knock on the door and open it. And they are inside, and they are over in a corner up against the wall. And she is crying. And he has a headlock on her. And she is screaming. And he is speaking Spanish, and she is speaking Spanish. He is Mexican, and she is a white girl, and she is [speaking Spanish] better than him almost. And we break them up, and she says, "Yeah, he has been hitting me."

So we decide we better remove him from the house for a little while and take him to jail for six hours so he has time to cool off and they can work out their problems. And we take him out of the house, and he is screaming her name and not wanting to go, and we have to struggle with him out of the house. And we get him outside, and he is saying. "Lorraine, Lorraine." And that is the only English he knows, and that is not even her real name: it is, like, Mary.

We go to having to restrain him and I said, "Shut up." And he says, "Okay."

Well, he speaks perfectly good English, but he is just faking it, like so many do, when they come into contact with the police. And when we get to the car, we ask him if he has any weapons on him, and he does not speak English.

So we take things out of his pocket, and I pull out a huge block of methamphetamine. And I'm thinking, "Okay, great. He is under arrest for battery and in the search, which is legal at this point, I find a big old rock of methamphetamine."

So I am like, "Oh man, paperwork the rest of the night. That is my reward." So he has like three IDs. So I put him in the back of the car and the drugs in the trunk. And we sit there and play the guessing game on what his name is, when is his date of birth, and how you spell all of it. And I take him to jail. And it is that short."

The boyfriend is a "bad guy." He beat his girlfriend, resisted arrest, and had a "big rock of methamphetamine" in his pocket. The story includes no mitigating details. The boyfriend is not, as in similar stories in which the offender receives a break, hardworking or trying to cope with a difficult situation. He does not cooperate with the police or show repentance. He uses meth rather than marijuana. He solicits no compassion and is reduced to a stereotype of a hotheaded Latino who fakes not knowing English, "like so many do," to try to avoid responsibility. The arresting officer prepares to spend the night doing the paperwork to assure that the abusive boyfriend is punished as harshly as possible.

The "bad guys" are, in many ways, the mirror image of the worthy. From street-level workers' perspective, those deemed unworthy may receive minimal, even harsh, treatment and, when available, severe punishment. From this perspective, this minimal help or maximum punishment is nonetheless fair and just. In general, we think of "fairness" as a positive, but fairness and justice have a different meaning for these citizen-clients. In these cases, fairness does not imply equal or even good treatment. Fairness for the unworthy corresponds to the concept of just desserts. They may be treated poorly, but they are treated as their behavior and character warrant. Street-level workers make moral judgments about individuals' bad character and then reinforce definitions of good character by punishing the bad guys. The decision norms applied by workers to classify someone as a bad guy are similar, although in the inverse, to those used to identify the worthy. These norms differ markedly in tone, however.

Street-level workers are often highly critical of the school, social service, or criminal-justice systems in which they work. Nonetheless, workers will classify citizen-clients who try to exploit or cheat the system as unworthy of help. Workers often tell of, even brag about, manipulating "the system" to help worthy clients yet have little tolerance for citizen-clients who themselves try to manipulate the system—and, not incidentally, the street-level workers.

A midwestern vocational rehabilitation counselor tells of a woman who goes from state to state looking for services. This is her fourth state. According to the counselor, the woman has been diagnosed with a "personality disorder" that makes her "difficult to treat, and the prognosis is fairly poor." She wanted training for clerical work, but "she couldn't keep it together to get through a one-week evaluation. Training was not recommended for her." The client wanted extra services for job placement but never followed through, more evidence of bad character. The counselor concludes that "she is just using the system for extra money and services" and closes her case "for failure to cooperate." But the story doesn't end with this minimal, by-the-rules bureaucratic response. The counselor tells fellow workers to watch out for this manipulative client. The counselor punishes the woman by trying to prevent her from getting future services.

> And sure enough, she called in two or three times after that. When I get clients like her, I become the watchdog for the taxpayers' money. . . . So I'm going to make sure she doesn't come back here and con somebody else into spending money when there aren't going to be any results. I don't approve of people taking advantage of services and tax money. . . . So I guess I can say I blacklisted her from the agency. I felt this was necessary.

In the interview after telling this story, the counselor admitted that his client did show some independence and initiative: "Actually, after I closed her case, she got some kind of loan or grant and did go to school." This positive effort was, however, not enough to transform the client into someone worthy of assistance: the moral judgment was set and unchanging. The counselor concludes, "She had one of the administrators call to ask me to provide money for transportation. . . . And I said, 'No, no, no. Training is not recommended. She is no longer an open case. There isn't anything I can do for her.'"

For those in the helping professions, like vocational rehabilitation counselors and teachers, clients who do not try, who do not follow through, and who are seen as lazy have not earned the help provided. They do not do their part and are unlikely to change. "The Squeaky Wheel Is the One That Won't Shut Up" included no descriptive details about John's struggle with his quadriplegia—no information about the hours of physical therapy, about how hard it must have been for him to do his schoolwork, or just about the daily struggles of someone so disabled. The story is silent on these issues—details of pain, suffering, and struggle that must have been present, at least to some degree, in John's life. Stories speak even when silent. The details omitted by the storyteller give voice to norms just as clearly as the details included. This is true in part because stories are not factual presentations but rather are intentionally created to tell a moral. The story presents John's life as one of leisure—with "minimum-wage slaves" attending to his every need, including his marijuana habit—and of luxury beyond what "most people ever dreamed of." When John is hospitalized for painful recurrent bed sores, a plague of the wheelchair bound, it is because he is too lazy to properly take care of himself and, therefore, undeserving of sympathy.

Laziness plays a different role in police stories because cops do not require citizen-clients to cooperate to achieve results. In police stories, work and being a hard worker are a core characteristic of morality. Citizens who work—especially those who work hard just to help their families scratch by—are forgiven numerous transgressions that would lead to harsh treatment for people who do not work. Nowhere is this distinction clearer than in the details that distinguish Francisco, the good drug dealer, from Steve and Cory, the bad dealers, in "Bad Dealers, Good Dealers, and Stray Bullets" (story 8.2). Francisco was a hard worker—he had scars on his arms and back from carrying a chemical weed sprayer—trying to support his family. Although he was a small-time drug dealer who sprayed the neighborhood with bullets during a gunfight, he was never charged. Steve rarely worked, and "when he did have a job, he would steal from the employer." He and his equally lazy accomplice, Cory, were arrested and punished for their role in the same incident.

The unworthy, therefore, are not just people who have done bad things. Many of those considered worthy and given special treatment and second and third chances have, like Francisco, done illegal and wrong actions. The unworthy are those citizen-clients classified or identified as bad people. This identification goes beyond behavior to include character. The unworthy are unlikely to change, bad guys who will remain bad guys. They deserve whatever ill treatment they get because this ill treatment serves and protects society by reinforcing dominant norms of good behavior and good character.

In addition to the issues of identity, "Watching the Prostitute from a Distance" (story 7.1) tells of a police officer's efforts to punish an "immoral" prostitute. It is not the prostitution that troubles the officer but that she is drunk and pregnant. The storyteller's descriptions of her are unsympathetic: she is thirty-nine years old, has no teeth, is a chronic alcoholic, and is pregnant. The prostitute's disregard for her fetus outrages the officer, who is unwilling to acknowledge the difficulty of her life circumstances. He contrasts her irresponsibility to his wife's proper behavior as if the vast difference in their life circumstances made no moral difference. The storyteller laments that the laws that fail to protect the fetus allow this immorality to continue, and to enforce his definition of morality, the officer is reduced to harassing this drunk prostitute. The storyteller cannot let go. Every detail in this story underscores the immorality of the drunk prostitute and the moral struggle of the police officer trying to protect the innocent fetus. There is no question about who is bad and deserving punishment and who is innocent deserving protection. The story exaggerates the moral distinctions to highlight the central point: street-level workers see their jobs as enforcing moral judgments, not just rules and laws.

Although rare, the stories also admit to the dangers of the role of morality enforcer. In "Remembering My First Arrest" (story 6–2), a veteran and high-ranking officer recalls how, many years earlier, his training officer had instructed him to "initiate contact" with an African-American guy "walking along drinking a Miller beer." The senior officer was passing to his young apprentice the tradition of harassment of citizens deemed marginal. This enforcement of a minor violation—a policy that is now officially sanctioned as "zero tolerance"—leads to a confrontation, which in turn leads to an arrest. The officer tells the story to suggest how racism had previously guided cops' moral judgments; he introduces the story by stating that his young daughter had recently been asking about the civil rights movement.

This story also suggests an additional criterion in determining who deserves punishment. Especially in police work, but also in social services and teaching, citizen-clients who do not accept or, even worse, challenge workers' authority are often categorized as bad guys. In the stories, street-level workers rarely back off when challenged but typically escalate the conflict until citizen-clients are overpowered. When the quadriplegic, John, challenges the counselor by calling the senator and by failing to report a hospital stay, the worker retaliates, "slapping his wrists" by removing services. In "Paperwork the Rest of the Night," as soon as the abuser resists arrest, punishment escalates. The pattern repeats in story after story. In the following tale, this pattern of conflict escalates beyond the initial confrontation and ends in the courts.

Story 11.3.   Midwestern Police Department
"Sued for $52 Million"

I'm going to tell you one about getting sued for $52 million. How does a guy get sued for $52 million? Well, I was on the SCORE unit, that's our SWAT team, and we, well I, have done over eight hundred drug raids on houses. And one night we went to do a drug raid on a house that was on Eighteenth Street. And after we kicked the house in, then the narcotics guys go inside and wave it secure. We surround the house to keep the bad guys from going in while the narcotics [unit] is in [the house].

Well, we had our SCORE van, which is our van, and all of our equipment is in there—extra smoke and stun grenades and all that. And it was parked on the street.

Well, I was standing outside, and I had the front of the house to watch. I saw a guy walking up the street from a Cadillac, and he walked around the van three times, looking over it real closely.

And I'm watching this guy. The doors are still open, and it's not illegal to look at it, but it sure worries us to death because there is a lot of stuff in it.

So I went over there, and I said, "What are you doing?"

And he looked at me and said, "Fuck you." And he started to walk away.

At this point the story is unremarkable. The SCORE and narcotics units are conducting a routine drug bust, one of eight hundred. A local citizen—the stereotypical drug-dealer-type who drives a Cadillac—scrutinizes the police van, which is suspicious though not illegal. On the lookout for bad guys, the storyteller initiates contact, and the suspicious local insults the cop but walks away. The events could have ended here, but the story continues because the police officer could not let the insult stand without response. He escalates.

Story 11.3, *Continued*

I said, "No, that's not going to work. Come back here." And he walked back to his car. About that time [another officer] saw I was having trouble, and he walked over to me.

I met [the suspicious] guy at his car and forcibly put his hands down on his hood and started patting him down. Well, we found crack cocaine in his pocket, and I asked who he was. He mumbled something, and I just put my ear closer to him so I could hear, and I said, "Who are you?"

He pushed me out of the way and took off running, and we're still in full SWAT gear, which weighs well over sixty pounds. [Another officer] was running after this guy. They both fell and tripped in this same hole. It was dark and nobody could see it. This hole was about six foot around and two foot deep. They both fell in. [The officer] landed on top of this guy and bounced like a turtle, just rolled right back off of him. By that time, I had caught up.

Well, this guy jumped back up out of the hole and took off running again. Well, I was close enough to get a piece of him, but what I didn't know yet was that he was already high on crack, which means you have to handle him different because they're terribly strong. I didn't realize that yet, until he started dragging me across this yard, and he was still running and I was hanging on. So [the other officer] ran around and got in front of me and stopped him.

[The other officer] got ahold of him, and it took both of us to stop him, but he would not go down. I could not get him handcuffed. So he threw [the other officer] off of him and started hitting him and kicking him. So I pulled the guy back—I was still behind him—I pulled him backwards a ways and spun him around, and I was getting ready to hit him, and [the other officer] grabbed his leg to try to tackle him like a football player does.

Well, that didn't work either. This guy was running with [the other officer] attached to his legs. Now, [the other officer] is six foot two and weighs almost two hundred pounds, and this guy is running with him hooked to his leg.

It took a while. I punched him about three times and that didn't work, so I gave him a karate kick to the ribs, and that finally dropped him. He went to the ground, and we had to lay on him. And it took both of us to get his hands close enough to handcuff him. We processed the drugs, of course, and got him booked.

Well, about a week later, his attorney called me and said he was in the hospital. He had a broken liver, spleen, kidney, three ribs. . . . I forgot what all else was done to this guy.

And I said, "Well, I didn't do it. All I did was hit him a couple of times and kicked him once" and explained that to her. . . . She hates policemen. She sued lots of them and never won. So about three years later this goes to court. . . .

The story continues to describe the court case. Because of a technical error, the storyteller was found "nonnegligent." A nurse on the jury discovered that the expert defense witness inaccurately described the injuries: the doctor's exhibit of the X rays was backward. In this story, a flippant but mild and everyday challenge to police authority transforms a suspicious-acting local into a bad guy. The officer, not the local, escalates the conflict, leading to a violent encounter. The violence is retold in video-game style, with two SWAT-geared cops battling a superhuman, crack-empowered bad man. The good guys win, but the victory is tarnished by the lawsuit against the officer, which only heightens the storyteller's sense of injustice and conflict. He summarized the story: "I did my job. I did not overreact. I reacted to the situation that I had, and it ended up in federal court anyway." He does not acknowledge that he could easily have ignored the insult and avoided the entire conflict.

Just as street-level workers will bend the rules, give second chances, and greatly extend themselves and state benefits to those deemed worthy, those considered unworthy receive the least possible service or the greatest possible punishment. Street-level workers become harsh and unforgiving state agents when they believe that citizen-clients are trying to con the system, are unresponsive or lazy, are immoral and unlikely to change, and are challenging or even questioning street-level workers' authority.

From the perspective of the state-agent narrative, the use of discretion to get the bad guys is deeply ironic. In these circumstances, street-level workers become stringent rule followers, trying to limit services to the minimum allowable. Rather than cutting corners, they follow every procedure. They use the rules to discourage and harass citizen-clients—for example, using a lengthy evaluation process to get rid of a troublesome client. In these cases, workers express more concern for the state's interests than for those of citizen-clients. Workers worry about budgets and taxpayers' dollars, concerns quickly discarded when helping worthy clients. Front-line workers become the proper agents depicted in principal-agent theory, defining their jobs as following rules and placing fiduciary responsibility to the state above service obligations to citizens.

These street-level workers can, conversely, become rogue agents when responding to those deemed unworthy. Though morally justified in their own minds (and stories), these workers use procedures and standards to punish and at times abuse citizens. In the police stories that involve violent encounters, the storytellers are quick to add details about how their manner of restraining the citizen or using their batons followed procedures. Their abuse is by the book, but the line between using a baton to restrain and to injure is razor thin. In the stories about "getting the bad guys," street-level workers describe their motives and actions, however dismissive or violent, as acting for the state.

The workers justify their abuse of bad guys as service to the community: the community and its values take on the role of the worthy citizen-client, whereas individual citizen-clients deemed unworthy become dehumanized caricatures of immoral behavior, deserving abuse rather than help. Many of these stories also include an ironic subtheme: when street-level workers take risks to punish the bad guys and protect the community, the result is often punishment by the state. The system punishes workers for taking risks to preserve the social order. A midwestern police officer tells of a domestic violence call in 1984, long before the current policy of automatic arrest in domestic-violence calls. The first two officers on the scene let the drunk and violent man go, but then the storyteller looked toward the house, "and sitting on the outside steps was this lady holding two little bitty kids—one of them was less than a year old, and the other one was maybe two—crying her eyes out. And this guy was headed towards them." The storyteller steps between the drunk abuser and his helpless family. A fight and an arrest follow. But the story does not end with the brave cop protecting the abused mother. The drunk files a brutality complaint, and the storyteller is suspended: "For two weeks prior to Christmas and two weeks after Christmas, I was without a job. Now that's the most embarrassing, degrading, god-damned thing that could ever happen to you." The justification for the suspensions was not so much the brutality but that the storyteller sub-stituted his judgment for that of the other two officers who had let the abuser go. He questioned the authority of the other cops and, like unworthy citizen-clients, was punished.

12. Streetwise Workers and the Power of Storytelling

Street-level stories are powerfully descriptive: they take us into the storytellers' worlds, both real and imagined. Through the storytellers' words, we experience the physical and emotional context of their work. We meet the students, clients, criminals, victims, bystanders, coworkers, and bosses who populate these story worlds. Street-level stories, like other narratives both grand and mundane, help us understand how sense and meaning are made and how norms are conveyed and enforced. Whether the story is of Odysseus on his mythic voyage or a voc rehab counselor confronting a difficult client, stories reveal moral reasoning as the storyteller navigates through the shoals of ambiguity and conflict. In describing decisions and actions, street-level stories also reveal acts of governing. "Mundane stories of daily life," write Sanford Schram and Philip Neisser, "execute a sort of narrative statecraft by reinforcing the banal truths by which political institutions operate."[1] These banal or mundane truths are central to understanding street-level work and the modern state, for they reveal governing at its most elemental, the interaction of the state and citizen.

These stories make clear that street-level work is as much a process of forming and enforcing identities—of both citizen-clients and street-level workers—as of delivering services and implementing policy. More than bureaucratic politics, identity politics shape the citizen-clients' outcomes.[2] The street-level work world is ambiguous and marked by conflicting signs, leaving the worker to determine how to respond. Two spoiled rich girls caught committing credit card fraud: one recalcitrant, the other repentant. Two small-time drug dealers: one a hardworking Mexican immigrant trying to support his family, the other a lazy miscreant. Two students from a tough neighborhood: one is seen as a threat, the other as deserving extra help. Two vocational rehabilitation clients: one, a tough-looking injured upholsterer, elicits needed but unauthorized service; the other, a demanding and uncooperative quadriplegic, receives as little help as the rules allow. Two more voc rehab clients: for one, the counselor sues her agency to get services; for the other, she conspires with her coworkers to limit services.

In these and many more cases described in their stories, street-level workers first establish citizen-clients' identities and then respond. Forming and fixing identities may involve careful evaluation, as in the case of vocational rehabilitation, or snap judgments, as with police officers patrolling a neighborhood. Once fixed, these identities shape the nature of street-level workers' responses, from bending the rules and providing extraordinary assistance to allowing only begrudging and minimal help and at times to abuse.

Some of these identities—"troublemaker," "personality disorder," "nice lady"—are indelible and define, for better or worse, the ongoing relationship between workers and citizen-clients. Other identities are fluid and change as ongoing interactions challenge preconceived stereotypes: the hapless drunk who is trying to turn his life around, the offender who admits responsibility, the client with a violent history who proves cooperative. Sustained interaction, as in the classroom or when working on a voc rehab case, fosters changes in perceptions of identities, and teacher and rehab worker stories are full of surprises about unpredictable students and clients. Brief interactions, as commonly occur in police work, tend to reinforce stereotyped identities, but police stories also reveal incidents of surprise and change.

Whether identities are fixed or fluid, two important observations stand out. First, workers fix the identity of citizen-clients. Identity marking and enforcing are fundamental exercises of power by street-level workers. Citizen-clients are not entirely passive in this process: how they respond to workers greatly influences the labels they receive. Citizens who show deference to police officers, students who demonstrate motivation, and clients who respect their counselors' expertise are deemed more worthy than individuals who do not. Nonetheless, street-level workers exercise their power over citizen-clients by asserting definitions of citizen-client identities.

Second, how workers respond to citizen-clients reveals the workers' identities, at least at the moment of interaction: Do they define themselves as enlightened or hard-nosed cops? Do they see themselves as compassionate or by-the-book teachers or counselors? Over time, these identities can become as rigid as the workers' stereotypes of the citizen-clients. Moreover, street-level workers bring to this process their occupational identities, which are formed largely in their interaction with peers and the bureaucratic settings of their work. Each interaction with citizen-clients either confirms or questions this occupational identity. The identity-making process is, therefore, mutual in the sense that it involves and affects both workers and citizen-clients. Identity fixing is, however, not mutual in the sense that both sides are equal partners. The workers alone retain the power to define and fix, and to unfix and redefine, citizen-clients' identities. This power affects the interactions between worker and client and, by extension, defines the relationship between state and citizen.

Fixing and enforcing citizen-client identities forms the premise for street-level workers' judgments. Their stories reveal how street-level decision making is complexly moral and contingent rather than narrowly rule bound and static. Cops, teachers, and counselors first make normative judgments about offenders, kids, and clients and then apply, bend, or ignore rules and procedures to support the moral reasoning. Identity-based normative judgments determine which and how rules, procedures, and policies are applied. Morality trumps legality in terms of which rules, procedures, and policies are acted on; who gets what services and who is hassled or arrested; and how rules, procedures, and policies are enacted.

As expressed in these stories, street-level moral judgments are couched as statements about group belonging and people's character—their identity. As a storytelling convention, these judgments of the characters in the stories are stated as empirical observations. The details in the stories about appearance, history, actions, and interactions that make the characters vivid are the textual embodiments of the storytellers' moral judgments about the characters. In stories, details are representations of beliefs. To recall one of many examples, in "Bad Dealers, Good Dealers, and Stray Bullets" (story 8.2), an officer provides physical details about the Mexican immigrant (the chemical scars on his back from years of farm labor) to justify implicitly the decision not to arrest this struggling, hard worker for his part in a drug-related shootout. The details describe character, and character shapes response. As Thomas McCollough observes, "Moral judgments are not simply 'emotive' expressions of how people feel, but cognitive claims about how things are, that is, moral knowledge. In this regard, moral judgments are similar to scientific judgments. Both represent our considerable beliefs about reality."[3]

A fundamental belief about the reality of street-level work expressed in the stories is that the needs and character of the citizen-clients (as defined by workers) and the demands of rules, procedures, and policies (as understood by workers) exist in unresolvable tension. In many instances, workers cannot respond to the needs of individuals and follow the dictates of law and policy. Workers must continually make judgments about citizen-clients to determine how to apply rules and procedures and to determine their meaning and value.

To our storytellers, fairness and justice require providing citizen-clients services or treatment based on perceived character, not on acts. Indeed, acts are important primarily as they reveal enduring character, which in turn affects response. If deemed evidence of an enduring character trait, good or bad, an act will elicit a different response than if the act is seen as an isolated incident, an aberration with no implications for character. Contrary to current views, street-level workers will risk careers, reduce the bureaucratic measure of their success, and make their jobs more difficult and more dangerous to provide extraordinary and often unauthorized help to citizens deemed worthy. For this select group, workers break or ignore rules. If street-level workers judge citizen-clients as unworthy—as "bad guys"—then rules are used to protect the workers and to withhold or minimize services or at times to punish, even to be brutal. When police officers describe using their batons to "subdue" resisting "perpetrators," the cops do it "by the book."

Even though street-level workers reject or refuse to acknowledge their role as powerful state agents responsible for implementing government policies, the workers base their normative judgments on the presumption that they know what is best for the citizen-clients they encounter—that "father (or mother) knows best." Their experience-tested, practical reasoning is, in their view, superior to the abstract and ideological decisions of upper-level policymakers. Moreover, experience and expertise make workers' judgments superior to their citizen-clients' insights and preferences. Street-level workers' pragmatism and experience undergirds their moral reasoning and justifies (or to the critic, rationalizes) their assertions of power and authority relative to both their hierarchical superiors and their citizen-clients. Street-level workers clearly "take" responsibility to act based on their own judgments, but taking responsibility is not enough to make them responsible actors. For this, we must look beyond the street-level workers' stories.

Stepping back from the specific details of plot and character, these street-level accounts tell a larger story of the tension—perhaps unresolvable—between the view of street-level work summarized in the state-agent narrative and the workers' views that comprise the citizen-agent narrative. This interpretive tension articulates a profound challenge to the modern state. The previously recognized barrier between supervisors and front-line staff, between policymakers and policy implementers, goes well beyond hierarchy, rules, and routines: it is embedded in the social norms and culture of street-level work.

Listening to street-level accounts, we can and should recognize and sympathize with the difficulties of this work. Street-level workers are the coal miners of policy: they do the hard, dirty, and dangerous work of the state. Nonetheless, understanding cannot eclipse concern. In their often flattering self-portraits, street-level workers describe themselves as citizen agents enforcing moral standards and norms, but they are also and unavoidably state agents.[4] They cannot reject the state-agent role and the demands and tensions it brings to their work. Street-level workers cannot shed the responsibility that comes with the state-assigned power over others. This state-authorized power—best symbolized by the police officer's uniform and weapon but also apparent in how a voc rehab counselor allocates services and how a teacher responds to a class—is the source of much help and compassion during countless everyday interactions between workers and citizen-clients. Nevertheless, the potential for harm and abuse always lurks.[5] Racial and ethnic profiling is just one example of how stereotyped identities and misguided moral judgments can lead to the misuse of state power.

Most scholars acknowledge that the nature and norms of street-level work diminish the prospects for bureaucratic and democratic control over front-line workers' judgments and actions.[6] Furthermore, most scholars recognize what the stories reveal: workers' beliefs and values are formed in rough-and-tumble interaction with peers and citizen-clients, not in regulated, formal interaction with supervisors.[7] Our close reading of street-level work stories offers little help for reconciling these dilemmas and tensions—indeed, they may be unreconcilable.[8]

Moreover, the unresolvable tensions between the demands and expectations expressed in the state-agent and citizen-agent narratives profoundly shape street-level work. It is not possible to understand street-level work or workers without referencing both narratives and the conflict between them. Like savvy urban kids who must accommodate strict rules at home while navigating the dangers and ambiguity of the streets, street-level workers must continually balance the demands of the state and the needs and potential of the individuals encountered.[9] These workers must learn when to act as advocates and when to go by the book. In the words of the midwestern middle school teacher quoted in chapter 1, they must know when to act for the kids and when to conform to the building. Front-line workers must recognize subtle cues and know when and how far to stretch the rules.

The continual and successful balancing of the tension between the expectations of the state and law abidance and individuals' perceived identities and moral character—what we have termed cultural abidance—is the essence of workers' much-valued street smarts. Streetwise workers know when and how to adapt the rules of the state and when and how to pay attention to citizen-clients' identities. Such workers operate effectively in the state setting as well as in the street setting. Streetwise workers respond to the different demands and conflicting expectations of both. Like all juggling acts, there are times when balls are dropped and times of total collapse, but the other moments—when cops, teachers, and counselors make sound judgments despite the tension and ambiguity of their work—are the markers of successful street-level work.

Hard as we may look, there may be no resolution to the tensions evident in the state-agent and citizen-agent narratives, especially if we address the problem at the broad level of policy. At the much smaller scale of the individual street-level worker and the even smaller scale of worker-citizen interaction, the stories themselves, however, suggest some hope—not promise—for guiding the successful navigation of the ambiguous, tension-filled, and ever-changing terrain of street-level work. Our research and this book depend on the descriptive power of stories to reveal the moral reasoning and normative order of street-level work. Stories are powerfully descriptive, but they are also profoundly normative: they shape and alter the views and beliefs of the teller and the listener; they simultaneously reveal and modify preferences and reasoning. Telling and hearing stories can contribute to street-level responsibility and to the development of streetwise workers.

Narratives are not passive artifacts reflecting organizational culture but active elements in forming and reforming organizational culture. When captured in a specific rendition or text, as in this research, narratives become a form of cultural history: they show what sense was made, what social meanings were constructed. This past-tense meaning may and typically does frame future sense making and norm defining, but stories told within organizations change with each telling, as plot and character details are deleted or embellished and words and emphasis change. Some old stories are dropped from the repertoire, while new ones are added. Retelling, forgetting, and inventing stories continues to modify the socially constructed world of the storyteller and listener. And, most importantly, these retellings, forgettings, and inventions simultaneously confirm and challenge the storytellers' and listeners' assumptions, thinking, and identity. Storytelling is often conservative in that it reinforces established norms and beliefs, but stories can also voice challenges to hegemonic assumptions; they provide, in Patricia Ewick and Susan Silbey's phrase, "openings for creativity and invention in reshaping the social world."[10] Living narratives have present and future tense meaning. As John Hall writes,

> Narratives are kinds of social action. . . . Narrative is used not only to describe action (e.g., the activities of work as an unfolding sequence), but also to construct meaningful models of action (procedures and practices of work), and to coordinate action (accounts about how to handle situations as work unfolds). . . . Narrative is a formative discourse infused with both superadded moral principle and life worldly capacities to mediate meanings.[11]

Thus, beyond stories' descriptive power to reveal the assumptions and beliefs that comprise organizational cultures (and subcultures), the formative power of stories offers the potential to strengthen and channel street-level workers' moral reasoning. It has long been recognized that organizational stories, such as those collected and examined here, play a key role in the initial and continuing socialization of organizational actors.[12] Moreover, as John Brehm and Scott Gates conclude, organizational culture, not hierarchy, supervision, or accountability, is of "overwhelming importance" in "determining the subordinates' levels of compliance."[13] The functioning state, therefore, does not depend on a web of principal-agent relations that connects, link by link, the core democratic "principals" with remote street-level "agents." The state rests on a foundation of social norms that at least in part is simultaneously revealed and re-created in stories, including street-level stories.[14]

Narrative's formative role suggests an approach (but not a solution) to confronting the problems inherent in street-level discretion and judgment. In his insightful examination of these issues, Joel Handler argues that the inevitability of street-level discretion requires that it "ought to be approached positively and creatively; but ways have to be sought to assure that power advantages [of street-level workers over citizens] are not exploited."[15] Retelling, forgetting, and inventing stories may enhance but cannot assure street-level responsibility.

Responsible action requires the critical examination of meanings, motives, and actions. Responsible action cannot be based on the mindless rule following of the functionary or the mindless norm following of the conformist. Responsible action demands analysis of both the self and the context. Much—too much—street-level normative judgment operates at what Terry Cooper calls the expressive level.[16] The stories collected for this research provide a multidimensional self-portrait of street-level moral reasoning, but it is a self-portrait on which street-level workers rarely gaze. Ironically, the stories express more than the storytellers analytically know, yet the meaning is there, awaiting self-reflection. Street-level workers learn from peer accounts, observations, and conversations how to intuitively navigate the moral dilemmas of their work. While essential, this moral intuition is not enough.

Philip Jos writes that responsible action must meet three criteria: "(a) moral sensitivity, the ability to recognize the moral implications of ambiguous situations . . . ; (b) moral understanding, the ability to reason about these implications; and (c) moral courage, the willingness to confront and act on moral issues even where there is substantial pressure to do the contrary."[17] Many teachers, vocational rehabilitation counselors, and police officers we met during our several years of fieldwork expressed moral courage: they were ready to act on their beliefs even at some personal cost. Moral sensitivity and understanding are more difficult to judge, but the stories are replete with both characteristics. The act of telling and retelling work stories has the potential for heightening moral sensitivity and deepening moral understanding, which are, in our view, the most promising avenues for confronting the ever-present danger of irresponsible (even "evil") street-level action. We agree with Lawrence Lessig that "regulating social meaning is at the core of regulating . . . social problems" and that meaning can change through inadvertent or deliberate changes in either text or context.[18]

There are no simple solutions to the problems of street-level responsibility through tightening rules, regulations, and supervision or through strengthening moral reasoning. Moreover, stories will never conform to management pressures or preferences: imposed stories from hierarchical supervisors will be ignored, just as are top-down rules and other dictates. Only stories told by street-level workers to street-level workers have the potential to deepen moral reasoning and heighten moral responsibility. From our observations, these stories and interactions already contribute to teachers', counselors', and police officers' levels of responsible action. Deepening the workers' readiness and ability to analyze their own and others' normative judgments involves augmenting a naturally occurring organizational process.

Streetwise Workers and the Powers of Storytelling

These natural social processes, like storytelling, can be suppressed or encouraged even if they cannot be managed in the traditional, hierarchical sense of that term. When storytelling is suppressed, it does not disappear but becomes less publicly available for critical examination. "Cut the Power" (story 10.2) describes a police officer's successful effort to silence a noisy neighbor by shutting off the electricity to his apartment. At the end of the story, the teller, still upset, describes how he told this story at a training class as an example of creative judgment in responding to a difficult situation. But rather than encouraging the analysis of the moral reasoning behind the officer's judgment, the superior dismissed and suppressed the story as not what he wanted. The street-level story was not valued, not worthy of attention.

The first step, therefore, in augmenting the formative potential of storytelling is simply to take stories and storytelling seriously rather than viewing them as mere diversions from work.[19] Street-level work is guided by many texts; cops, teachers, and counselors spend much time divining and learning the meanings of the rules, regulations, and procedures that infuse their work. Workers' stories are also texts that call out for examination and thought, a process that should be encouraged, not belittled, as was done in "Cut the Power."[20]

Taking stories seriously requires that storytelling be given time and place. In contrast to the stories told in the police departments and vocational rehabilitation offices, the middle school stories collected in this research were generally thin and undeveloped. Teaching has become an isolated profession, with teachers interacting more with students than peers. There is little opportunity to share stories, and teacher stories remain private and not constitutive of organizational culture. Police departments tend to foster subversive stories in part because the opportunities for public storytelling tend to occur at supervisor-dominated meetings at the beginnings and ends of shifts. The shift-change meetings suppress street-level stories that do not conform with official views.

In contrast to schools and police departments, the two vocational rehabilitation sites offered positive models of constructive group storytelling and story analysis. In these agencies, supervisors chaired regular meetings with counselors to discuss cases. Case descriptions often took the form of stories—stories much like and in some cases identical to those discussed here—and group discussion centered on analyzing the best way to respond to client needs given policy constraints. Storytelling and analysis were routine parts of managing these agencies, as the supervisors created a context in which stories were told, dilemmas were discussed, and moral reasoning was critically examined. Story analysis did not eliminate moral dilemmas or assure appropriate treatment, but group storytelling heightened the possibility for responsible action. So we will end where we began—with a story.

Story 12.1. Western Police Department
"The Annual Windy Acres Super Bowl Parade"

The beat that I work in is predominantly Hispanic, or used to be, and the residents there were mostly Dallas Cowboy fans. So every year, when Dallas was winning, they would have celebrations in the park or in their neighborhoods in the block. Everybody would come over and drink beer and just bring their kids over, and everybody would be dressed up in Dallas Cowboys jackets and hats.

So, last year, when Dallas won the NFC East Championship, I figured I'd stop by at the house where everybody met after a game and talk to them because they knew I was a New York Giants fan, and Dallas played the Giants. Of course, the Giants would lose. I'd be at work and I'd see them and, you know, they'd all say, "Ah, we told you."

So I stopped by, and there must have been about twenty people at the house, and they were all excited. So, one of the residents there I knew said to me, "[William], how about taking us around the neighborhood to celebrate?"

I'm thinking, "That's never been done before, and I'm on duty in the police car." I thought a second and then it dawned on me, "Well, this would be a good public relations thing to do something like this to show that police are involved in the community and that we do like to share in the community's happiness or help them at bad times." So I told them, "Okay, I'll just take you around a few blocks around the neighborhood."

So everybody got in their cars and lined up. I was the lead car, and I turned on my overhead lights, and I led a parade of about five or six cars through the neighborhood. They were all honking car horns, and people would come up and raise their fists, [yelling] "Dallas Cowboys." So it only lasted maybe five minutes. We drove up and down a few blocks, and then we came back to the house, and everyone that was in this little parade came over to me and said, "Gee, thanks. You know, you're the only one that would do something like that."

I said, "Well, I know it's never been done before, but I'm going to be the first one to do it, and I don't suspect I would get into any trouble for it. Everything was orderly. Nobody got out of hand, no accidents or anything."

So they thanked me for it. So, jokingly, I said, "Well, if they win the Super Bowl, we'll drive through the whole neighborhood, okay?"

That came back to haunt me. I was working the day of the Super Bowl, and I was over at the beat trailer listening to the game on the car radio, and it was down to the last quarter. The game was just about over, so I remembered my promise, and I said, "Well, better go get it over with."

Well, I didn't know this, but the group had already assembled and was waiting for me. I drove down the 2500 block of East Seneca Street, and they apparently had been over at another house. When I drove up there, there were about twenty vehicles waiting. They were all parked, engines running. Everybody had on their Cowboys' outfits. They were waiting for me. I said, "Well, I promised it to them. This is too big. Dallas has won the Super Bowl." Okay, so I said, "Okay, let's line up. Everybody stay in line." And we went over the route that we were going to take.

So we started. We drove down—we started at the north end of the neighborhood and slowly went through the blocks there, and again the residents came out. They were running out, yelling "Dallas Cowboys." People were coming out with their Dallas flags and waving the flags. So as we got to one street, we turned left on Casablanca, and I noticed these garbage cans lined across the street to block us. Well, I stopped the parade, and I saw a woman out there. She was with her family. They were related to some of the people in the parade. It turns out they couldn't stand Dallas. They didn't care who won. They just could not stand Dallas. So they had saw that, you know, I was leading the parade, and they just put the garbage cans there to block our way. So I got out of my car, and I told the woman, "Okay, move these garbage cans." And so there was one Hispanic guy across the street. It was obvious he'd been drinking. So he went to move the garbage cans. He struggled and pushed it out of the way. So I gave the sign, "Let's continue."

Well, people were coming out, and someone actually videotaped the whole thing. Well, as we go by one house, and I see this lady and she comes out on the telephone right after she sees the police car with the overheads on—the lights—and the caravan of twenty cars following it. So, I'm thinking, "Well, she's going to call the station, wanting to find out what is that police car doing driving around the neighborhood with twenty cars following it." Well, apparently she wasn't calling the station. She was calling a relative to tell her, "Hey, we're having a parade over here."

Well, just about that time we're driving down another block and a police helicopter comes over us and is hovering above us. I'm thinking, "Uh-oh, I wonder if that officer thinks I'm in trouble, seeing all those cars and just one police car." Well, that officer didn't call, so there was no problem.

During the time we're having this parade through the neighborhood, we didn't have one call for service—not one. So I led the group back to our original starting point, and as I'm getting ready to leave, a couple people who were involved came up to me and they said, "You know, William, we really appreciate what you did. You kept your promise, and we really appreciate that. We have something for you." Well, they gave me a New York Giants football team desk calendar, a big one, in appreciation for just taking a few minutes out of my day to lead them on a little parade through their community to express their joy over the football game.

So after it was all over—I mean, everything was orderly and everything—they said, "Well, let's make this an annual event, provided the Cowboys win it." I said, "You know what?" I said, "Next time I'll get a motor officer to pull up the rear, you know, and make it look like a real escort." And they said, "Thanks."

So that was a story that I hold very dear. Like I said, it's never been done before, and if it was even mentioned, I don't think it would have been taken to heart. Because of the time it sets up in the community when I do things like that for the people in the community, they are really grateful.

So I just wanted to share that story with you about what happened with the Super Bowl parade. So it will be called the Annual Windy Acres Super Bowl Day Parade. After the parade was over, I mentioned it to the supervisor, and the supervisor mentioned it to the commander. . . . She heard about it, and she came to me and said, "That is a great example of community policing. Keep up the good work." So I felt good about that,

that the commander would accept the decision I made to do something in the community like that.

"The Annual Windy Acres Super Bowl Parade" tells of small acts that build community and link people, in this case disenfranchised poor people, to the state. In this story a police officer ignores regulations— all the time fretting that he will be caught and sanctioned—to fulfill an offhand promise to a neighborhood. The tension between state-agent rule following and citizen-agent improvisation is evident throughout but is wonderfully resolved by the supervisor's acceptance of the street-level worker's judgments and actions. To the storyteller's surprise and in contrast to the police officer's experience in "Cut the Power" (story 10.2), the supervisor lauds rather than punishes this act of "pragmatic improvisation." In these small acts of responsibility and of the system allowing, even reveling in, the constructive exercise of practical reasoning, the tensions between the state-agent and citizen-agent narratives are momentarily—only momentarily—resolved. Although holding the potential for great harm, such small acts of normative improvisation by forgotten streetwise workers sustain the state: they are acts of statecraft on which the institutions of governing depend.

Appendix A: Methodology

Three years of fieldwork undergird the interpretations and observations reported in this book. We spent six to ten months in five research sites, each of which is described in chapter 4. Chapter 3 discusses, in general terms, our narrative methodology, although we did not rely exclusively on narratives but employed the multiple methods that are common practice in field research. This appendix also describes these methods.

Our extensive time in the field enabled us to put the narratives into a larger interpretive context. As part of the field research, we completed semistructured entry and exit interviews with each participant, took notes on observations, and collected relevant agency documents about policy and process. During the exit interviews, each participant also completed a questionnaire. Our methodology is best described by detailing the process used to gain entry, collect data, conduct data analysis, and arrive at interpretations. Although some variation occurred in specifics, the overall process was replicated in each successive site.

We began by selecting three very different types of street-level work: police, vocational rehabilitation counseling, and teaching. The differences between these types of workers are described in chapter 4. We chose these three types because their differences strengthen and discipline generalizations: we identified observations and themes that cut across these different types of work yet isolated the distinctive characteristics of the different forms of street-level work.

Getting permission to study street-level workers is labyrinthine because they occupy the bottom of large and often tangled government bureaucracies. Getting permission for research follows, by necessity, the same top-down path of rules and procedures that circumscribes street-level work. With vocational rehabilitation, we started with the state commissioners and followed the chain of command to the super-visors of the community voc rehab centers where we would work. With police, we began with the chiefs of police in the two cities, and in one city we also needed permission from the city administrator. To gain permission to work in the middle school, we started with the district superintendent before we identified a particular school and discussed the project with its principal. When asking for permission from the top administrators, we also informally interviewed them on issues of policy and street-level influence on policy implementation.

The next major hurdles were permission from the voc rehab and police supervisor and the school principal. We made it clear to these individuals that participation had been authorized but not required. We also stressed that we would not report findings to higher adminis-trators and that individual workers would have the ultimate right to choose or reject participation. We promised to report observations back to the participants and work teams and shared the hope that the project would prove to be a learning experience for the participants as well as the researchers.

After gaining agency-level approval, we identified work groups of approximately ten individuals. The work group for the middle school was the eighth-grade team, including all the core and special-service teachers. Police work is organized temporally and geographically, and we chose teams or squads that patrolled particular beats. The voc rehab sites were community-based centers. Focusing on work groups provided an ample number of street-level workers and an intact work subculture: these individuals routinely interacted with and relied on each other in the course of completing their work. They also shared a supervisor.

After gaining permission from the supervisors, we set up a group meeting with all of the street-level workers on the targeted team. We reiterated that participation was authorized but not required. We asked for both collective and individual permission. Without dis-cussing our theoretical frames and questions, we presented our research procedures to the group and asked if its members would, as a group, permit us to proceed. It was important that the entire group accept our presence, even if individuals chose not to participate. After their questions were answered, we left the room to allow them to make a collective judgment.

Once we received work-group permission, we then asked individuals for written consent to participate. We again stressed that group approval did not require individual approval. In several sites, a few work-group members declined to participate but remained welcoming of our presence. As table A1 shows, forty-eight street-level workers distributed across five sites in two states participated in interviews and story collection. We concluded the group meeting by scheduling individual interviews with those workers who had agreed to participate.

Data collection began with the entry interview. This interview served two purposes: to gather background information on the storytellers and to explain and schedule the story-collection process. The entry interview flexibly followed the protocol reproduced in appendix B. We began by asking the storytellers about their work history and then asked about their current job and their relations with citizen-clients, coworkers, and supervisors. We asked them to describe which citizen-clients proved the easiest and which the most difficult. With some prodding, the storytellers described their various personal, professional, and group identities and how their social identities related to those of the citizens with whom they interacted. We ended by asking them to describe any critical incidents in the history of the agency, such as a public scandal or change of administration, that influenced the work environment.

When the entry interview was completed, we scheduled our initial story collection approximately one month in the future and handed out pamphlet-sized storybooks that included instructions adapted slightly for the three different agency types and room for text or notes on three stories. The instructions for the two voc rehab sites read:

> Over the next several weeks, we would like you to use this sketch book to write down a rough outline of 2 to 3 different stories. These stories should describe situations that take place within your agency during this time, or that you might recall from the past. The rough outlines will help you remember the

TABLE A1. Distribution of Street-Level Worker Participants

	Site Location	
Agency Type	Southwest	Midwest
Police Dept.	9	10
Vocational Rehab	9	10
Middle School	—	10
Total	18	30

story when you tell it to us later; you will not be required to share these notes with us.

We are interested in stories about how or when your own beliefs about fairness or unfairness help you make decisions. At times your beliefs may have conflicted with the department's formal and informal policies; at other times, policies may have facilitated your reliance on your own beliefs.

Stories can involve an encounter between you and clients, be about encounters between you and your agency, or among you and other members of your agency. You may also retell a story that happened to someone else, even if you are not a character in the story.

The stories should, as much as possible: (1) have a plot or storyline with a beginning, middle, and end; (2) tell us who the characters are; (3) explain the relationships among the characters; (4) describe the feelings of the characters toward each other and the events; and (5) include a description of the setting and circumstances in which the event(s) occurred.

At the appointed time, the researcher and storyteller would find a private place to meet. To initiate story collection, we merely asked the street-level worker to tell his or her stories, which were tape-recorded. During the initial storytelling, the researchers interrupted as little as possible but asked questions at the conclusion to encourage the storyteller to fill in missing or unelaborated details. We collected one to three stories during the first session and then scheduled a second session for one month later. A third session was also typically held.

The tape-recorded stories were transcribed verbatim, with the "ums" and other verbal utterances included. We also transcribed the probes and responses. These transcripts were lightly edited for clarity and to introduce the responses to the researcher's probes into the body of the text. The goal of this editing was to strengthen the narrative order in the text. We shared these edited versions with the storytellers, who could suggest changes. We gave the storytellers the final say on the stories to assure them and us that these were the stories they wanted to tell. No storyteller made significant changes, but some further embellished their stories, and a few eliminated verbalisms.

The story collection and revision process transforms stories from an oral to written form, and the change in form could alter interpretation. In oral stories, inflection and gesture convey meaning that is often lost when written down. Oral stories are also less fixed in content and form.

We did not ask the street-level workers to write stories because we did not want to base our data collection on our storytellers' writing skills. Moreover, writing demands more work than telling. We transformed the stories from oral to written form to facilitate the analysis and communication of stories. This transformation was done to minimize changes in the spoken structure of the stories, but nuances of the oral presentation were inevitably lost.

Interviews and story collection provided opportunities for extended observations, although the observations took different forms in the different agencies. Like voc rehab clients, we waited in anterooms before appointments, and like voc rehab counselors, we chatted in the halls and break rooms before and after interviews. We became familiar with routines and the support staff. At the school site, as in the voc rehab sites, we often arrived early for appointments. We waited outside the principal's office—usually sharing the waiting room with students lined up for disciplining—and walked the halls. We did not routinely observe teaching but usually held interviews and story-collection sessions in vacant classrooms, giving us a chance to observe student-teacher interactions as previous classes filed out and some students delayed their exit to have individual moments with teachers.

In the two police sites, we did some interviews and story collections at the station, but the primary opportunity to interact with and observe the police was during ride-alongs. Spending time in patrol cars as officers cruise their beats has become a staple of police ethnography. Police officers often insist that outsiders ride along to see the world as the cops see it. We were in the voc rehab offices, middle school, and police departments one to two days a week for three to four months.

Immediately after spending time in the field, the researcher would take notes of observations. Since our primary method of analysis is a close and interpretive reading of the stories, these field observation notes were used to enrich our understanding of the ways storytellers act on citizen-clients, to learn how storytellers represent themselves in relation to the citizens encountered, and to hear expressions of storytellers' beliefs and values. For example, the officer who told "Watching the Prostitute from a Distance" (story 7.1) was frequently in touch with his wife in the suburbs via a cell phone, talked often about the differences between his neighbors and the citizens he encountered on patrol, and aggressively pursued contacts with people whose attire and/or possessions suggested that they were not "mainstream" citizens.

For each site, we also collected relevant documents that described the rules, procedures, and organizational structure of that site. These documents were used in part to describe the settings (see chapter 4) and to provide a backdrop for the stories. For example, a new procedure requiring central-office approval for high-speed chases provides context for a police story about turning off the radio during an unauthorized pursuit.

The exit interview involved a structured questionnaire and a brief open-ended interview. It is important to note that our small, nonrandom sample of forty-eight street-level workers does not allow statistical inference. These data are used to describe our storytellers. The exit questionnaire and interview included the only time we directly asked the street-level workers about discretion and justice. We waited until the end to avoid channeling the stories in researcher-defined directions. The questionnaire (see appendix C) asked a series of standard questions on task authority, task variety, frequency of work exceptions, applicability and clarity of rules, and percentage of time working directly with citizen-clients. We also asked about the adequacy of resources, workload, loyalty, job satisfaction, and perceptions of fairness at work. We concluded with a series of questions on ideology and political orientation. To get the storytellers' views of justice, we asked a hypothetical question regarding distribution rules:

Which of the following should be taken into account in deciding how to distribute scholarship money to applicants to medical school?

- Scholarships should be given to applicants according to how much they need the money in order to attend medical school.
- Scholarship money should be given to applicants according to how hard they have tried to get prepared for medical school.
- Scholarship money should be given to applicants based on their grades and medical school admission test scores.
- Scholarship money should be given to applicants in such a way that the smallest scholarships are not much less than the largest awards.

The brief exit interview involved three questions. First we asked, "What does the word *justice* mean to you?" Responses to this question underscored the power of stories: the same street-level workers who told richly textured narratives about fairness offered only flat, standard, and socially acceptable answers to this direct question. To get at questions of ideology, we asked whether the workers felt that some groups in America are treated unfairly. We concluded by asking about fairness at work and if any of the rules or procedures struck them as unfair.

The exit questionnaire serves two purposes. First, we ascertain how closely our storytellers align with dominant depictions of street-level workers as occupiers of jobs that require discretion, cannot be reduced to following rules and procedures, and are involved in face-to-face contact with citizen-clients. Second, we compare answers across the three types of street-level workers and two regions. Unless specifically discussed, there are no statistically meaningful differences in type or regions.

As shown in figure A1 and consistent with expectations, the street-level workers in our study score in the middle to high range of the discretion scales. These front-line workers who lack the authority of high position claim considerable authority over determining their own work: the overall mean was nearly 4 on a 5-point scale. They claim slightly less authority in establishing rules and procedures (mean = 3.6) and in determining how exceptions are handled (mean = 3.1). Although their work is moderately repetitive—most responded "to some extent" to the question "To what extent do you perform the same tasks from day to day?"—exceptions are commonplace. When asked, "During a normal week, how frequently do exceptions arise in your work?" 8 percent responded "constantly" and an additional 45 percent responded "quite or very often." Police work and teaching are more routine than voc rehab counseling (see figure A2), but there are no differences in the frequency of exceptions among our three types of street-level workers.

Confirming other accepted characteristics, only 23 percent of our teachers, VR counselors, and police officers report that the written rules and procedures provide specific guidance about how to accomplish their work (see figure A3). We also asked what percent of the worker's time was spent in face-to-face contact with citizen-clients. As expected and as figure A4 shows, 26 percent responded "all of my work," and an additional 38 percent said that three-quarters of their work involved direct contact. There were no differences in our three very different types of workers on these variables.

When asked the hypothetical questions (we deliberately chose to use an example that was not related to the work of our study participants) about how to distribute medical school scholarships, 48 percent stressed need, 24 percent stressed effort, 24 percent stressed performance, and only 5 percent based their judgment on equity (see figure A5).

Discretion, Authority, and Rules

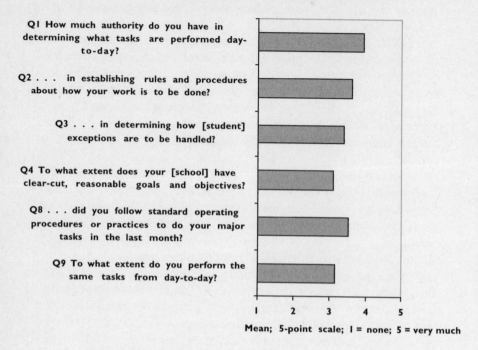

Q1 How much authority do you have in determining what tasks are performed day-to-day?

Q2 . . . in establishing rules and procedures about how your work is to be done?

Q3 . . . in determining how [student] exceptions are to be handled?

Q4 To what extent does your [school] have clear-cut, reasonable goals and objectives?

Q8 . . . did you follow standard operating procedures or practices to do your major tasks in the last month?

Q9 To what extent do you perform the same tasks from day-to-day?

Mean; 5-point scale; 1 = none; 5 = very much

Fig. A1.   Mean scores of all street-level workers on discretion scales

Q9 To what extent do you perform the same tasks from day-to-day?

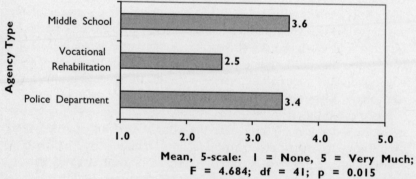

Mean, 5-scale: 1 = None, 5 = Very Much;
$F = 4.684$; $df = 41$; $p = 0.015$

Fig. A2.   Routine work by type of worker

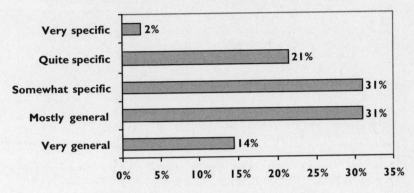

Q7 How precisely do these written rules and procedures specify how your major tasks are to be done?

Very specific — 2%
Quite specific — 21%
Somewhat specific — 31%
Mostly general — 31%
Very general — 14%

(0% 5% 10% 15% 20% 25% 30% 35%)

Fig. A3. Guidance provided by rules and procedures

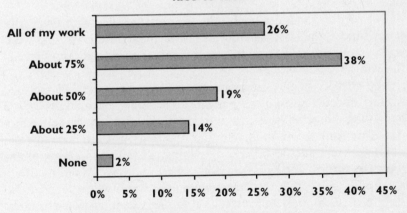

Q11a How much of your work deals directly with people face-to-face?

All of my work — 26%
About 75% — 38%
About 50% — 19%
About 25% — 14%
None — 2%

(0% 5% 10% 15% 20% 25% 30% 35% 40% 45%)

Fig. A4. Prevalence of face-to-face contact with citizen-clients

Q22 Which of the following should be taken into account in deciding how to distribute scholarship money to applicants to medical school?
Scholarships should be given to applicants . . .

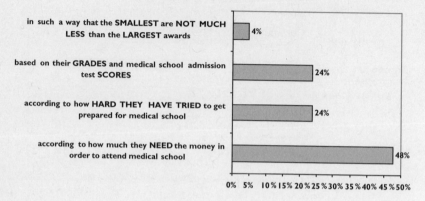

Fig. A5.   Distribution rules

Voc rehab counselors tend to be the most satisfied with their jobs, police officers the least. There were few regional differences, but western workers had more resources and a lighter workload than those in the Midwest.

The analysis of the stories relied primarily on close and repeated reading, supplemented by note taking and coding. The analysis looked first at the individual stories and then for common themes across stories. This book's core argument and observations were derived from this iterative, inductive process of reading, abstracting interpretations from the stories, and cross-checking interpretations. Much of this is irreducibly subjective, but throughout the book we have provided story texts to support our interpretations and to show that our interpretations ring true with the texts offered by the storytellers. Other interpretations are plausible and can exist concurrently with those we derived.

To facilitate collaborative interpretation within the research team, we began our analysis by completing a detailed description of each story on a "story cover page" (appendix D). We identified the story type, narrator's role, social identity of the storyteller (taken from the entry interview), story characters, and time frame. Each cover page included a brief synopsis and a list of the themes.

Appendix A

We then divided the stories among the four members of the research team. After our initial reading, we developed a specific set of codes covering a range of issues relevant to the nature of the stories and street-level judgment (appendix E). Codes include: story structure, decision norms, decision rules, worker and client identities, relational dynamics at work and on the street, and characteristics of the workplace. A member of the research team would read the story, block off sections of the text that reflected an individual code (some were double-coded), and mark the code in the margins. A second researcher from a different field site would then review the coding for completeness and accuracy. Disagreements were resolved by the coders and code checkers. We decided against blind double-coding because our goal was not interrater reliability but rather completeness and consensus.

We used the codes to create indexes to locate key discussions and to focus our interpretations. We did not count the frequency of mention of various coded statements or, as is common, examine out-of-context phrases with similar codes. Although we experimented with this approach, we found that the coded phrases lost meaning when "disembodied" from the story. Words, phrases, and passages are most meaningful in the specific context of the story, not as statements of observations or beliefs taken out of the narrative. The need to keep the text intact may be a stronger requirement in narrative analysis than in other forms of interpretive research.

The primary values of the coding and code checking were that they contributed to the close reading of the text and facilitated our own memory of text elements. The codes also provided a means for the research team to discuss varying interpretations of the text and to more easily locate stories and story passages across our relatively large collection of stories. In many ways, the most important analysis process was the drafting of this book: the themes and arguments grew out of our close reading of the stories and the placement of our reading in the context of our fieldwork, but these observations, themes, and arguments were refined by the writing process. In narrative analysis, writing is itself a methodology.

Appendix B: Entry Interview

These interviews should, if possible, be tape-recorded and transcribed verbatim.

Introduction:

Thank you for taking the time to talk with me.

Before we begin, let me explain a little about our research project:

This is academic research funded by the National Science Foundation. Although we have permission from [the director's name] to do the research, we are not reporting to him [or her] or anyone else in the government. What you tell us is confidential and anonymous. We will use what we learn for scholarly writing but will not link specific observations with individuals. We will, however, identify the type of agency and the city.

Our purpose is to gain a greater understanding of decision making of front-line public employees, such as yourself. The study focuses on police officers, schoolteachers and disability-claims processors working in two metropolitan areas.

Our research involves field observation, interviews, and the collection of stories from front-line staff about work experiences.

The stories will be our primary source of information about decision making, but today I'm not asking for stories

My purpose today is to get to know a little more about the nature of [name of organization] and about you.

Do you have any questions?

May I proceed?

First, can you tell me a little about yourself?

Why are you in this job? What made you decide to become a [police officer, teacher, or disability-claims worker]?

How long have you been working at [name of organization]?

Can you tell me a little about other jobs that you have had?

What's it like working here?

Probe: feelings about the work (e.g., scary, boring, overwhelming, etc.)

Probe: relations with other workers (e.g., cooperative, contentious, friendly, cold, etc.)

Probe: relations with supervisors (e.g., cooperative, "bossy," appreciated, unappreciated, etc.)

Probe: relations with clients [or citizens or whatever is appropriate to the setting] (e.g., friendly, unpleasant, scary, rewarding, matter-of-fact or businesslike, etc.)

Can you describe the typical client [or citizen] you serve?

How are they similar to you? How are they different?

Who are the easiest to serve? Who are the most difficult?

Are their any complaints from particular groups of clients [or citizens]?

Social identities assessment

We are all members of different groups or social affiliations. Some of these groups pertain to your sex, race, ethnicity, or social class. We are also members of different occupational groups.

Describe the social or occupational group that is **most** important to your sense of what kind of person you are.

Identify critical incidents

Thinking back over the history of your agency, are there any specific events that changed the way you do things? These events could be anything: a court case, an investigation, a well-publicized success, or whatever.

When did these things happen?

How did they change how you do things?

Thank you very much. We will be in your office from time to time for the next six months. If you think of anything else or just want to talk, just let me or [other member of the team] know. Thanks again.

Appendix C: Questionnaire
and Exit Interview

(Example: Teacher Site)

Please fill out the following questionnaire.

1. How much authority do you have in determining what tasks to perform day to day?

    None
    Little
    Some
    Quite a bit
    Very much

2. How much authority do you have in establishing rules and procedures about how your work is to be done?

    None
    Little
    Some
    Quite a bit
    Very much

3. How much authority do you have in determining how student exceptions are to be handled?

    None
    Little
    Some
    Quite a bit
    Very much

4. To what extent does your school have clear-cut, reasonable goals and objectives?

> To a very small extent
> To a little extent
> To some extent
> To a great extent
> To a very great extent

5. During a normal week, how frequently do student exceptions arise in your work?

> Very rarely
> Occasionally
> Quite often
> Very often
> Constantly

6. When considering the various situations that arise in performing your work, what percentage of the time do you have written procedures for dealing with them?

> 0–20%
> 21–40%
> 41–60%
> 61–80%
> 81–100%

7. How precisely do these written rules and procedures specify how your major tasks are to be done?

> Very general
> Mostly general
> Somewhat specific
> Quite specific
> Very specific

8. To what extent did you follow standard operating procedures or practices to do your major tasks in the last month?

> To no extent
> To little extent
> To some extent
> To great extent
> To very great extent

9. To what extent do you perform the same tasks from day to day?

    To no extent
    To little extent
    To some extent
    To great extent
    To very great extent

10. In performing your major task, how different are the day-to-day situations?

    Completely different
    Very much different
    Quite a bit different
    Mostly the same
    Very much the same

11a. How much of your work deals directly with people face to face?

    None
    About 25%
    About 50%
    About 75%
    All of my work

11b. When it comes to working with [students], how different are the day-to-day situations?

    Completely different
    Very much different
    Quite a bit different
    Mostly the same
    Very much the same

12a. How easy is it for you to know whether you did your work correctly?

    Very difficult
    Quite difficult
    Somewhat easy
    Quite easy
    Very easy

12b. What percentage of the time are you generally sure of what the outcomes of your work efforts will be?

> 40% or less
> 41–60%
> 61–75%
> 76–90%
> 91% or more

13. To what extent are the resources you have to work with adequate?

> To a very small extent
> To a little extent
> To some extent
> To a great extent
> To a very great extent

14. How heavy was your workload in the past month?

> Light
> A bit light
> Just about right
> Heavy
> Too heavy to keep up with

15. How much feeling of loyalty do you have toward this [school]?

> No feeling at all of loyalty
> Very little
> Some
> Quite a bit
> Very strong feeling of loyalty

16. I feel the compensation I receive for my work is fair.

> Strongly agree
> Somewhat agree
> Somewhat disagree
> Strongly disagree

17. I believe that administrators in my organization are paid fairly.

> Strongly agree
> Somewhat agree
> Somewhat disagree
> Strongly disagree

18. I am concerned about the differences in pay between the teachers and administrators in my organization.

    Strongly agree
    Somewhat agree
    Somewhat disagree
    Strongly disagree

19. I am concerned about the differences in pay between front-line staff and managers in society in general.

    Strongly agree
    Somewhat agree
    Somewhat disagree
    Strongly disagree

20. I am more concerned about fair compensation than about fair treatment at work.

    Strongly agree
    Somewhat agree
    Somewhat disagree
    Strongly disagree

21. All in all, how satisfied are you with your job?

    Unsatisfied
    Somewhat unsatisfied
    Satisfied
    Quite a bit satisfied
    Very satisfied

22. Which of the following should be taken into account in deciding how to distribute scholarship money to applicants to medical school?

    Scholarships should be given to applicants according to how much they need the money in order to attend medical school.
    Scholarship money should be given to applicants according to how hard they have tried to get prepared for medical school.
    Scholarship money should be given to applicants based on their grades and medical school admission test scores.
    Scholarship money should be given to applicants in such a

way that the smallest scholarships are not much less than the largest awards.

23. The role of government should be to help people.

   Strongly agree
   Somewhat agree
   Somewhat disagree
   Strongly disagree

24. When government provides welfare benefits such as disability, unemployment compensation, and early retirement pensions, it only makes people not want to work.

   Strongly agree
   Somewhat agree
   Somewhat disagree
   Strongly disagree

25. It is the responsibility of government to meet everyone's needs, even in case of sickness, poverty, unemployment, and old age.

   Strongly agree
   Somewhat agree
   Somewhat disagree
   Strongly disagree

26. If someone has a high social or economic position, that indicates the person has special abilities.

   Strongly agree
   Somewhat agree
   Somewhat disagree
   Strongly disagree

27. Would you like to live in a society where the government does nothing except provide for national defense and police protection so that people could be left alone to earn whatever they could?

   Strongly agree
   Somewhat agree
   Somewhat disagree
   Strongly disagree

28. Please choose the category that best describes your political
    views.

      Extremely liberal
      Liberal
      Slightly liberal
      Moderate, middle of the road
      Slightly conservative
      Conservative
      Extremely conservative

The following open-ended questions will be asked once the questionnaire has been handed back.

1. What does the word *justice* mean to you? Are there groups or types
   of people who are treated unjustly in America today? (If yes) Who?

2. Do you feel that there are any kind of people who get special treatment by your agency? Is that fair? Are there others who are discriminated against by your agency?

3. Are there any agency rules or procedures that you feel are unfair?

Appendix D: Story Cover Page

Site:
Storyteller: (Number)
Story ID:

1. **Story Type** (circle one)
   a. Official ("those that our boss, our government, our parents, or anyone in authority instructs us to tell"; stories that present a "public relations" view of the organization; tell how the organization would like to see itself or be seen)
   b. Firsthand experiential (narrator tells story about personal experience)
   c. Secondhand (narrator tells story that someone else told him or her)
   d. Culturally common (common stories of the organization; no one person tells them, and no one person makes them up; clue is if more than one storyteller tells the same story)
2. **Role of the Narrator**
   a. Job: (detailed description of the job of the person telling the story)
   b. In story: (same as above, or as described in story, such as narrator, bystander, actor)
3. **Social Identity of Storyteller** (taken from first interview)
4. **List of Characters with Descriptive Details** (using the name or identifier from the story)
5. **Time of Story**
   a. Present (within 1 yr/ongoing)
   b. Near past (1–3 yrs)
   c. Past (More than 3 yrs)
   d. Indeterminate

6. **Synopsis** (one- or two-line summary of the story)
7. **Meta Themes**
    a. Triumph of goodwill
    b. Being reformed
    c. Who are the worthy?
    d. Getting the bad guys
    e. Justifying action, "Father Knows Best"
    f. Self-aggrandizement
    g. Street-level worker vs. management
    h. Other

Appendix E: Story Codes

Instructions: For story and thematic codes, mark with brackets on the right margin the text segments that are coded. Mark any and all codes that apply to that text. First coder uses red; second uses blue. Mark all disagreements by circling the code and flag the text area.

Story Codes

Interrupts (INT): A premature halt in the action sequence or a shift from one action sequence to another. An interrupt is often but not always associated with change of place and characters.

Repetition: (REP): A restatement of a descriptive or action detail with or without variation.

Symbols/Signs/Artifacts (SYM): Objects or words that are presented in the story that connote meaning beyond their narrow meaning (e.g., bullet-wound scars, accommodation ribbons, pictures).

Causation (CAU): Causal attribution, statement that infers "if/then" relationships between actions, motives, etc. (e.g., police officer justifies use of deadly force, "if he wouldn't have come so close to me, I wouldn't have had to shoot"; "being on crack gave him super powers").

Thematic Codes

Decision Norms (DN): Reason from the perspective of: following the rules or **legality/rules (DN-LAW)**; doing what was equitable, fair, impartial or **justice (DN-JUS)**; acting to protect the good, acting against the bad or **morality (DN-MOR)**; looking out for me or **self-interest (DN-SIN)**; protecting the profession, seeing to the reputation of the organization or **organizational interest (DN-ORG)**; and doing what the situation calls for, or **pragmatism (DN-PRAG)**.

Decision Rules (DR): follow the rule **(DR-FOL)**; ignore the rule **(DR-**

IGN); bend the rule **(DR-BND);** subvert or take action against the rule **(DR-SUB).**

Consequence to SLW (CON): What happens to the worker as a result of decision or action (e.g., nothing, punished, rewarded).

Worker Affect (WA): Worker depictions of feelings in the context of being a member of a profession, working the streets, interacting with others, including expressions of fear, satisfaction, bitterness.

Worker Self-Identity (WI): Who one is, or depicting oneself as an American, as a worker, as gendered, as family oriented, as sexualized, as racialized, as ethnically embedded, as religiously inclined.

Worker Self-Worth (WW): Characterization of one self as virtuous, flawed, brave, caring.

Client Identity (CI): Who the client is as an American, as a worker, as family oriented, as gendered, as sexualized, as racialized, as ethnically embedded, as religiously inclined.

Client Worth (CW): Characterization of the client as deserving, lazy, flawed, caring.

Workplace Relational Dynamics (WD): Depicting relations and interactions in the workplace between subject/storyteller/interviewee and: **subordinate (WD-SUB); supervisor (WD-SUP); fellow worker (WD-WKR); other organizations (WD-ORG).**

Street Relational Dynamics (SD): Depicting, at times stereotypically, relations and interactions on the job between subject/storyteller/interviewee and: **client (SD-CLT); student (SD-STD); suspect (SD-SUS); victim (SD-VIC); groups** of citizens such as rich, poor, women, etc. **(SD-GRP); media (SD-MED); advocacy groups** such as Independence Inc. **(SD-ADV); public,** as in protecting the public **(SD-PUB);** and another governmental entity, such as state agency, "the feds," the mayor, etc **(SD-GOV).**

Organizational Culture (OC): The work atmosphere, as collegial, as conflicted, as divided, as in transition, and the relation of worker to organization.

Place/Space (PS): Depictions of setting where one is doing work, including expressions about doing work in public places (e.g., street corners) as distinct from private places (e.g., a citizen's home).

Resources (RES): The characterizations of resources available to do job, including time, how workers cope with deficiencies in resources, and engage in rationing.

Critical Events (CE): Changes in key personnel, in organizational process; dramatic news about the organization or particular workers as reported in the media.

Notes

Chapter 1

1. For a review of the literature and a description of these tensions, see Marcia K. Meyers and Susan Vorsanger, "Street-Level Bureaucrats and the Implementation of Public Policy," in *Handbook of Public Administration,* ed. B. Guy Peter and Jon Pierre (Thousand Oaks, CA: Sage, forthcoming).

2. See David A. Harris, "The Stories, the Statistics, and the Law: Why Driving while Black Matters," *Minnesota Law Review* 84, no. 2 (1999): 265–326.

3. For a discussion of the discomfort associated with scholarship that operates between competing ideas and the desire for conceptual unity related specifically to inquiry of law and culture, see David Goldberg, Michael Musheno, and Lisa Bower, "'Shake Yo' Paradigm: Romantic Longing and Terror in Contemporary Sociolegal Studies," in *Between Law and Culture: Relocating Legal Studies,* ed. David Goldberg, Michael Musheno, and Lisa Bower (Minneapolis: University of Minnesota Press, 2001), ix–xxv.

4. For an earlier version of the state-agent and citizen-agent narratives, see Steven Maynard-Moody and Michael Musheno, "State-Agent or Citizen-Agent: Two Narratives of Discretion," *Journal of Public Administration Theory and Research* 10, no. 2 (2000): 329–59.

5. For an overview of police abuse of authority, see David Barlow and Melissa Hickman Barlow, *Police in a Multicultural Society: An American Story* (Prospect Heights, IL: Waveland Press, 2000), 3–78; and Neil Websdale, *Policing the Poor: From Slave Plantation to Public Housing* (Boston: Northeastern University Press, 2001). Austin Sarat describes legally abusive powers of social workers and how welfare workers deploy law to resist abuse in "'. . . The Law Is All Over': Power, Resistance, and the Legal Consciousness of the Welfare Poor," *Yale Journal of Law and Humanities* 2, no. 2 (1990): 343–79. David Engel explores the intimidation that parents of children living with disabilities experience in school meetings with teachers, social workers, and other professionals in "Origin Myths: Narratives of Authority, Resistance, Disability, and Law," *Law and Society Review* 27, no. 4 (1993): 785–826.

6. Two meanings of the word *character* merge in story interpretation: the "nice lady" is a character in a story, but the characterization provided by the storyteller indicates judgments about her essential and distinguishing nature—her character.

7. What characteristics and actions a worker "notices" or overlooks can have profound consequences. See Ann Arnett Ferguson, *Bad Boys: Public Schools in the Making of Black Masculinity* (Ann Arbor: University of Michigan Press, 2001), 88.

8. The relationship between worker and citizen-client, if often personal and direct, is not a relationship of equal power. Street-level workers make judgments about who is helped and who is hassled or threatened and control access to state resources and opportunities, especially for the poor. See Joel F. Handler, *Law and the Search for Community* (Philadelphia: University of Pennsylvania Press, 1990), 18. Other scholars have focused on the broader implications of street-level decision making, including works by Barbara Yngvesson on the importance of court clerks and other front-line judicial employees in the construction of community and social order. See Barbara Yngvesson, *Virtuous Citizens, Disruptive Subjects: Order and Complaint in a New England Court* (New York: Routledge, 1993), and "Making Law at the Doorway: The Clerk, the Court, and the Construction of Community in a New England Town," *Law and Society Review,* 22, no. 3 (1988): 409–48.

Chapter 2

1. The legitimacy of the modern state is substantially entwined with the rule of law. For an overview and critique of the rule of law, see David Kairys, "Introduction," in *The Politics of Law: A Progressive Critique,* ed. David Kairys (New York: Pantheon, 1982), 1–17. In addition, according to Michel Foucault, the modern state hinges on its capacity to "foster civil respect and public morality" ("The Political Technology of Individuals," in *Technologies of the Self,* ed. Luther H. Martin, Huck Gutman, and Patrick H. Hutton [Amherst: University of Massachusetts Press, 1988], 155). For a focus on the culturally productive role of the police, see Trish Oberweis and Michael Musheno, *Knowing Rights: State Actors' Stories of Power, Identity, and Morality* (Burlington, VT: Ashgate/Dartmouth, 2001), 1–10. It is important to emphasize that law and culture are interwoven. For example, Naomi Mezey focuses on law as culture, emphasizing that "law's power is discursive and productive as well as coercive" ("Law as Culture," *Yale Journal of Law and the Humanities* 13, no. 1 [special issue 2001], 47). Further, we recognize that some scholars would take the view that both the culturally and legally productive judgments of street-level workers are ultimately about legality. See, for example, Sarat, " . . . 'The Law Is All Over.'" Still, we take the position that it is important to trace how front-line workers embrace and act on law, rules, and

bureaucratic procedures distinctly from their embrace and use of identity, relational dynamics, and morality to structure judgments and decisions. This is particularly important because the prevailing conceptualization of street-level work—the state-agent narrative—gives very little attention to the cultur-ally productive engagement of front-line workers. Other sociolegal scholars do make the distinction between legal and moral normativity in tracing the deci-sional dynamics of state workers and of citizens while recognizing their inter-connectivity. See Steve Herbert, *Policing Space: Territoriality and the Los Angeles Police Department* (Minneapolis: University of Minnesota Press, 1997); John Conley and William M. O'Barr, *Rules versus Relationships: The Ethnography of Legal Discourse* (Chicago: University of Chicago Press, 1990); Sally Engle Merry, *Getting Justice and Getting Even* (Chicago: University of Chicago Press, 1990). We follow in their footsteps and embrace Mezey's claim: "While I agree that law and culture do not exist independently of each other, I disagree that their necessary interconnections make them indistinguishable from one another" ("Law as Culture," 47).

2. Marcia K. Meyers, Bonnie Glaser, and Karin MacDonald, "On the Front Lines of Welfare Delivery: Are Workers Implementing Policy Reforms?" *Journal of Policy Analysis and Management* 17, no. 1 (1998): 13.

3. John Brehm and Scott Gates, *Working, Shirking, and Sabotage: Bureaucratic Response to a Democratic Republic* (Ann Arbor: University of Michigan Press, 1997), 199; Søren C. Winter, "Information Asymmetry and Political Control of Street-Level Bureaucrats: Danish Agro-Environmental Regulations," paper presented at the annual research meeting of the Associa-tion for Public Policy Analysis and Management, Seattle, 2–4 November 2000.

4. John Van Maanen, "Observations on the Making of Policemen," in *Policing: A View from the Street,* ed. Peter K. Manning and John Van Maanen (Santa Monica, CA: Goodyear, 1978), 304.

5. Janet Coble Vinzant and Lane Crothers, *Street-Level Leadership: Dis-cretion and Legitimacy in Front-Line Public Service* (Washington, DC: Georgetown University Press, 1998), 10.

6. Michael K. Brown, *Working the Street: Police Discretion and the Dilemmas of Reform* (New York: Sage, 1981); Michael Lipsky, *Street-Level Bureaucracy: Dilemmas of the Individual in Public Services* (New York: Sage, 1980).

7. H. George Frederickson, *The Spirit of Public Administration* (San Francisco: Jossey-Bass, 1997), 99.

8. Joel F. Handler, *The Conditions of Discretion: Autonomy, Community, Bureaucracy* (New York: Sage, 1986), 8.

9. For an excellent review, see John A. Rohr, "The Administrative State and Constitutional Principle," in *Centennial History of the American Adminis-trative State,* ed. Ralph Chandler (New York: Free Press, 1987), 113–59.

10. Dwight Waldo, *The Administrative State: A Study of the Political The-*

ory of American Public Administration, 2d ed. (New York: Holmes and Meier, 1984); James Q. Wilson, *Bureaucracy: What Government Agencies Do and Why They Do It* (New York: Basic Books, 1989).

11. During this period, some scholars suggested a broader view of implementation. See Michael Musheno, "The Justice Motive in the Social Policy Process: Searching for Normative Rules of Distribution," *Policy Studies Review* 5 (1986): 697–704.

12. Brehm and Gates, *Working, Shirking, and Sabotage.*

13. Brown, *Working the Street;* Handler, *Conditions of Discretion;* Lipsky, *Street-Level Bureaucracy;* Meyers and Vorsanger, "Street-Level Bureaucrats"; Richard Weatherley, "Implementing of Social Programs: The View from the Front Line," paper presented at the Annual Meeting of the American Political Science Association, Washington, DC, 1980; Wilson, *Bureaucracy.* Ann Chih Lin, *Reform in the Making: The Implementation of Social Policy in Prison* (Princeton: Princeton University Press, 2000).

14. Jeffrey M. Prottas, *People-Processing: The Street-Level Bureaucrat in Public Service Bureaucracies* (Lexington, MA: Lexington Press, 1979).

15. Many of these bulletproof barriers were built after the bombing of the federal office building in Oklahoma City. Social Security Administration offices tend to be located on the first floor because they serve the disabled; they are literally on the front line.

16. Lipsky, *Street-Level Bureaucracy,* xii.

17. Our notion of clashes of law and culture resembles Mezey's idea of "slippage," or moments "in which specific cultural practices or identities coincide or collide with specific legal rules or conventions, thereby altering the meanings of both. In the slippage between a law's aims and effects, you often see this collision of cultural and legal meaning" ("Law as Culture," 58).

18. Andrew J. Polsky, *The Rise of the Therapeutic State* (Princeton: Princeton University Press, 1991), 21.

19. Brehm and Gates, *Working, Shirking, and Sabotage,* 3.

20. Brown, *Working the Street;* Evelyn Z. Brodkin, "Inside the Welfare Contract: Discretion and Accountability in State Welfare Administration," *Social Service Review* 71 (March 1997): 3–4.

21. Names and other identifying information have changed throughout to assure anonymity. The first time a name is changed, it appears in brackets to alert the reader.

22. Steve Herbert, "Morality in Law Enforcement: Chasing 'Bad Guys' with the Los Angeles Police Department," *Law and Society Review* 40, no. 4 (1996): 803. See also Steven Maynard-Moody and Michael Musheno, "Morality over Legality: Invoking Norms from the Front-Lines of Government," paper presented at the Annual Meeting of the Law and Society Association, Chicago, 27–30 May 1999.

23. This phrase is drawn from Conley and O'Barr's study of litigants, "Rules versus Relationships."

24. Carol Gilligan, "Re-Mapping the Moral Domain: New Images of the Self in Relationship," in *Reconsidering Individualism: Autonomy, Individuality, and the Self in Western Thought,* ed. Thomas C. Heller, Morton Sosna, and David E. Wellenberg (Stanford, CA: Stanford University Press, 1986), 239.

25. For an in-depth treatment of these identity dynamics based on the narratives and fieldwork of two sites from this research project, see Oberweis and Musheno, *Knowing Rights.* For a detailed examination of the issues of race, gender, and occupational identity in another front-line government service, see Carol Chetkovich, *Real Heat: Gender and Race in the Urban Fire Service* (New Brunswick, NJ: Rutgers University Press, 1997).

26. Joel Handler and Ellen Jane Hollingsworth, *The "Deserving Poor": A Study of Welfare Administration* (New York: Markham, 1971), 18–19.

27. For a discussion of the need for pragmatic improvisation in a functioning state, see James C. Scott, *Seeing Like a State: How Certain Schemes to Improve the Human Condition Have Failed* (New Haven: Yale University Press, 1998).

28. Yngvesson, "Making Law at the Doorway," 444.

29. The state-agent narrative portrays the decisions of front-line workers as threatening the state's legitimacy by interrupting democratic accountability. The citizen-agent narrative, with its emphasis on the culturally as well as materially productive work of street-level workers, recognizes their importance in constituting citizenship as they distribute the benefits and burdens associated with state resources and power. A similar perspective is developed in Vinzant and Crothers, "Street-Level Leadership," 19.

30. Some scholars use the concept of "reproduction" in that the strategies of street-level workers are "conceived as deriving from social structure, and their use in interaction serves to reproduce dialectically social structure" (Richard Ericson, *Reproducing Order: A Study of Police Patrol Work* [Toronto: University of Toronto Press, 1982], 9).

Chapter 3

1. Joshua Foa Dienstag, *"Dancing in Chains": Narrative and Memory in Political Theory* (Stanford, CA: Stanford University Press, 1997), 2.

2. Livia Polanyi, *Telling the American Story: A Structural and Cultural Analysis of Conversational Storytelling* (Norwood, NJ: Ablex, 1985), 2.

3. John R. Hall, *Cultures of Inquiry: From Epistemology to Discourse in Sociohistorical Research* (New York: Cambridge University Press, 1999), 72–73.

4. Dienstag, *"Dancing in Chains,"* 10. Others make a different distinction, calling the phenomenon the "story" and the inquiry the "narrative." "Thus, we can say that people by nature lead storied lives and tell stories of those lives, whereas narrative researchers describe such lives, collect and tell stories of them and write narratives of experience" (F. Michael Connelly and D. Jean

Clandinin, "Stories of Experience and Narrative Inquiry," *Educational Researcher* 19, no. 4 [1990]: 2).

5. Herbert M. Kritzer, "The Data Puzzle: The Nature of Interpretation in Quantitative Research," *American Journal of Political Science* 40 (February 1996): 1–32.

6. See also Paul Atkinson, *The Ethnographic Imagination: Textual Construction of Reality* (New York: Routledge, 1990), 105.

7. Paul Ricoeur, "Narrative Time," in *On Narrative,* ed. W. J. T. Mitchell (Chicago: University of Chicago Press, 1980), 168.

8. For example, see David M. Boje, "The Storytelling Organization: A Study of Story Performance in an Office-Supply Firm," *Administrative Science Quarterly* 36 (March 1991): 106–26.

9. William Labov, *Language in the Inner City* (Philadelphia: University of Pennsylvania Press, 1972), 354–55.

10. Gary Bellow and Martha Minow, eds., *Law Stories* (Ann Arbor: University of Michigan Press, 1996), 1.

11. Molly Patterson and Kristen Renwick Monroe, "Narrative in Political Science," *Annual Review of Political Science* 1 (1998): 316.

12. Dvora Yanow, *How Does a Policy Mean? Interpreting Policy and Organizational Actions* (Washington, DC: Georgetown University Press, 1996), 5.

13. John C. Meyer, "Tell Me a Story: Eliciting Organizational Values from Narratives," *Communications Quarterly* 43, no. 2 (1995): 210–24; Charles L. Briggs, ed., *Disorderly Discourse: Narrative, Conflict, and Inequality* (New York: Oxford University Press, 1996), 14.

14. Emery Roe, *Narrative Policy Analysis: Theory and Practice* (Durham, NC: Duke University Press, 1994), 2.

15. Patterson and Monroe, "Narrative in Political Science," 316–17.

16. Ibid., 320–21.

17. Elinor Ochs, Carolyn Taylor, Dina Rudolph, and Ruth Smith, "Storytelling as a Theory-Building Activity," *Discourse Processes* 15 (January–March 1992): 44–45.

18. Dienstag, *"Dancing in Chains,"* 7.

19. Bellow and Minow, "Introduction: Rita's Case and Other Law Stories," in *Law Stories,* ed. Bellow and Minow, 18.

20. Steven Maynard-Moody and Marisa Kelly, "Stories Public Managers Tell about Elected Officials: Making Sense of the Politics-Administration Dichotomy," in *Public Management Theory: The State of the Art,* ed. Barry Bozeman (San Francisco: Jossey-Bass, 1993), 71–90.

21. Steven Maynard-Moody and Suzanne Leland, "Stories from the Front-Lines of Public Management: Street-Level Workers as Responsible Actors," in *Advancing Public Management: New Developments in Theory, Methods, and Practice,* ed. Jeffrey L. Brudney, Laurence O'Toole Jr., and Hal J. Rainey (Washington, DC: Georgetown University Press, 1999), 109–23.

22. Labov, *Language in the Inner City,* 370–71.

23. Trish Oberweis and Michael Musheno. "Policing Identities: Cop Decision-Making and the Constitution of Citizens." *Law and Social Inquiry* 24, no. 4 (1999): 897–923.

24. Anthony V. Alfieri, "Welfare Stories," in *Law Stories,* ed. Gary Bellow and Martha Minow (Ann Arbor: University of Michigan Press, 1996), 39.

25. Patricia Ewick and Susan B. Silbey, "Subversive Stories and Hegemonic Tales: Toward a Sociology of Narrative," *Law and Society Review* 29, no. 2 (1995): 212.

26. Story 6.3 was, however, told in an agency that proved more hospitable to lesbian workers and subculture than might be expected. While still an organizational subculture, homosexuals are not a powerless and silenced subculture.

27. In the process of our research, we discovered that we could not ask storytellers to record their stories on paper. Many were embarrassed by their poor spelling and uncertain about the grammar. They would readily tell stories but were reticent writers.

28. See, for example, David M. Engel and Frank Munger, "Rights, Remembrance, and the Reconciliation of Difference," *Law and Society Review* 30, no. 1 (1996): 7–54. The authors of this insightful article claim that they approached their story collection "with no preconceptions" (8).

29. Conley and O'Barr, *Rules versus Relationships,* 171.

30. Gary King, Robert O. Keohane, and Sidney Verba, *Designing Social Inquiry: Scientific Inference in Qualitative Research* (Princeton: Princeton University Press, 1994), chap. 6.

Chapter 4

1. The image of the "super crip" is a double edged-sword for the disabled. As Joseph P. Shapiro writes, "But the change in [the disabled] mind-set is powerful enough to win rights and perhaps eventually convince a nation and the world that people with disabilities want neither pity-ridden paternalism nor overblown admiration. They insist simply on common respect and the opportunity to build bonds to their communities as fully-accepted participants in everyday life" (*No Pity: People with Disabilities Forging a New Civil Rights Movement* [New York: Times Books, 1993], 332).

2. See William Lyons, *The Politics of Community Policing* (Ann Arbor: University of Michigan Press, 1999).

3. Herbert, *Policing Space.*

4. Peter Manning, *Police Work* (Cambridge: MIT Press, 1997), 319; Herbert, "Morality in Law Enforcement," 800.

5. For a description of police language, see Marcus Laffrey, "The Word on the Street: What a Cop Says and How He Says It Can Matter More Than His Stick or His Gun," *New Yorker,* 10 August 1998, 36–39.

Part 2

1. For more treatment of our particular conceptualization of identity, see Oberweis and Musheno, "Policing Identities." For other treatments of identities and the structuring of subject positions that have informed ours, see Stuart Hall, "Introduction," in *Questions of Cultural Identity,* ed. Stuart Hall and Paul Du Gay (London: Sage, 1996), 1–17; Ernesto Laclau and Lillian Zac, "Minding the Gap: The Subject of Politics," in *The Making of Political Identities,* ed. Ernesto Laclau (London: Verso, 1994), 11–39; Judith Butler, *Gender Trouble: Feminism and the Subversion of Identity* (New York: Routledge, 1990); Michael Walzer, *Spheres of Justice* (New York: Basic Books, 1983). For an alternative view of social identity grounded in social psychology, see Michael A. Hogg and Dominic Abrams, *Social Identification: A Social Psychology of Intergroup Relations and Group Processes* (London: Routledge, 1988).

2. See Samuel Walker, *Police Accountability: The Role of Citizen Oversight* (Belmont, CA: Wadsworth, 2001), 109–11.

3. "Politics of difference" traditionally references urban identity-based social movements that embrace a positive self-definition of group difference in the pursuit of emancipatory political goals. See Iris Marion Young, *Justice and the Politics of Difference* (Princeton: Princeton University Press, 1990), 156–83. We use this concept to depict the identity-based politics that the stories and fieldwork reveal as operating internal to the work sites of public agencies, particularly the western police department. The internal struggles we uncovered may be connected to urban-based identity politics operating in the larger political landscape of the urban municipality, but further research would be required to uncover these connections.

4. See also Susan L. Miller, *Gender and Community Policing* (Boston: Northeastern University Press, 1999).

5. See John Van Maanen, "The Asshole," in *Policing: A View from the Street,* ed. Peter K. Manning and John Van Maanen (Santa Monica, CA: Goodyear, 1978), 221–37.

Chapter 5

1. Few stories focused on the collective pursuit of grievances among workers. Individual workers told stories of being wronged by their supervisors and managers, usually indicating that workers lump these wrongs together. For an overview of how people handle grievances, see Tom R. Tyler, Robert J. Boeckmann, Heather J. Smith, and Yuen J. Huo, *Social Justice in a Diverse Society* (Boulder: Westview, 1997), 153–78.

2. See John M. Conley and William M. O'Barr, *Just Words: Law, Language, and Power* (Chicago: University of Chicago Press, 1998); Yngvesson, *Virtuous Citizens, Disruptive Subjects.*

3. For insights into citizen-clients' struggles against workers and public service agencies, see Mezey, "Law as Culture," 35–67.

4. Earlier field ethnographies of policing as an occupation have noted similar traits. See, for example, John Van Maanen, "Kinsmen in Repose: Occupational Perspectives of Patrolmen," in *Policing: A View from the Street,* ed. Peter K. Manning and John Van Maanen (Santa Monica, CA: Goodyear, 1978), 115–28.

5. Some scholars who focus on inner-city schools claim that teachers have abandoned coercive powers and the responsibility for disciplining youth that teachers historically held, turning these tasks over to security guards and municipal police agencies. See esp. John Devine, *Maximum Security: The Culture of Violence in Inner-City Schools* (Chicago: University of Chicago Press, 1996).

6. Indeed, persuasion is about the exercise of power but is based more on reason and reasoning than on brute force. For an elaboration of this distinction, see Steven Lukes, *Power: A Radical View* (London: MacMillan, 1974).

7. For a treatment of appeals to substantive justice in public service work, see Musheno, "Justice Motive." The significance of procedural justice to public agencies is taken up by Tom R. Tyler, *Why People Obey the Law: Procedural Justice, Legitimacy, and Compliance* (New Haven: Yale University Press, 1990).

Chapter 6

1. This perspective on the police work environment is detailed in Elizabeth Reuss-Ianni, *Two Cultures of Policing: Street Cops and Management Cops* (New Brunswick, NJ: Transaction Books, 1983).

2. Community policing is the dominant reform strategy of urban municipal police departments. The broad intent is to have police officers work more closely with urban residents, focusing on quality-of-life and social-order issues. For the orthodoxy of this reform strategy, see Herman Goldstein, *Problem-Oriented Policing* (New York: McGraw-Hill, 1990); and James Q. Wilson and George L. Kelling, "Broken Windows," in *Critical Issues in Policing,* ed. Roger G. Dunham and Geoffrey P. Alpert (Prospect Park, IL: Waveland Press, 1993), 395–407. For a critical look at this strategy, see the essays in Jack R. Greene and Stephen D. Mastrofski, eds., *Community Policing: Rhetoric or Reality?* (New York: Praeger, 1991).

3. For a treatment of identity enclaves in urban communities, see Young, *Justice and the Politics of Difference,* 226–56.

4. See also Ferguson, *Bad Boys,* 95, 230.

5. This contrasts with the related occupation of urban fire fighters. Despite continual pressure to hire more women, the fire service remains a largely male dominated profession. See Chetkovich, *Real Heat.*

Chapter 7

1. The VR worker provided the title of this story and said that Janet was the counselor's sunshine lady. The vocational rehabilitation worker revealed the origins of her title—"the caregiver said she used to call [Janet] the Sunshine Lady because every day, Janet would walk to the same street corner and stare up at the sun all day long. As a result, Janet now has retina damage." In an interview, the counselor revealed that she also has a physical disability related to an eye injury sustained early in her life.

Chapter 8

1. The counseling was justified not because it was authorized or even an appropriate service from a voc rehab counselor but because the citizen-client needed it.

2. Jennifer L. Hochschild, *Facing up to the American Dream: Race, Class, and the Soul of the Nation* (Princeton: Princeton University Press, 1995).

Chapter 9

1. Exaggeration is a common storytelling technique. We do not know if the actual credit card bill was $12,000 or if the amount was inflated for narrative impact. This $12,000 bill underscores both the wealth of the families and the seriousness of the offense. The storyteller also uses repetition to highlight his points and his frustration with the two girls.

2. The storyteller is aware of the implausibility of much of his story and adds such statements to give credibility to the entire tall tale.

3. For a detailed analysis of street-level workers' coping behaviors, see Lipsky, *Street-Level Bureaucracy,* pt. 3.

4. Repetition is a salient element in many of the street-level stories. This story shares many of the same rhetorical devices as "Borrowed Pants and a $12,000 Credit Card Bill" (story 9.1), told in a different state by a different type of street-level worker.

5. This is a most revealing sentence construction: when the street-level worker responds bureaucratically, he refers to himself as "the system," which is treated like an individual who can "say" things to the client.

Chapter 10

1. Storytellers often provide an "abstract" of the story in the first few sentences. In this instance, the storyteller has some difficulty getting started but is clear about the intended message.

2. The storyteller exaggerates the gap between the client's abilities and aspirations to reinforce the "street-level worker knows best" message.

3. This story contrasts to those discussed in the next chapter. This kind of challenge to authority, especially of the police, often leads to escalating conflict, even violence. This is a story of restraint.

4. "Doing movement" is police jargon for potentially dangerous actions, like going for a gun. The subject's passivity is one reason this officer overlooked his noncompliance.

Chapter 11

1. The storyteller is referring to himself in the third person.

2. For those considered worthy, cases of pot smoking and selling are overlooked because pot is not considered a hard drug. But every infraction, however slight, is used in the battle of worker versus unworthy citizen-client.

3. In 1998, federal law was changed to disallow disability claims for substance abuse and addiction.

Chapter 12

1. Sanford F. Schram and Philip T. Neisser, eds., *Tales of the State: Narrative in U.S. Politics and Public Policy* (Lanham, MD: Rowman and Littlefield, 1997), 10.

2. Oberweis and Musheno, "Policing Identities."

3. Thomas E. McCollough, *The Moral Imagination and Public Life: Raising the Ethical Question* (Chatham, NJ: Chatham House, 1991), 11.

4. Oberweis and Musheno, *Knowing Rights.*

5. Guy B. Adams and Danny L. Balfour, *Unmasking Administrative Evil* (Thousand Oaks, CA: Sage, 1998). See also Susan Bandes, "Patterns of Injustice: Police Brutality in the Courts," *Buffalo Law Review* 47 (fall 1999): 1275–1341.

6. For a recent treatment, see Brehm and Gates, *Working, Shirking, and Sabotage.*

7. See also Brodkin, "Inside the Welfare Contract."

8. Emery Roe suggests that one way out of polarizing disputes, such as are evident in the state-agent and citizen-agent views of street-level work, is to articulate a new "metanarrative" that "underwrites and stabilizes assumptions" for an alternative view (*Narrative Policy Analysis,* 4). Roe acknowledges, however, that reconciling metanarratives cannot always be articulated and, if articulated, may not always change the discourse. Such is the case with street-level work.

9. Elijah Anderson, *Code of the Street: Decency, Violence, and the Moral Life of the Inner City* (New York: Norton, 1999).

10. Ewick and Silbey, "Subversive Stories," 222.

11. John R. Hall, *Cultures of Inquiry,* 97.

12. For example, see Van Maanen, "Observations," 292–308.

13. Brehm and Gates, *Working, Shirking, and Sabotage,* 146. See also John Brehm, Scott Gates, and Brad Gomez, "Donut Shops, Speed Traps, and Paperwork: Supervision and the Allocation of Time to Bureaucratic Tasks," paper presented at the annual meeting of the Midwest Political Science Association, Chicago, 23–25 April 1998.

14. For the general point, see Amitai Etzioni, "Social Norms: Internalization, Persuasion, and History," *Law and Society Review* 34, no. 1 (2000): 157–78.

15. Handler, *Law and the Search for Community,* 18–19. See also Yeheskel Hasenfeld, "Power in Social Work Practice," *Social Service Review* 61 (1987): 469–83; and Yeheskel Hasenfeld and Dale Weaver, "Enforcement, Compliance, and Disputes in Welfare-to-Work Programs," *Social Service Review* 70 (June 1996): 235–56.

16. Terry L. Cooper, *The Responsible Administrator: An Approach to Ethics for the Administrative Role,* 3d ed. (San Francisco: Jossey-Bass, 1990).

17. Philip H. Jos, "Administrative Responsibility Revisited: Moral Consensus and Moral Autonomy," *Administration and Society* 22 (1990): 242.

18. Lawrence Lessig, "The Regulation of Social Meaning," *University of Chicago Law Review* 62 (1995): 997, 1034.

19. Clifford Shearing and Richard Ericson, "Culture as Figurative Action," *British Journal of Sociology* 42 (1991): 482–506.

20. Karl E. Weick, *Sensemaking in Organizations* (Thousand Oaks, CA: Sage, 1995).

References

Adams, Guy B., and Danny L. Balfour. *Unmasking Administrative Evil.* Thousand Oaks, CA: Sage, 1998.

Alfieri, Anthony V. "Welfare Stories." In *Law Stories,* edited by Gary Bellow and Martha Minnow, 31–49. Ann Arbor: University of Michigan Press, 1996.

Anderson, Elijah. *Code of the Street: Decency, Violence, and the Moral Life of the Inner City.* New York: Norton, 1999.

Atkinson, Paul. *The Ethnographic Imagination: Textual Construction of Reality.* New York: Routledge, 1990.

Bandes, Susan. "Patterns of Injustice: Police Brutality in the Courts." *Buffalo Law Review* 47 (fall 1999): 1275–1341.

Barlow, David, and Melissa Hickman Barlow. *Police in a Multicultural Society: An American Story.* Prospect Heights, IL: Waveland Press, 2000.

Bauman, Richard. *Story, Performance, and Event: Contextual Studies of Oral Narrative.* Cambridge: Cambridge University Press, 1986.

Bellow, Gary, and Martha Minow, eds. *Law Stories.* Ann Arbor: University of Michigan Press, 1996.

Boje, David M. "The Storytelling Organization: A Study of Story Performance in an Office-Supply Firm." *Administrative Science Quarterly* 36 (March 1991): 106–26.

Box, Richard C. "The Administrator as Trustee of the Public Interest: Normative Ideals and Daily Practice." *Administration and Society* 24 (1992): 323–45.

Brehm, John, and Scott Gates. *Working, Shirking, and Sabotage: Bureaucratic Response to a Democratic Republic.* Ann Arbor: University of Michigan Press, 1997.

Brehm, John, Scott Gates, and Brad Gomez. "Donut Shops, Speed Traps, and Paperwork: Supervision and the Allocation of Time to Bureaucratic Tasks." Paper presented at the annual meeting of the Midwest Political Science Association, Chicago, 23–25 April 1998.

Briggs, Charles L., ed. *Disorderly Discourse: Narrative, Conflict, and Inequality.* New York: Oxford University Press, 1996.

References

Brodkin, Evelyn. "Inside the Welfare Contract: Discretion and Accountability in State Welfare Administration." *Social Service Review* 71 (March 1997): 1–30.

———. "Investigating Policy's Practical Meaning: Street-Level Research on Welfare Policy." Paper presented at the Annual Meeting of the Association for Public Policy Analysis and Management, Washington, DC, 4–6 November 1999.

———. "Street-Level Research: Policy at the Front Lines." Paper presented at the Annual Meetng of the Association for Public Policy Analysis and Management, Washington, DC, 4–7 November 1999.

Brooks, Peter, and Paul Gewirtz, eds. *Law's Stories: Narrative and Rhetoric in the Law.* New Haven: Yale University Press, 1996.

Brown, Michael K. *Working the Street: Police Discretion and the Dilemmas of Reform.* New York: Sage, 1981.

Bruner, Jerome. *Actual Minds, Possible Worlds.* Cambridge: Harvard University Press, 1986.

Burke, John. *Bureaucratic Responsibility.* Baltimore: Johns Hopkins University Press, 1986.

Butler, Judith. *Gender Trouble: Feminism and the Subversion of Identity.* New York: Routledge, 1990.

Chaney, Carole Kennedy, and Grace Hall Saltzstein. "Democratic Control and Bureaucratic Responsiveness: The Police and Domestic Violence." *American Journal of Political Science* 42 (July 1998): 745–68.

Chetkovich, Carol. *Real Heat: Gender and Race in the Urban Fire Service.* New Brunswick, NJ: Rutgers University Press, 1997.

Conley, John M., and William M. O'Barr. *Just Words: Law, Language, and Power.* Chicago: University of Chicago Press, 1998.

———. *Rules versus Relationships: The Ethnography of Legal Discourse.* Chicago: University of Chicago Press, 1990.

Connelly, F. Michael, and D. Jean Clandinin. "Stories of Experience and Narrative Inquiry." *Educational Researcher* 19, no. 4 (1990): 2–14.

Cooper, Terry L. *The Responsible Administrator: An Approach to Ethics for the Administrative Role.* 3d ed. San Francisco: Jossey-Bass, 1990.

Demorest, Amy P., and Irving E. Alexander. "Affective Scripts as Organizers of Personal Experience." *Journal of Personality* 60, no. 3 (1992): 645–63.

Devine, John. *Maximum Security: The Culture of Violence in Inner-City Schools.* Chicago: University of Chicago Press, 1996.

Dienstag, Joshua Foa. *"Dancing in Chains": Narrative and Memory in Political Theory.* Stanford, CA: Stanford University Press, 1997.

Ellickson, Robert. *Order without Law: How Neighbors Settle Disputes.* Cambridge: Harvard University Press, 1991.

Engel, David M. "Origin Myths: Narratives of Authority, Resistance, Disability, and Law." *Law and Society Review* 27, no. 4 (1993): 785–826.

Engel, David M., and Frank Munger. "Rights, Remembrance, and the Rec-

References

onciliation of Difference." *Law and Society Review* 30, no. 1 (1996): 7–54.

Ericson, Richard. *Reproducing Order: A Study of Police Patrol Work.* Toronto: University of Toronto Press, 1982.

Etzioni, Amitai. "Social Norms: Internalization, Persuasion, and History." *Law and Society Review* 34, no. 1 (2000): 157–78.

Ewick, Patricia, and Susan S. Silbey. *The Common Place of Law: Stories from Everyday Life.* Chicago: University of Chicago Press, 1998.

———. "Subversive Stories and Hegemonic Tales: Toward a Sociology of Narrative." *Law and Society Review* 29, no. 2 (1995): 197–226.

Feldman, Martha S. "Social Limits to Discretion: An Organizational Perspective." In *The Uses of Discretion,* edited by Keith Hawkins, 163–83. New York: Oxford University Press, 1992.

Ferguson, Ann Arnett. *Bad Boys: Public Schools in the Making of Black Masculinity.* Ann Arbor: University of Michigan Press, 2000.

Foucault, Michel. "The Political Technology of Individuals." In *Technologies of the Self: A Seminar with Michel Foucault,* edited by Luther H. Martin, Huck Gutman, and Pattrick H. Hutton, 145–62. Amherst: University of Massachusetts Press, 1988.

Frederickson, H. George. *The Spirit of Public Administration.* San Francisco: Jossey-Bass, 1997.

Garofalo, Charles, and Dean Geuras. *Ethics in the Public Service: The Moral Mind at Work.* Washington, DC: Georgetown University Press, 1999.

Gergen, Kenneth. *The Saturated Self: Dilemmas of Identity in Contemporary Life.* New York: Basic Books, 1991.

Gergen, Kenneth J., and Mary M. Gergen. "Narrative Form and the Construction of Psychological Science." In *The Storied Nature of Human Conduct,* edited by Theodore R. Sarbin, 22–44. New York: Praeger, 1986.

Gilligan, Carol. *In a Different Voice.* Cambridge: Harvard University Press, 1982.

———. "Re-Mapping the Moral Domain: New Images of the Self in Relationship." In *Reconsidering Individualism: Autonomy, Individuality, and the Self in Western Thought,* edited by Thomas C. Heller, Morton Sosna, and David E. Wellberg, 237–52. Stanford, CA: Stanford University Press, 1986.

Giroux, Henry, Colin Lankshear, Peter McLaren, and Michael Peters. *Counternarratives: Cultural Studies and Critical Pedagogies in Postmodern Spaces.* New York: Routledge, 1996.

Glenn, Brian J. "The Shifting Rhetoric of Insurance Denial." *Law and Society Review* 34, no. 3 (2000): 779–808.

Goldberg, David. "Modernity, Race, and Morality." In *Race Critical Theories: Text and Context,* edited by Philomean Essed and David Goldberg, 283–306. Oxford: Blackwell, 2001.

Goldberg, David, Michael Musheno, and Lisa Bower. "'Shake Yo' Paradigm: Romantic Longing and Terror in Contemporary Sociolegal Studies." In *Between Law and Culture: Relocating Legal Studies,* edited by David Gold-

References

berg, Michael Musheno, and Lisa Bower, ix–xxv. Minneapolis: University of Minnesota Press, 2001.

Goldstein, Herman. *Problem-Oriented Policing.* New York: McGraw-Hill, 1990.

Greene, Jack R., and Stephen D. Mastrofski, eds. *Community Policing: Rhetoric or Reality?* New York: Praeger, 1991.

Hall, John R. *Cultures of Inquiry: From Epistemology to Discourse in Sociohistorical Research.* New York: Cambridge University Press, 1999.

Hall, Stuart. "Introduction." In *Questions of Cultural Identity,* edited by Stuart Hall and Paul Du Gay, 1–17. London: Sage, 1996.

Hammond, Kenneth R. *Human Judgment and Social Policy: Irreducible Uncertainty, Inevitable Error, Unavoidable Injustice.* New York: Oxford University Press, 1996.

Handler, Joel F. *The Conditions of Discretion: Autonomy, Community, Bureaucracy.* New York: Sage, 1986.

———. *Down from Bureaucracy: The Ambiguity of Privatization and Empowerment.* Princeton: Princeton University Press, 1996.

———. *Law and the Search for Community.* Philadelphia: University of Pennsylvania Press, 1990.

Handler, Joel, and Ellen Jane Hollingsworth. *The "Deserving Poor": A Study of Welfare Administration.* New York: Markham, 1971.

Harris, David A. "The Stories, the Statistics, and the Law: Why Driving while Black Matters." *Minnesota Law Review* 84, no. 2 (1999): 265–326.

Hasenfeld, Yeheskel. "Organizational Forms as Moral Practices: The Case of Welfare Departments." *Social Service Review* 74 (September 2000): 329–51.

———. "Power in Social Work Practice." *Social Service Review* 61 (1987): 469–83.

Hasenfeld, Yeheskel, and Dale Weaver. "Enforcement, Compliance, and Disputes in Welfare-to-Work Programs." *Social Service Review* 70 (June 1996): 235–56.

Herbert, Steve. "Morality in Law Enforcement: Chasing 'Bad Guys' with the Los Angeles Police Department." *Law and Society Review* 40, no. 4 (1996): 799–818.

———. *Policing Space: Territoriality and the Los Angeles Police Department.* Minneapolis: University of Minnesota Press, 1997.

Hochschild, Jennifer L. *Facing up to the American Dream: Race, Class, and the Soul of the Nation.* Princeton: Princeton University Press, 1995.

Hogg, Michael A., and Dominic Abrams. *Social Identification: A Social Psychology of Intergroup Relations and Group Processes.* London: Routledge, 1988.

Holland, Dorothy, William Lachicotte, Debra Skinner, and Carole Cain. *Identity and Agency in Cultural Worlds.* Cambridge: Harvard University Press, 1998.

Johnson, David T. "The Organization of Prosecution and the Possibility of Order." *Law and Society Review* 32, no. 2 (1998): 247–308.

References

Jos, Philip H. "Administrative Responsibility Revisited: Moral Consensus and Moral Autonomy." *Administration and Society* 22 (1990): 228–48.

Kairys, David. "Introduction." In *The Politics of Law: A Progressive Critique,* edited by David Kairys, 1–17. New York: Pantheon, 1982.

King, Gary, Robert O. Keohane, and Sidney Verba. *Designing Social Inquiry: Scientific Inference in Qualitative Research.* Princeton: Princeton University Press, 1994.

Kinsey, Karyl A., and Loretta J. Stalans. "Which 'Haves' Come Out ahead and Why: Cultural Capital and Legal Mobilization in Frontline Law Enforcement." *Law and Society Review* 33, no. 4 (1999): 993–1024.

Kritzer, Herbert M. "The Data Puzzle: The Nature of Interpretation in Quantitative Research." *American Journal of Political Science* 40 (February 1996): 1–32.

Labov, William. *Language in the Inner City.* Philadelphia: University of Pennsylvania Press, 1972.

———. "Narrative Analysis: Oral Versions of Personal Experience." In *Essays on the Verbal and Visual Arts,* edited by June Helm, 12–44. Seattle: University of Washington Press, 1967.

Laclau, Ernesto, and Lillian Zac. "Minding the Gap: The Subject of Politics." In *The Making of Political Identities,* edited by Ernesto Laclau, 11–39. London: Verso, 1994.

Laffrey, Marcus. "The Word on the Street: What a Cop Says and How He Says It Can Matter More Than His Stick or His Gun." *New Yorker,* 10 August 1998, 36–39.

Lessig, Lawrence. "The Regulation of Social Meaning." *University of Chicago Law Review* 62 (1995): 943–1045.

Lin, Ann Chih. *Reform in the Making: The Implementation of Social Policy in Prison.* Princeton: Princeton University Press, 2000.

Lipsky, Michael. "Standing the Study of Public Policy Implementation on Its Head." In *American Politics and Public Policy,* edited by Walter Dean Burnham and Martha Wagner Weinberg, 391–402. Cambridge: MIT Press, 1978.

———. *Street-Level Bureaucracy: Dilemmas of the Individual in Public Services.* New York: Sage, 1980.

Lukes, Steven. *Power: A Radical View.* London: MacMillan, 1974.

Lyons, William T. *The Politics of Community Policing: Rearranging the Power to Punish.* Ann Arbor: University of Michigan Press, 1999.

Manning, Peter K. *Police Work.* Cambridge: MIT Press, 1997.

———. *Semiotics and Fieldwork.* Newbury Park, CA: Sage, 1987.

Mashaw, Jerry L. *Bureaucratic Justice: Managing Social Security Disability Claims.* New Haven: Yale University Press, 1983.

Maynard-Moody, Steven, and Marisa Kelly. "Stories Public Managers Tell about Elected Officials: Making Sense of the Politics-Administration Dichotomy." In *Public Management: The State of the Art,* edited by Barry Bozeman, 71–90. San Francisco: Jossey-Bass, 1993.

References

Maynard-Moody, Steven, and Suzanne Leland. "Stories from the Front-Lines of Public Management: Street-Level Workers as Responsible Actors." In *Advancing Public Management: New Developments in Theory, Methods, and Practice,* edited by Jeffrey L. Brudney, Laurence O'Toole Jr., and Hal G. Rainey, 109–23. Washington, DC: Georgetown University Press, 1999.

Maynard-Moody, Steven, and Michael Musheno. "Morality over Legality: Invoking Norms from the Front-Lines of Government." Paper presented at the Annual Meeting of the Law and Society Association, Chicago, 27–30 May 1999.

———. "State-Agent or Citizen-Agent: Two Narratives of Discretion." *Journal of Public Administration Research and Theory* 10, no. 2 (April 2000): 329–58.

McCollough, Thomas E. *The Moral Imagination and Public Life: Raising the Ethical Question.* Chatham, NJ: Chatham House, 1991.

Merry, Sally Engle. *Getting Justice and Getting Even.* Chicago: University of Chicago Press, 1990.

Meyer, John C. "Tell Me a Story: Eliciting Organizational Values from Narratives." *Communications Quarterly* 43, no. 2 (1995): 210–24.

Meyers, Marcia K., Bonnie Glaser, and Karin MacDonald. "On the Front Lines of Welfare Delivery: Are Workers Implementing Policy Reforms?" *Journal of Policy Analysis and Management* 17, no. 1 (1998): 1–22.

Meyers, Marcia K., and Susan Vorsanger. "Street-Level Bureaucrats and the Implementation of Public Policy." In *Handbook of Public Administration,* edited by B. Guy Peter and Jon Pierre. Thousand Oaks, CA: Sage, forthcoming.

Mezey, Naomi. "Law as Culture." *Yale Journal of Law and the Humanities* 13, no. 1 (special issue 2001): 35–67.

Miller, Susan L. *Gender and Community Policing.* Boston: Northeastern University Press, 1999.

Musheno, Michael. "The Justice Motive in the Social Policy Process: Searching for Normative Rules of Distribution." *Policy Studies Review* 5 (1986): 697–704.

Oberweis, Trish, and Michael Musheno. *Knowing Rights: State Actors' Stories of Power, Identity, and Morality.* Burlington, VT: Ashgate/Dartmouth, 2001.

———. "Policing Identities: Cop Decision-Making and the Constitution of Citizens." *Law and Social Inquiry* 24, no. 4 (1999): 897–923.

Ochs, Elinor, Carolyn Taylor, Dina Rudolph, and Ruth Smith. "Storytelling as a Theory-Building Activity." *Discourse Processes* 15 (January–March 1992): 37–72.

Patterson, Molly, and Kristen Renwick Monroe. "Narrative in Political Science." *Annual Review of Political Science* 1 (1998): 315–31.

Peters, Michael, and Colin Lankshear. "Postmodern Counternarratives." In *Counternarratives: Cultural Studies and Critical Pedagogies in Postmodern*

References

Spaces, edited by Henry Giroux, Colin Lankshear, Peter McLaren, and Michael Peters, 1–9. New York: Routledge, 1996.

Polanyi, Livia. *Telling the American Story: A Structural and Cultural Analysis of Conversational Storytelling.* Norwood, NJ: Ablex, 1985.

Polkinghorne, Donald E. *Narrative Knowing and Human Sciences.* Albany: State University of New York Press, 1988.

Polsky, Andrew J. *The Rise of the Therapeutic State.* Princeton: Princeton University Press, 1991.

Prottas, Jeffrey M. *People-Processing: The Street-Level Bureaucrat in Public Service Bureaucracies.* Lexington, MA: Lexington Press, 1979.

Reeher, Grant. *Narratives of Justice: Legislators' Beliefs about Distributive Justice.* Ann Arbor: University of Michigan Press, 1996.

Reuss-Ianni, Elizabeth. *Two Cultures of Policing: Street Cops and Management Cops.* New Brunswick, NJ: Transaction Books, 1983.

Ricoeur, Paul. "Narrative Time." In *On Narrative,* edited by W. J. T. Mitchell, 165–86. Chicago: University of Chicago Press, 1980.

Roe, Emery. *Narrative Policy Analysis: Theory and Practice.* Durham, NC: Duke University Press, 1994.

Rohr, John A. "The Administrative State and Constitutional Principle." In *Centennial History of the American Administrative State,* edited by Ralph Chandler, 113–59. New York: Free Press, 1987.

Sarat, Austin. ". . . 'The Law Is All Over': Power, Resistance and the Legal Consciousness of the Welfare Poor." *Yale Journal of Law and Humanities* 2, no. 2 (1990): 343–79.

Schank, Roger C. *Tell Me a Story: A New Look at Real and Artificial Memory.* New York: Scribner's, 1990.

Schneider, Anne L., and Helen Ingram. *Policy Design for Democracy.* Lawrence: University Press of Kansas, 1997.

Schram, Sanford F., and Philip T. Neisser, eds. *Tales of the State: Narrative in U.S. Politics and Public Policy.* Lanham, MD: Rowman and Littlefield, 1997.

Scott, James C. *Seeing Like a State: How Certain Schemes to Improve the Human Condition Have Failed.* New Haven: Yale University Press, 1998.

Scott, Patrick G. "Assessing Determinants of Bureaucratic Discretion: An Experiment in Street-Level Decision Making." *Journal of Public Administration Research and Theory* 7 (January 1997): 35–57.

Shapiro, Joseph P. *No Pity: People with Disabilities Forging a New Civil Rights Movement.* New York: Times Books, 1993.

Shearing, Clifford, and Richard Ericson. "Culture as Figurative Action." *British Journal of Sociology* 42 (1991): 482–506.

Soss, Joe. *Unwanted Claims: The Politics of Participation in the U.S. Welfare System.* Ann Arbor: University of Michigan Press, 2000.

Toulmin, Stephen. *Return to Reason.* Cambridge: Harvard University Press, 2001.

References

Tyler, Tom R. "Justice, Self-Interest, and the Legitimacy of Legal and Political Authority." In *Beyond Self Interest,* edited by Jane Mansbridge, 171–79. Chicago: University of Chicago Press, 1990.

———. *Why People Obey the Law: Procedural Justice, Legitimacy, and Compliance.* New Haven: Yale University Press, 1990.

Tyler, Tom R., Robert J. Boeckmann, Heather J. Smith, and Yuen J. Huo. *Social Justice in a Diverse Society.* Boulder, CO: Westview, 1997.

Van Maanen, John. "The Asshole." In *Policing: A View from the Street,* edited by Peter K. Manning and John Van Maanen, 221–37. Santa Monica, CA: Goodyear, 1978.

———. "Kinsmen in Repose: Occupational Perspectives of Patrolmen." In *Policing: A View from the Street,* edited by Peter K. Manning and John Van Maanen, 115–28. Santa Monica, CA: Goodyear, 1978.

———. "Observations on the Making of Policemen." In *Policing: A View from the Street,* edited by Peter K. Manning and John Van Maanen, 292–308. Santa Monica, CA: Goodyear, 1978.

Vinzant, Janet Coble, and Lane Crothers. *Street-Level Leadership: Discretion and Legitimacy in Front-Line Public Service.* Washington, DC: Georgetown University Press, 1998.

Waldo, Dwight. *The Administrative State: A Study of the Political Theory of American Public Administration.* 2d ed. New York: Holmes and Meier, 1984.

Walker, Samuel. *Police Accountability: The Role of Citizen Oversight.* Belmont, CA: Wadsworth, 2001.

———. *Taming the System: The Control of Discretion in Criminal Justice, 1950–1990.* New York: Oxford University Press, 1993.

Walzer, Michael. *Spheres of Justice.* New York: Basic Books, 1983.

Weatherley, Richard A. "Implementing of Social Programs: The View from the Front Line." Paper presented at the Annual Meeting of the American Political Science Association, Washington, DC, 1980.

———. *Reforming Special Education: Policy Implementation from State Level to Street Level.* Cambridge: MIT Press, 1979.

Websdale, Neil. *Policing the Poor: From Slave Plantation to Public Housing.* Boston: Northeastern University Press, 2001.

Weick, Karl E. *Sensemaking in Organizations.* Thousand Oaks, CA: Sage, 1995.

White, Hayden. "The Value of Narrativity in the Representation of Reality." In *On Narrative,* edited by W. J. T. Mitchell, 1–23. Chicago: University of Chicago Press, 1980.

White, Jay D. *Taking Language Seriously: The Narrative Foundation of Public Administration Research.* Washington, DC: Georgetown University Press, 1999.

Wilson, James Q. *Bureaucracy: What Government Agencies Do and Why They Do It.* New York: Basic Books, 1989.

References

Wilson, James Q., and George L. Kelling. "Broken Windows." In *Critical Issues in Policing,* edited by Roger G. Dunham and Geoffrey P. Alpert, 395–407. Prospect Park, IL: Waveland Press, 1993.

Winter, Søren C. "Information Asymmetry and Political Control of Street-Level Bureaucrats: Danish Agro-Environmental Regulations." Paper presented at the annual research meeting of the Association for Public Policy Analysis and Management, Seattle, 2–4 November 2000.

Yanow, Dvora. *How Does a Policy Mean? Interpreting Policy and Organizational Actions.* Washington, DC: Georgetown University Press, 1996.

Yngvesson, Barbara. "Making Law at the Doorway: The Clerk, the Court, and the Construction of Community in a New England Town." *Law and Society Review* 22, no. 3 (1988): 409–48.

———. *Virtuous Citizens, Disruptive Subjects: Order and Complaint in a New England Court.* New York: Routledge, 1993.

Young, Iris Marion. *Justice and the Politics of Difference.* Princeton: Princeton University Press, 1990.

Index